Given for life

A guide to motivational gifts

A N D Y   R A I N E

kevin mayhew

kevin mayhew

First published in Great Britain in 2004 by Kevin Mayhew Ltd
Buxhall, Stowmarket, Suffolk IP14 3BW
Tel: +44 (0) 1449 737978 Fax: +44 (0) 1449 737834
E-mail: info@kevinmayhewltd.com

www.kevinmayhew.com

9 8 7 6 5 4 3 2

ISBN 978 1 84417 271 9
Catalogue No. 1500712

Edited by Katherine Laidler
Typesetting by Richard Weaver
Cover design by Jonathan Stroulger

Printed and bound in Great Britain

Contents

Acknowledgements

Thank you . . .

- to all other teachers and exponents of Motivations, some of whom I know, and some whose notes I have devoured or interacted with.
- to Dave Reynolds who pressed me to get this material out ('because you've got it all there in you') into book form, and did most of the hard work of beginning the process.
- to Mo Jowett for taking over in the later stages when it had ground to a halt, and encouraging me to complete.
- to those whose stories punctuate these pages, and who have agreed to let these anecdotes appear.
- to Anne Cope for encouragement and typing as I worked on the new enlarged version of the chapter on life and work.
- to Jim Thwaites for necessitating a rewrite of that chapter.
- to friends in the Northumbria Community, and beyond, who have lived and owned this material as it developed and grew.

We arranged that my wife, our children and I would stay from Monday to Friday with Mike and Mo and their kids Sarah and Dan at their house in Harrogate, so that Mo and I could work on the computer to get this book finished. Both of us sensed an urgency about this with no real notion why. It was a good time just all being together.

Two weeks to the day from our completion of the rewrite of this text, Mo suffered a sudden brain haemorrhage. In the course of the next two weeks she fought her way back, and spoke with visitors excitedly about her plans to work with motivational gifts – especially with people with leadership responsibilities, or with couples in their marriages.

Then a second bleed came which took her life.

Hopefully, the book can still touch those Mo wanted to share the material with, and they will realise why she was so excited about it.

Mo, here it is; now the book is for you.

Prologue

This was going to be a very difficult letter to write. There were so many important things to say; there was so much to explain which was crucial to their survival. Who would hear the letter? A very mixed group of people in Rome. Some of them Jews, but most of them not. Some rich, influential and well educated; others would be craftsmen, tradesmen, smallholders or visiting merchants. Then there were household servants, and, of course, many slaves – slaves of every conceivable ability and rank. Many of his hearers had already borne the unpopularity and stigma of the name 'Christian', as followers of the Way were now seemingly called. Others were not confessed believers at all, but interested onlookers prepared to listen whenever what they heard seemed to make sense of their own busy lives. Any gathering of the devout community would always attract such inquirers, as well as their friends or family members. To these the name of Paul of Tarsus carried no particular weight of reputation: his words alone must act as advocate. So how was he to begin? What had they all in common that already reached in and tugged at their hearts? They all could see the beauty and bigness of the sky. All of them recognised the joy and cruelty of human existence in one way or another. Each of them faced the question of how they, as one human being, could begin to relate to the universe around them. What is my purpose for existing? What do I mean? How am I to relate to the people I bump up against day after day?

He looked around the room at an imaginary gathering of people – people like any others, like those he had encountered in every place on his various journeys. People gifted in different ways, often intolerant of others because of their differences – or, worse still, their similarities!

Some of you are the clear-sighted, radical, impulsive ones – and so you should be.

Some of you are the ones who get on with the job while everyone else is still sitting around talking about it. If you are still there and listening, this won't take long . . .

Some of you want to take it all in, and to think it all through; whatever I say will require further explanation and mulling over. Think about it.

Some of you can hardly listen for watching other people's reactions to what I am saying, and hoping it will really do them good. What I have to say to you is this: use your gift of encouragement.

Some of you feel you have little to give, to contribute, to anyone, but what a heart you have to do so! Give . . . what you can . . .

Some of you are already assessing the value of my input, and have mentally sketched out plans for implementing the parts you consider relevant. Good.

Some of you are more aware of feelings, and may even be sensing the strength of someone else's reaction to what they are hearing; or, right now, it is your own responses that are concerning you. Don't get too overwhelmed.

I have something to say to each of you. I have met people not unlike you before.

CAPTAIN'S LOG *circa* AD 57, Corinth
Your reference: Romans 12:6-8

About the author

Writer, dancer and facilitator for various groups, Andy Raine lives on Holy Island (Lindisfarne) in Northumberland with his wife Anna and their two young children, Joel and Martha. He was author/editor of *Celtic Daily Prayer* and one of the founders of the Northumbria Community. When he's not writing he talks on the phone and appreciates interruptions. At home or travelling, he may explore questions about Celtic monasticism over coffee, does dance workshops or motivations seminars, and likes to give Guinness and friends his undivided attention.

Introduction

The essence of teaching on motivational gifts is simple. Each person is born with a gift: a basic take on life, and a number of aptitudes and abilities that are innate. To develop these is to do what comes naturally. These are the *why* we do what we do, the motivation for how we are. There are seven of these different motivational gifts. Each of us has only one of them as our starting point, though we may also develop some outward aspects or traits of other people's gifts and priorities that we admire and emulate. Whatever we aspire to, or receive additional training for, the original gift always remains integral and will often explain the particular insights or approach that we bring to each new task or situation.

This book seeks to identify and contrast these seven distinct motivations and recognise them as 'gift' – each one valid, necessary and insightful. These are introduced and explained in Chapter 3 and then one by one in Chapters 4 to 10. Chapters 11 to 18 go on to develop and apply an understanding of motivational gifts, as well as giving further help in their recognition.

Some aspects of this will be familiar to people who have worked with other models of personality profile such as Myers-Briggs or Enneagram, but a fundamental difference of this approach is that it recognises giftedness rather than compulsion as the root of personality, and is not surprised to discover a fascinating diversity of unique individuals within each motivational grouping.

The gift of a person's motivation is only one element in the consideration of giftedness, for there are insights and abilities we experience from time to time as help from beyond our own capability. (These are considered in Chapter 1.) Another aspect of 'gifting' is the sense of vocation many individuals experience in moving into a new phase of life that challenges them to reach beyond the present level of their abilities, knowing that somehow they will be enabled to be equal to what this new vista demands. (This is considered in Chapter 2.)

None of this reflection, and process of taking inventory of a person's abilities, aptitudes and first responses, can ever take place in a vacuum, and I have increasingly considered it helpful to 'set the scene' by allowing space for the individual to take stock of five basic aspects of their life:

1. What is my present 'state of life'? (married/single/celibate/bereaved/divorced)
2. What does 'family' mean for me?
3. What do I get to do? (work/other involvements/vocation?)
4. What is my cultural identity? (background, present reference points, interests and passions)
5. Who are my friends?

Chapter 2 invites you to consider these questions about your life-context before embarking on an exploration of motivational gifts.

I hope and trust that this whole process will be a fascinating undertaking for you, and that it will yield new understanding of your *why*, also helping you to recognise some aspect of your particular inherent wisdom.

Andy Raine

How it began for me

In 1978 on a School of Creative Ministry (affectionately designated 'Sock 'em!') in Dunham, Quebec, I sat at a desk, irritated and unreceptive, notebook closed, and pen firmly not in hand, for a lecture entitled, 'Motivational Giftings'. More talk about spiritual gifts, I thought. I can do without this, and, besides, what I already teach works perfectly adequately; I don't care if this is true, there's no way I'm going home to re-teach anything!

With this promising attitude, I listened absent-mindedly to sketched-out descriptions of people of different 'motivations'.

Some way down the list I suddenly became very attentive. What I was hearing was the description of a person that was everything I had always hated about myself, known but not admitted, and even told lies about. I had wanted so much to be 'like everyone else', but now this was telling me that I was different in some ways precisely for the benefit of everyone else. What I had hated was the gift of who I was.

The lecture was over and was never referred to again. This left me confused. I had discovered myself, but was given no opportunity to hear the response of anyone else on the School. I was left, through my inattention, with inadequate notes, no integration and no follow-up. This was probably an oversight in a busy lecture schedule – I should perhaps be grateful that the topic was introduced at all, however cursorily it was explained!

Returning home from Canada about three months later, I moved, not back to Holy Island as I had expected, but into a large house in Berwick-upon-Tweed with John

11

and Linda Skinner. Our time there together lasted nine months, and quite early on I mentioned the experience I had had in the classroom, hearing myself described so accurately. We looked at the notes and soon discovered John and Linda's respective giftings. A steady stream of people came through that house as visitors. Real steps of friendship were taken . . . walls dismantled, miracles experienced . . . and there were not a few tears. Quite often, all three of us would be there with, or for, the people who came to us, and we recognised how our differing giftings complemented each other. A caricature of it would be something like this: John confronts and challenges, after cutting through the small talk; Linda empathises and cries with the person; I produce a timely cup of coffee and urge them that 'It'll be worth it in the end!' On an occasion when the same response was called for, but John happened to be absent, Linda and I would look at each other and wonder which of us needed to step into John's shoes as well as fulfilling our normal role. This way of thinking proved so helpful to the three of us that we began to teach what notes we had (one and a half A4 sheets!), and what little we had learned ourselves, to the Sunday night group who met with us in the house. Immediately it bore fruit in reducing conflict and basic misunderstanding. There was much to learn, but we had started.

Whilst visiting my friends Paul and Mary Cullity in New Hampshire, the subject of 'motivations' came up again. They were also familiar with the teaching and saw its value, though they were hesitant to claim conclusively which motivations were their own. (The reasons for this later became apparent. Not being hurried into drawing premature conclusions is characteristic of Paul's 'explaining' motivation, and Mary had yet to find an acceptable role model of the tender-hearted 'mercy' her insides knew she was.) We began to rewrite and add to the notes, in words that seemed less clumsy. Many of the phrases in those lecture notes which I began with were inflatedly 'spiritual'. 'Where did all this come from, anyway?' was the question I was now asking. (The irony was, it had taken me months and years to reach this point – my motivation only cares if a thing *works* in people's experience, not whether it is 'the truth' or not!) Paul was clear: motivations was taught as part of the package at one of the courses in Bill Gothard's Institute of Basic Youth Conflicts. Whoever had taught each of us had got the material indirectly from there. Its source was a list in Chapter 12 of the letter to the Romans from the apostle Paul. (My comment? The most boring book by the most aggravating and boring and long-winded writer in the Bible.)

I had been very selective until now about who would be exposed to 'motivations' through me. It was close to my heart and had radically changed my own life in the area of self-acceptance; but I couldn't have coped with anyone who wanted to argue about its validity – what I had experienced was too significant to be dirtied by callous analysis. But if all this was true, and was so basic a part of our thinking and sensitivity, and had just jumped out of Romans 12, why did it take Bill Gothard in America and in the late twentieth century to pull the rabbit out of the hat? The simplest things are not always true, but the truest things are invariably simple, once you boil them down.

In order to explain what happened next, I need to tell you that I avidly read and collect novels by Amy le Feuvre, who wrote prolifically during the late nineteenth and early part of the twentieth century. Great excitement: a 'new' second-hand Amy le Feuvre turned up as a birthday present. *Robin's Heritage* was as good as most of her novels, but contained a short story, not entirely consistent with the drift of the rest of the book, but an amazing window into the whole idea of motivational gifts, drawn entirely from her own reading of Romans 12, without the benefit of Bill Gothard's work on it some two generations later. (The short story 'Heritages' is reproduced in full in Chapter 13 of the book you are now reading.)

Remember, by now I was growing in confidence with this material. When I taught it to three families from the Earl Shilton area, that was essentially the beginning of what would become 'The Vine Community' in Leicester-shire. (They had connected with me very strongly on our initial meeting, then travelled a couple of hundred miles to be with me on my birthday a month later.) So, one summer I was on holiday on a campsite in Norfolk with four families from The Vine. That particular day we all sat under the awning of Kev and Ellen's caravan and watched the rain persisting hour after hour. Cathy remarked that she'd had a surprise the other day when she turned up, not terribly enthusiastically, for the annual Women's World Day of Prayer. The scripture reading had been from Romans 12, and she was amazed to realise how many of the familiar phrases from their notes on motiv-ations were sitting there in that one chapter. With nothing better to do, we reached for the nearest NIV and listened, as if for the first time, to the fateful chapter. All of these people knew each other well, knew each other's motiv-ations well, were very familiar with the teaching of it, and in their relationships with each other relied on it already as the bread and butter of their interaction. So we were not exactly disinterested listeners.

Paul in his letter begins to list the kinds of people he is addressing, identifying them, and initially saying little

14

more to them than, 'Go for it; be yourself.' We see each of the company under the dripping awning nodding firmly at the appropriate signal. Next, Paul goes round the room again, in exactly the same order, giving each in turn a word of challenge, an exhortation. Again, thoughtful nods – recollection but no big surprises. As Paul turns to each group in order for the third and final time, the response from all of us at the campsite was more dramatic, for *this* word was an uncomfortable word that made each motivation in turn go 'Ouch!' rather loudly. Also it seemed that in the previous few days on holiday we had had clear object lessons illustrating why these words of caution were necessary and important. *We* call these the BUTs, the word we probably don't want to hear. It was another key in our growing understanding of motivations.

All this time, I never actually had copies of any Bill Gothard notes on the subject; but we did play a card game bought at one of the seminars, and that was all about character qualities and how people of differing motivations want to collect different qualities. The principle is similar to Happy Families, but a bit more mind-boggling. A year later, we photocopied the cards; and John Skinner and I tentatively began to incorporate this new material, without shuffling it too much, into our counselling.

One friend who was in severe hot water at the time went through the new sheet with John. (John by now did motivations with anyone he was counselling before he started anything else, as it made it so much simpler for him to proceed.) Martyn had no difficulty at all in recognising the character qualities that would appeal to his particular (ruling) motivation; they were all things he had reached out for, and sought to develop and make his own. It was only when John read him the corresponding list of see-saw qualities that he blanched entirely. What John had read out was a description identical to the list of accusations being hurled at him by his second wife as the reasons why she was now in the process of divorcing him.

Eventually, we have come across not only the full Bill Gothard notes but also those of Don and Katie Fortune, Darrelle Marshall, and many others who have lived with and taught about motivational gifts. The similarities of our discoveries are staggering; the fresh insights are exciting; and, after what is now over 25 years, I feel in some ways still at the beginning of the process of un-wrapping the significance of part of that one small chapter.

In the film *Fahrenheit 451** a totalitarian regime has removed all books, ostensibly to store their contents on computer for posterity, but in fact to control the dangerous impact that uncontrolled exploration of thought might have. Once on computer, the words may vanish mysteri-ously. In the far corner of a forest is the meeting of some who have recognised the danger, the threat of destruction to an entire culture. These people have each systematically committed to memory a book or a portion of a book. As long as they live, that book will not be destroyed or lost.

From parts of Eastern Europe, where access to Bibles was dangerous and their cost on the black market prohibi-tive, have come reports of whole copies of scripture torn apart, page by page, and memorised tirelessly. Only when each word was imprinted flawlessly on their minds would they then exchange the weathered sheet for another precious fragment.

My friends and I are among those who have swallowed this particular page and it has become part of us. If you decide it is worth listening to, we have only to tell it. What happens then is up to the words themselves and to you.

---

* From the book by Roy Bradbury (1954, Hart-Davies)

Chapter 1
A box of tools

The primary task of this book is to describe, identify, and show the advantages of recognising the various motivational gifts. To do this it will be helpful to set these in the context of other gifts and supernatural/God-given abilities. Imagine a pile of three boxes (of gifts) placed one on top of the other. When we look at the whole pile of gifts, what is it that we will see?

The top box is the most visible and we may be tempted to see it as the measure of the whole pile, or even, since it is on the top, as being the most important. It is not. It is actually the most superficial of the three, and were it removed the others that support it would still stand in the same place. This top box has a fancy name written across the top: 'Manifestational Gifts by the Spirit of God'. On the side, where there isn't room for such a pretentious name, is printed the word 'Tools'.

If you have ever been around small children at home you will have noticed a small child's fascination with their dad's heavy toolbox. It seems the source and symbol of all kinds of power and mysterious things, and the child drags the toolbox along, scuffing their ankles and the skirting board in the process. The wise father at this point may intervene. One of those jobs that was waiting to be done sometime or other suddenly requires urgent attention. Perhaps it is a plug that needs changing. Small child's hand goes round screwdriver, father's hand goes round small child's hand, and – after much perseverance – the plug is changed . . . 'Daddy, Daddy, look what I did!'

To an impartial observer it would seem obvious that the father could have accomplished the task much more quickly and efficiently without the 'help' of the child. But, little by little, the child comes to learn that tools are not there to play with, that they don't need carrying around all the time, and that whenever they are needed to do a job, you need only reach into the toolbox to find what you need. The same child given a screwdriver to play with would probably have damaged the wallpaper or stuck it in the dog. It is also perfectly possible that someone could have become proficient in the use of all the tools without knowing the name of a single one of them. The only usefulness of knowing their names is that it can save time if you are talking with someone else who also uses similar tools.

The list of probable supernatural manifestational tools in the box runs something like this (according to the manufacturer's inventory):

- The wise word
- The knowing
- Discerning of spirits

- Gifts of healings
- Defying the nature of things
- Believing without the power to doubt
- Speech in other tongues
- Interpreting
- Prophecy

You may now want to skip the rest of this chapter,
or pursue it later.

If you want to move to the next box,
then proceed to Chapter 2.

We will now examine each of the aforementioned tools and their usefulness.

The wise word

What we are referring to here is not accumulated wisdom but the sense of being 'given' the right words to say in a situation. This will not usually be a general sense of inspiration, but almost the sense of words coming out of our mouth that we have not had any chance to think: we will be speaking, with a sureness, exactly the right thing, sometimes without even knowing why that would be the right thing . . .

> When my friend Steve was deeply upset and disturbed, and I was responding to something he said, I opened my mouth to say, 'Of course not,' and heard myself instead say, 'Why not?' (which meant the exact opposite). This different question unleashed from him years of excuses pouring out of his mouth, things he had never resolved and had avoided facing.

This rather convinced me that I had been given the right words to say in spite of my own ideas at the time. I was so impressed by the effectiveness of these two words that I dropped my guard enough to be open for this process to continue. (That also proved to be a dangerous move. At the time God was a concept I'd not been speaking to for three years . . .)

It is important to check the source of this kind of intervention. If its net result is to diminish someone's responsibility, proper self-esteem and true freedom within affective relationships, the source may properly be questioned. (For example, be wary of any book that the author claims has been 'channelled' from spirit guides.)

The knowing

This is something slightly more specific than a hunch! 'I just knew . . .' without knowing how I knew. It is very useful in counselling, tricky diagnosis or getting to the heart of a situation.

One of the funniest examples of this was when Jesus was talking to a woman alone by a well. 'Where's your husband?' he said. 'I haven't got a husband,' she said. 'You're too right you haven't – you've been married five times already and the bloke you're with now isn't your husband.' The woman was so impressed she brought the whole town out to meet . . . a new kind of man. *(John 4:16-29)*

Discerning of spirits

This gift has the disadvantage of usually only cropping up to make you uncomfortable. When something is going badly wrong and there is falsehood or deceit or a presence of evil of some kind, this discerning gift will manifest itself in some form of physical and/or emotional distress. This signal may be unpleasant, but is infinitely preferable to the greater unpleasantness of whole webs of deception or dangerous influences being given a platform by mistake. It's a little bit like a car alarm. It may be very annoying when it goes off, but it's less aggravating than a break-in would be! The danger in this would obviously be to make too much of someone's subjectivity. The gift is operating only as an early warning system which should set off more than one alarm.

> As a student in north London years ago, during a meeting I was leading I momentarily felt slightly uneasy. It was enough to raise a question mark in me about the appropriateness of what the person speaking was saying. I was already aware of who in the group could be depended upon as 'detectors', so although everyone's eyes were closed I glanced over at little Christina Goh, who, sure enough, was shaking and tearful, obviously beginning to be distressed, and I also saw big Steve Ford frowning uneasily – both with their eyes still closed, and no conferring. The situation was immediately able to be resolved.

There may not always be two independent witnesses.

> Some years ago a girl we knew used to walk to work each morning. She couldn't understand why suddenly as she was walking she would want to throw up some days, but not on other days. And it always happened when she wasn't feeling ill at all. Eventually she spotted the connection. It was always when she happened to walk past a particular man on her way. Subsequent enquiries revealed that he was a spiritualistic medium.

A similar recognition occurs when the Holy Spirit is strongly at work. The gift of discerning of spirits may draw your attention to something that God is doing, so that you can appreciate this and align with it. We are reminded that when the pregnant Mary visited the pregnant Elizabeth, the baby John leapt in his mother's womb, recognising that Jesus was nearby.

Gifts of healings

Exaggerated claims and sensational journalism make many uneasy and wary of 'miracle mongering'. Much that is said about healing is highly emotive and inappropriate. Yet people hope against hope for miracle cures, and the severely distressed are especially vulnerable to exploitation.

There are many sorts of healings, and many gifts that facilitate these. Opinions vary as to what proportion of modern ailments are psychosomatic, or partly psychosomatic, in their causes. Prayer ministry and the laying on of hands are often scorned as effective only as 'mind over matter' in the case of psychosomatic illnesses. Since no one else seems to have any solutions for these either, even that would be a start . . . Could it also be a symptom of increased dis-integration in our day, that so much attention seems to need to be given to the area of inner healing – for example, the healing of traumatic memories, etc?

To give someone your time and availability, the love and focus of prayer, can often occasion their healing through dramatic improvement in their physical or emotional condition. The words attributed to Francis of Assisi say, 'Lord, make me an instrument of your peace: where there has been hatred let me sow love, and pardon where there has been injury. Grant that I may not so much seek to be understood as to understand, to be loved as to show love.'

Gifts of healings are gifts through one person, the instrument, to another, and various tools may be employed in accomplishing the task. The gift of 'the knowing' of what is wrong, or what is the cause, will often precede attention to the problem.

Simplicity of trust may also allow the healing to happen.

> David Nellist remarked that in the Philippines when he talked about Jesus, and said God's power was still at work today, the people surged forward for prayer, and it was not unusual for 80 per cent to be healed immediately of whatever condition troubled them. Still more reported gradual recoveries. In the UK, the equivalent prayer ministry met with negligible results. He concluded that, here, we come equipped with all the reasons why we might not be healed, and take those same reasons, and our condition, back with us.

It seems that no one really understands healing. Sometimes, the person trying to bring healing does all they know to do but to no avail. The danger, then, is to conclude that God wants the person to be unwell, or that it is somehow their fault they have not been healed. Just because we haven't all the answers, should we refrain from reaching in the toolbox at all?

> In 1976 during the bicentennial events in Boston, New England, Kay was experiencing discomfort with her throat, and lost her voice. Since her task that day was to talk to people in the city she asked if I would pray with her for a healing. I 'laid hands' on her head briefly as we travelled in on the coach, and said to grab me later if she was no better. The sense for me subjectively was that she had been immediately made better, so I was surprised to have to repeat the exercise later. By the third time she approached me, in tears, I was thoroughly confused. 'As far as I know, you should be healed – it seemed to me like you were.' But her

body didn't seem to know anything about it. We were sitting on the steps behind the platform at Tremont Temple. The meeting was about to begin and the other musicians were waiting for me, so I had to leave her at that. George Otis Jr gave a talk about reconciliation between family members, and at the end of the meeting Kay shouted me over. 'I realised when he was speaking how I'd never forgiven my father for how he'd hurt me, and the moment I released that resentment my throat was completely better.'

It may be stating the obvious to say that healing itself will nearly always be a good thing, but true healing will not have any strings attached, any harmful side-effects, nor create inappropriate dependency or indebtedness.

Defying the nature of things

Many things that were once thought of as miracles can now be rationally explained. This does not mean they never happened, just that now we have analysed how. It was said to be a scientific impossibility for the bumble bee to fly, because its body was too heavy for its wings, but since the little bumble bee never read a book on science, it just kept on flying! In a similar way, things have a habit of happening, to some people who don't see them as improbable, that appear to disregard or bend natural laws. Sometimes a person is healed, and subsequent tests show not just an improved condition but organs whole and in place that had actually been surgically removed.

We were just about to eat, and it was Joe's turn to cook. The doorbell rang – with impeccably bad timing. 'Oh no,' he groaned, 'go and see who that is. I need to serve up. And whoever it is, I hope they've eaten already.' The visitors arrived – acquaintances of a friend of ours who had apparently arranged to meet up with them at our flat. They soon confided that they were grateful to be asked to share our evening meal, having had nothing since breakfast. I struggled to make conversation, but was much distracted by Joe appearing from the kitchen, and standing, looking very confused, behind the settee on which they were sitting, exiting and returning a while later, pan in hand, jumping up and down twice, leaving again, and eventually serving up sufficient quantities of food. 'What was all that about,' I asked him later, 'all that business with the pan?' 'Well, I asked God to make it all right, and to let there be enough to eat,' he said; 'then I started to serve up, and there seemed to be more than enough. That's funny, I thought. So I tried putting it back in the pan, and it wouldn't fit!' A similar thing happened for him a week or two later. It sounds improbable, but I do remember that I ate the meal.

Believing without the power to doubt

This is the power to believe that something is going to happen, to believe it so strongly that it is impossible to imagine anything else, any other outcome. All action will then be in harmony with this belief, but it is not the power of 'positive thinking', nor is it even a decision to believe; it is as if, in this instance, that belief has been given as a present which need only be unwrapped. No amount of struggling would have worked up belief of this kind: it is given, or it is not.

Speech in other tongues

This controversial phenomenon has always been a feature of Pentecostalism and of the charismatic movement in traditional churches of all kinds and those outside these denominations. It both offends and appeals precisely because it requires a non-rational jump, a 'leap of faith' that not only perceives it to be possible to experience in theory but requires an experimental opening up to the Holy Spirit in a way that is an affront to our self-sufficiency. It does not require us to be an irrational and unthinking person before, after or during this experience; rather, it allows the possibility of our thinking mind being by-passed as our 'spirit' itself is activated to pray. This comes from deeper within us than thought itself, groanings that could otherwise not be uttered. It is at all times our self – our deep self at a level in touch with, but deeper than, all thought, emotion or memory – that is speaking; the Spirit of God only activates this, unlocking a new voice within. We are not taken over or possessed. We are not in a trance-like state or unable to reflect calmly upon what is happening: mental awareness is, if anything, heightened and sensitised. The words we may then be speaking will be in language we would not naturally understand. Someone else may well understand what we are saying, if they happened to know the language. The language used may even differ from time to time, but the content will always be us expressing what is deep inside or addressing God on someone else's behalf.

My first visit to a liberal synagogue with a Jewish friend was a fascinating privilege, but I became frustrated at being unable to join in the sung service. The Hebrew text was considerately translated on the opposite pages of the service book which, of course, read from back to front, but it was difficult to follow how far through we were. I just turned the page too, whenever my friend did. Tentatively, I began to sing a little in tongues under my breath. The melody line of the sung service went all over the place without, as far as I could see, any recurring tune or predictable pattern. I only hoped my singing softly would not clash noticeably. It didn't seem to, so I grew a little bolder and for a while seemed to have found the trail of the melody. I broke off for a moment (to blow my nose), and inside me was aware of what I would have been singing in tongues (had I not been blowing my nose). Meanwhile, my friend Pete beside me and the man in front seemed to be singing the exact same words and tune as I would have been. I finished blowing my nose and with some confidence joined in. Pete looked at me quizzically: since when had I learned Hebrew?

Interpretation

When tongues are used, half of the value will be lost if the content is not then articulated in language that can be understood by the speaker and, especially, anyone else who has heard what was spoken. This, in itself, may be a profound sign to someone who has had no belief in a God who would intervene at such a level. It would be possible that what was spoken in another language/ tongue was on behalf of the hearer, and articulated the very secrets of their heart in a language not learned by the speaker but familiar to the hearer. More often it will be in language accessible to neither of them. The hearer may feel stirred, as if the emotional content of what is spoken is articulating something on their behalf. If the speaker or another person then speaks out that content in normal language, the hearer is doubly amazed and quite clear that that is what has happened. Whoever customarily prays in tongues should adopt the discipline of pausing periodically and articulating in their own language what- ever content was not there previously. With use this becomes equally fluent and offsets any confusion in the mind of anyone who may overhear by chance. There may be times when it is not appropriate to interpret, usually when praying for something intimate or confidential, or in direct conflict with demonic influences.

Prophecy

The screwdriver of the toolbox. Everybody should know how to use it. 'Would that you all might prophesy!' said Paul, and in the Old Testament there is a story which stresses the same idea:

> The elders of the tribes all were summoned to the Tent of Meeting. There the Spirit of God came down on all 70 of them, no, on 68 of them. The other two had the Spirit of God come down on them too, but they hadn't made it to the meeting, so it happened as they were crossing the campsite on their way! All 70 of them began to prophesy, speaking out what they felt God was saying, all the things that were on his heart. A messenger ran to the Tent of Meeting. 'Moses, Moses, come quick! Eldad and Medad are prophesying out there in the middle of the campsite.' Joshua, Moses' assistant, said immediately, 'You'd better go and tell them to stop it! I'll keep an eye on things here while you're gone.' 'Stop them?' said Moses. 'I wish all the people would prophesy like that!'
> (Numbers 11:24-29)

Prophecy is simply endeavouring to hear what is on God's heart for a person or situation. When appropriate, we may then share these insights directly or in conversation, by letter or phone. Sometimes these insights should be stored in our heart until the 'right' time. At no time should prophecy be directive – telling someone what to do in a way that is controlling or manipulative, or would undermine their own responsibility to discern a course of action and make decisions. Where such a 'word' is given it may appear directive, but it will only serve to confirm independently the decision or direction a person has already settled upon. They must have the freedom to:

i. reject the 'word' because they don't like it, even if it is right;

ii. not respond to the 'word' because it doesn't seem appropriate or in line with what has already been happening in their heart;

iii. ask you not to try to speak into their life and/or circumstances at this time. You may not have earned the right or been given the permission to do so.

Chapter 2

Odd jobs

When people are insecure and unsure of their identity, carrying expensive tools and equipment around might help them feel important for a while. But they soon see something deeper is required to bring them identity. They are likely to place all their expectation now upon the second box in the pile instead and try to get their identity from that. This box too has a fancy name. It says, 'Vocation – What do I get to do?' On the spine, where there is less room to write, we simply read 'Jobs'.

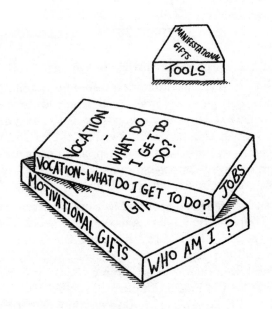

Pyramids or saucers?

One relevant factor in considering 'What do I get to do?' is my perception of the structures into which whatever I do get to do fits. Do I see it as part of some hierarchical structure where a privileged few are perched on high with status, responsibility and visibility? (The glory of the Pharaohs on the broken backs of many slaves.) Or do I see myself as part of a structure which is shaped to encourage reciprocal respect and mutual support?

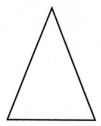

To use a clear example in a religious setting:

In the Roman Catholic tradition before the Second Vatican Council the pecking order was assumed to be God, acknowledged Saints of varying importance, then the Pope and Cardinals and Magisteria, Bishops and Priests, then the busy Nuns in the school or parish, and finally, under the weight of all this imposing authority, the company of the faithful – ordinary Christian people.

Vatican II changed all that, and its ripples are continuing to spread outwards to this day. A more useful model now, it was said, was to see the Church as one big saucer into which is thrown all the people of God in their varying giftedness. The Pope is in there and our Jimmy and his girlfriend and Sister Luke and Fred from down the street. The priest no longer has to be expected to do everything; other believers must also share in the task of evangelising and teaching and visiting and so on. The most strongly gifted in this model will not be imposing authority from above, but, if anything, will sink to the bottom of the saucer and undergird the company of the faithful and gently prod their gifts to the surface. They will be the servants of all.

There are many families, firms, and even non-denominational churches which are shaped far more like the pyramids of Egypt. This is not in itself necessarily a bad thing. But it does seem that in most of society there is a trend towards introducing saucer-structure expectations, or giving the illusion that management is less prescriptive, more inclined to listen.

Suddenly everyone is invited to contribute their skills and ideas, a process which becomes a delightful opportunity for some to put what they have to offer on to the table. Others lack the necessary confidence to share easily and are intimidated by other people's impressive contributions. Even pooling sandwiches for lunch makes them feel inferior. It is like wearing a big sign round their neck on which is written the word 'WORTHLESS'. Until they have the courage – or are given the permission – to tear up the sign and throw it away, they are unlikely to reach under the table for whatever they have brought with them in their own carrier bag and share their gift with anyone else. It may take someone else to act like a grown-up who takes charge and gets them to bring out what they have.

Have I got what it takes to contribute at my own initiative or will I always be waiting for someone else to prompt or reassure me? Will I finally get to be a 'grown-up' myself? Grown-ups can give direction, or can be self-directive; they can also accept direction.

Esteem and recognition

So, what do I get to do? – it seems we all want to know! Imagine the preparations for the school nativity play . . .

'. . . the cow had the best costumes, but I think I want to get to be a shepherd. I think I was *born to be* a shepherd.'

'What do I get to do?'

'You get to operate the sound desk . . . you make the sky light up . . . your picture got chosen for the poster design.'

'The shepherds had to be the ones with *very loud voices*, and I was the *first one chosen* . . .'

For the children it is important not just to be doing something, but in doing so to have esteem and recognition, a way of being included.

Roles

In practice most of us fulfil many jobs in the course of our daily life. The same person may be chief-cook-and-bottle-washer at home, boss in the office, an employee, a trade union member, a husband, a father, member of the local rugby club, a best friend, a next-door neighbour. He manages to juggle all these responsibilities, and usually doesn't have any problem relating differently in each of these distinct roles; should one of these discontinue the others remain. He may adopt a different attitude or tone of voice according to which role he is fulfilling. At a deeper level he remains himself. This truth we hold to be self-evident. What can be dangerous is if the one person actually only sees himself as the sum total of the roles he plays. If he has to be a different face to each person, who is he really when everyone else has gone away?

Decisions . . . decisions . . .

> We have a range of choices which for most of history would have been in the realm of mythological fantasy – choices of occupation, of place of residence, of marriage, or the number of one's children, in the manner of passing one's leisure time, in the acquisition of material goods . . .*

In his book *The Heretical Imperative*, Peter Berger contrasts the lifestyle of a modern passenger in a jet plane crossing the Indonesian archipelago with that of the Javanese villagers who glance up at the plane overhead:

> He moves on the same planet but in an altogether different world. His space is measured in thousands of miles, theirs by the distance a bullock cart can go. He moves with breath-taking speed, they move in the slow rhythms set long ago by tradition . . . With its multiplication of options, modern consciousness entails a movement from fate to choice. †

(It has always been theoretically possible to marry someone deemed unsuitable or to travel far away in search of a different life, to make friendships that cross cultural taboos or to challenge long-held beliefs and assumptions. But in primitive society most people will continue to live lives in harmony with what is expected of them.)

---

* Peter Berger, *The Heretical Imperative* (1979, Anchor Press, Garden City)
† Ibid.

In traditional societies marriage, family, work, culture and friendship are likely to be experienced in one location, overlapping and intensely contained, a rich culture reinforced by each experience. In contrast, it is not always easy for us to know what our context should be.

For us, the spheres are often stretched far apart so we may live far from our work, with widely dispersed families, different social networks, interests and pursuits. Frequently there is a huge divide between the worlds of work and leisure, public and private life.

With increased specialisation and increased separation of the varied spheres of life, it is easy to feel distanced from whoever is supposed to be protecting our interests, and feel confronted by faceless systems and anonymous decisions.

Many of us have felt alienated from the world of work, of government, systems and politics, and have looked to the world of home, family and leisure pursuits for our sense of well-being before venturing once more into increasingly hostile working environments or public institutions. If we opt just to withdraw to where we feel we already have a voice and some influence, at home or with our friends, we may have resigned ourselves by default to be publicly irrelevant, the victim of these systems, and not a questioning voice or organiser of change in the wider world.

Will I simply close the curtains on whatever is happening outside?

This is your life

At a big eighteenth birthday party it was interesting to see neighbours and family friends, a large group of extended family from different parts, and then the girl's own contemporaries from school or college with their dates, all gathered in one village hall, separate circles overlapping to include her and to toast her future. In a way, at this stage in her life, this is her world, gathered for an hour or two in one place, with her as its central focus. Each of us has a world like that, even if its components never overlap, even if it remains a 'notional world'.

At a funeral recently the church was packed out with people: friends, neighbours, relatives, work colleagues, and others who had arrived separately, stood and wept, then left. They were from different worlds to each other, and only one person linked them all.

What I do and how I am could affect any of the people I am connected with, or impact countless strangers in some way. This is true whether I am conscious of it or not. Each contact with me can be life-increasing or life-decreasing for someone else. It is important that I take my unique place and occupy it rather than abdicate responsibility for the influence I unconsciously exert.

Spheres of life (and stairways to heaven?)

Seeing how you spend your *self* in the intersecting spheres of your life could be much more crucial than any financial inventory. You need to be wiser than the lady in Led Zeppelin's song* who trusted that enough gold could buy 'a stairway to heaven'. Such stairways cannot be bought or sold, but their points of departure

* *Led Zeppelin IV* album, Jimmy Page / Robert Plant, 1971, Atlantic Records

may be discerned amongst the extraordinary/ordinary spheres of life which concern us all to some extent, spheres of marriage or relationships, family, work, culture and friendship. These are the places where often we long to derive meaning, have a sense of belonging, or feel we can make an impact. These spheres of possibility are each person's world; in some or all of them they invest their energies. Sometimes different spheres make conflicting demands. A deadline for work requires someone to put in extra hours, but their little daughter may not understand this. The market place seems adept at taking, but not giving. Maybe even one person could begin challenging some assumptions and set a series of small but significant changes in motion?

Still yourself for a moment. Take a deep breath, then take inventory of your circumstances in each of these

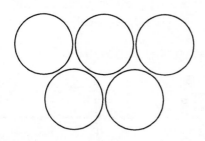

spheres, your achievements and failures, the labels and expectations other people try to put upon you, and your emotional responses to what is mentioned. It was when I heard Jim Thwaites from Australia speak about occupying these 'spheres' that I undertook a radical reappraisal of how I was investing my life and began challenging others to do the same.*

The gift of who I am will be expressed in the places where I live out my life. These broadly may be labelled: State of Life, Family, Work, Culture and Friendship.

So what is your life in each of these 'spheres'?

---

* Jim Thwaites, *The Church beyond the Congregation* (1999, Paternoster Press, Carlisle)

Where am I at? – personal inventory

There are no right or wrong answers at this juncture – only honest assessments of where you are right now.

1. State of life

How would you describe your present circumstances on the relationship front? For example:

single?
married?
widowed?
celibate?
outcome not yet determined?
presently licking wounds?
prefer own company?
serious serial heartbreaker?
other . . .

Our current marital status, be it elective or circumstantial, has huge knock-on effects and implications. The time, energy, finance and flexibility available in other areas of life are directly impacted.

2. Family

Who is family for me?

The family you started – children of your own?
Or the family you started with – parents, brothers, sisters?
Or the family that has adopted you – friends who accept you unconditionally and make room for you?

What was your immediate response?

3. What do I get to do?

For many people their paid employment is their work, what they get to do. For others that kind of work is not possible, or is simply not enough, and for them the question becomes 'What *else* do I get to do?'

Your answer may be a combination of these things, your employment, other involvements or projects.

4. What is your distinctive cultural identity?

What are your own interests, likes and dislikes? How do you choose to live your life? What makes you instantly recognisable or memorable? In what ways have you broken the mould of your upbringing, or resisted the pressures to conform to what people around you expect?

5. Who are my friends?

Who do I enjoy being with, and choose to share my life with?

The sections that follow are an opportunity to visit these questions more carefully. (In the next chapter we will begin to consider our *innateness* or motivation, but before that it is wise to take stock of our *involvements.)*

State of life

Marriage? celibacy? waiting? or whatever!

It has been said, 'When you love somebody all your saved-up wishes start coming out' and what happens then is up for grabs.

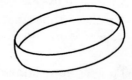

40

Is marriage my destiny? For someone at their eighteenth birthday party the question may not seem urgent. For someone already married for many years it may be crucial. The decision to marry might have been taken years ago, but the moment-by-moment decision to occupy or abdicate is ever-present.

> Marriage is an honourable institution, but who wants to live in an institution? *(Groucho Marx)*

A good marriage is a touching-place for two people, at times it can even seem like heaven on earth. (Some marriages are more like a living hell!)

In fabric design, where there is a gradual blending of one colour with another it is described as 'bleeding'. In a committed relationship both partners bring their unique colour and pattern to the fabric. But part of the design is that here heaven can bleed into earth, a distinctive shimmer is added that catches the light at each turn. I like the word 'bleeds' because of its other association of sustaining wounds. Even the best relationships require struggle and sacrifice and huge emotional investment to be aglow with energy and tenderness year after year. It is also true that addressing some crisis or painful circumstances can be the times we instinctively reach beyond ourselves and touch depths in relationship we did not know were possible. 'Heaven' is closer to us than our own hands and feet, as near as breathing, and where better to discover this than in a marriage?*

---

* Ben was delighted when Joyce 'became a Christian'. It did wonders for their marriage. He recommended it to his friends, and said that their wives should have a similar makeover. He widened the circle of their friends to include many of the new people she had met. But six and a half years later Ben was still touched by heaven only through Joyce. A persistent back problem and a work trip to Bristol took him to visit Ron McCatty, who was a practising qualified

Simply to maintain a touching-place in our relation-ship and to keep the sense of connection alive is attain-able, sustainable. To be too idealistic can bring blame and disappointment.

> 'What is it you want out of this relationship?' she said.*
>
> I replied ironically, 'What does anyone want out of a relation-ship? I want a placental relationship (like the baby has in the womb with its placenta) where the other mediates the world to me, is always there, meets all my needs and is everything!' I thought she'd understood me, until I got a letter from her saying, 'I've been thinking over what you said, and I think it's more than I can offer you . . .'
>
> Of course it was!

No one relationship can meet every need or be everything to us – it's too much to expect, even from the best of relation-ships. But most of us still want that significant other.

On one of her albums Kathy Mattea sings about a woman called Clare who had 'all but given up when she and Edwin fell in love'.† 'Where've you been?' she says. 'I've looked for you for ever and a day.' They never spent

---

osteopath, but also a preacher who prayed with people for healing. Joyce travelled with Ben to Bristol, and waited outside the room while Ben had his back worked on. 'They're a long time in there,' she thought. Ben was on the osteopathy couch. He was medium height, solid, very stubborn and very self-assured, but with a sore back. Ron was a big, tall black man with a very deep voice and a slight advantage. He was also working hard on Ben's back, saying, '*How* long you gonna hold out then? *How* long you gonna hold out then?' Ben emerged somewhat sheepishly to tell Joyce what had transpired. Afterwards he recounted the story to me, confidentially remarking, 'You've no idea how hard it is to accept God in your underpants!'

The more I think about that unforgettable statement the more my response is, 'If not there, then where?' If heaven touches us, it must be Access All Areas – accepted everywhere or not at all.

* My own early relationship with Anna!

† 'Where've you been?' by Jon Vezner and Don Henry © 1988, Wrensong Publ. Corp. Featured on Kathy Mattea, *Willow in the Wind* (1989, Mercury/Polygram Records) and *Kathy Mattea – A Collection of Hits* (1990, Mercury/Polygram)

a night apart; for years she always heard him snore. But then they're in a hospital 'in separate beds on different floors'. Clare never spoke another word until one day they wheeled him in beside her. He held her hand, stroked her hair. She opened her eyes, and in a fragile voice she whispered, 'Where've you been . . .?'

We expect the happily-ever-after we heard of as children (or aspire to the no-strings-attached popularity of a successful single person).

But together turns into 'alone again'.

For some 'alone again' is the ongoing pain of bereavement. For others it is the pain of abandonment or disappointment. Some will choose to not get involved again, to retain their emotional independence. Some bounce from one relationship to another, run from one encounter to the next. Part of them is given and taken with each experience, and as partner after partner walks away they feel increasingly spent and fragmented. The ties that bind them to past lovers need cutting if they are to be whole again. Reintegration or 'shalom': the Hebrew word is often translated as 'peace', but it conveys the sense of a much greater blessing – 'May all your bits come together in the right places.' We need to make peace with the past and where possible move on. The past cannot be made to *not happen*. As Ronald Rolheiser says in his book *Forgotten Among the Lilies*,* even God cannot unscramble an egg. But the prospect shalom speaks of is the possibility of 'living happily and with renewed innocence far beyond any egg we may have scrambled'.

For some people the challenge is to experience shalom in situations where they feel trapped, unheard or unloved.

---

* Ronald Rolheiser, *Forgotten Among the Lilies* (1990, Hodder and Stoughton, London)

Can we live beyond damage or 'creeping separateness' and find a touching place again? Do we really believe that promises are for keeps?

What does the sphere of marriage mean for the avowed celibate? Continuing in a promise is not enough – it must be chosen and renewed again and again.* Celibacy, like marriage, must be chosen, moment by moment, for life, not slow decay.

If we do not occupy, then we abdicate by default. It is too easy to live our lives in brackets, waiting for that relationship to be sorted, for someone to change everything, or the pain finally to go away. Whatever else happens, the decision must be made to live life fully, even in a waiting time.

Some people choose to be single: for others it is a decision that happens by default. Alone is not the same as lonely. An unhappy relationship can be lonelier than no relationship at all. But alone or together we can choose life in the now, and not waste a moment of it in regret.

Family matters

What does family mean to you?
Who is family for you?

There has never been a time in history when all families were happy. In truth, every family has bad and good in it, and each person in that family is a mixture of good and bad too. Sadly, some  youngsters' experience of family growing-up is one of

---

* I'll never forget a religious Brother talking about nuns, and saying that so many of them were like dried-up old prunes or a valley of dried bones! Then you meet others, he said, bright-eyed, radiant and fully present.

shame. For them it is not an option to bring friends home. They gaze longingly at the warmth they see in a more 'normal' family just as we on a cold winter's night might linger for a few moments if through some window we caught a glimpse of a cosy fireside.

A child who grows up knowing they have been adopted is usually given unconditional support and acceptance but often will face the eventual dilemma of whether to also seek contact with a birth parent.

When a couple split up it is as if a family photograph were torn down the middle. Their children become estranged from one parent or spend the rest of their lives travelling between the two, even if the parents settle more happily with new partners.

It may be that you were raised by one parent or have become a single parent now yourself.

People no longer have families as a matter of course. Today we take for granted that a couple can postpone the decision to 'start a family', then attempt to 'space' any children they do have. We expect sex without consequent pregnancy. Some happily married couples decide that children would disrupt their lifestyle irreversibly and opt to pursue their careers and still spend time with each other. They choose childlessness because either they don't want children of their own or they recognise there are only so many things you can do in one lifetime!

Others wait until they are in a secure relationship, have more financial stability, or even until they have already travelled extensively, before they think about becoming parents. Having waited until they were ready, some find that achieving pregnancy can be even harder than avoiding it, and may even discover that adoption agencies turn them away, favouring younger couples. Meanwhile, one more woman in the same town has agreed that it would be better to face a termination than an ill-timed pregnancy or giving birth to an 'unwanted' child.

Society has painful double standards. People can proudly pass around images of their scan during a pregnancy, and it is 'cool' to speak openly about sex. Yet in this same climate there is no general permission for anyone to talk about their experiences of abortion even years afterwards – they are expected to behave as if nothing ever happened.

The current fascination with researching family trees coincides with a time in history when more people feel adrift from any deep consciousness of their cultural roots and the continuity of family ties.

Often reaching a similar stage in our own lives gives us new insights or a real appreciation of what our parents went through, or what those in previous generations experienced, their strengths and sacrifices. Responsibility for children can awaken a sense of connectedness with our roots, childhood memories and the passing on of customs and traditions. Those without children may still look for significance in their past, finding their sense of how their family line has led to them.

Parenthood can be very demanding when children are small, and, as they grow, the responsibility changes rather than disappears. In trying to be good parents, the temptation is to begin seeing your children's achievements as an extension of your own, or an affirmation of their upbringing.*

The weight of your expectations can become an intolerable burden for them. A child needs to know they are unconditionally loved and accepted, even when their

---

* It is hard to find time and energy to be a couple when being a parent is so all-consuming. When the baby is finally asleep, and the couple have determined not to spend their child-free time talking about their child, they may suddenly look at each other and ask, 'What did we talk about before?'

behaviour or lack of achievement is disappointing. To be loved and believed in gives any individual a strong foundation of affirmation and self-worth. Somehow time must be carved out so that each child has opportunity to speak about whatever interests or concerns them. Too easily that time is deferred – 'Not now, I'm busy' – and the habit of sharing naturally is broken.

> If we listen to them when they are 5, 6 or 7, they may listen to us when they're 15, 16 or 17.*

A child is not a matching accessory, added on to our adult world like an afterthought, but a unique other person to know and be known by. Ironically, for many parents prioritising quality time with their kids is the consolation prize when a marriage breaks up and they see the danger of losing the children too. When you listen to someone enough to know them as who they are, you are less likely to imprison them in a web of your own expectations, the prison of who you would like them to be. Instead there comes acceptance and room to grow – parent *and* child.

When people have an extended family – aunts, uncles, grandparents, cousins – it is very probable that many of them live at a distance in other parts of the country, or even abroad. Involvement is harder to maintain than when relatives lived only a street away and babysitting was usually kept within the family. It is too easy to lose contact altogether.

In Jewish culture there is a particular emphasis placed on the importance of family ties, and in the Hebrew scriptures a key passage from Isaiah is a warning not to turn your back on your own flesh and blood. If you determine to take heed of this, it says, then your ruined

---

* Rob Parsons, *The Sixty-Minute Father* (1995, Hodder and Stoughton, London)

places shall be rebuilt, your light will dawn in obscurity, and your own springs will not fail (Isaiah 58). When family relationships have been a catalogue of pain, bitterness, accusation and quarrelling, it is often easier and more peaceful to withdraw completely. It is a remarkable achievement if parents and grown children are able to make the transition and find new relationships with each other as adults, unimprisoned by blame, nostalgia, projections or judgements. Yet it also seems true that the rewards are even greater when we persevere and maintain contact in spite of difficulties from the past: our own ruined places are able to be rebuilt; forgiveness, honour and respect finally begin to flow.

Part of the significance of family is the keeping of memories and the valuing of past experiences.* In some families a wonderful relationship develops between children and grandparents. Of course, they are natural allies, but more than that they can awaken in each other a sense of wonder – 'Were you little once, a long time ago?' The past is a different country; they do things differently there. Grandparents have travelled from the past, and carry its echoes inside them.

In today's culture youth is idealised and celebrated at the expense of seniority or experience.† Image quickly becomes everything, and respect for even inherent wisdom recedes. Our 'sell-by date' is pushed earlier and earlier. A

---

* In some cultures 'family' impacts every area of life – a family business, the people you meet, the choice of whom you marry, what everyone expects of you. Some people will do anything to stick up for their family. In extreme cases of family loyalty, animosity or an ongoing feud can continue from generation to generation!

† 'She wasted all her school time wanting to be the age she is now, and she'll waste all the rest of her life trying to stay that age. Her whole idea is to race on to the silliest time of one's life as quick as she can and then stop there as long as she can.' (C. S. Lewis, *The Last Battle*)

point can be reached where you expect to achieve little more in your own life, and where you expect more that is of interest to happen in the lives of your children (or grandchildren!).

We begin life dependent upon others, and if we survive long enough it is likely we will lose some of the independence we take for granted. Sometimes family can be relied upon to care for day-to-day needs; sometimes they are the ones who care and worry from a distance.

Family occasions such as Christmas (or Thanksgiving) can be times when those who have died or are at a distance are missed most keenly, and people on their own feel the most isolated.

Where family fails, is absent or non-existent, we do well to surround ourselves with neighbours, friends or others who care. These become our 'family', a place of belonging, a safe space to return to.

Jobs: What do you do?

Not long ago Joyce and Ben Williams were teaching a seminar about this material with over 40 people. Joyce placed three boxes one on top of the other as she spoke about giftedness. Then she would replace them with more vivid symbols of these areas of giftedness. She knew she would use a chocolate box to represent the innate motivational gifts which are the foundational box. She had recently won a box of chocolates, and was prepared to open it and share them out. For the top box she used Ben's metal concertina-style tool-box. But what could appropriately represent the middle 'Jobs' box? Finally it occurred to her: a very thick Yellow Pages directory. If you need a job doing, the Yellow Pages helps you to find the person able to help you.

Child-minding – Coffin-makers – Double glazing installers – Graffiti removal – Greyhound training – Grout injection – Hairpiece retailers – Haulage – Osteopaths – Plant and machinery hire – Self-defence – Solicitors – Systems analysis – Travel insurance: the range of entries is an education in itself.

The list of jobs and occupations is endless. These jobs vary in their degrees of difficulty and prestige.* Some jobs are well-paid, but not intrinsically satisfying. Also to be considered is the impact of the job on other spheres of a person's life. This can be considerable when it is necessary to travel, to work shifts or frequently be 'on call'.

It is ideal if we can sink into the happy tiredness at the end of the day which comes from a task completed, a job well done, the satisfaction of having worked hard at something worthwhile, but this is not our universal experience. No amount of social conditioning or engineering can guarantee this! The chief advantage of education may be to increase the range of possibilities a person may imagine. Ability, aptitude and training are also factors limiting the range of opportunities available, but the envisaging of possibilities may be crucial. Big risks may

---

* Fishing, farming and mining were always occupations where the ground or the sea yields up its produce as a return for worker's labours. George Mackay Brown in a passage from his novel *Magnus* extends this picture further to include many occupations: 'Man offers the first-fruits of his labour to the creator of everything in the universe, stars and cornstalks and grains of dust. This is not to say however that man is simply a brutish breaker of furrows, but he labours well in a variety of trades also, with stone and with loom and with oar and with harp and with law-book and with sweet ordering of words and with prism, towards some end which is likewise a kind of harvest. Well he knows that he could not call himself man at all unless he labours all his time under the sun to encompass the end for which his faculties were given to him. This end, whatever the nature of his occupation, is his harvest time (and he would be a poor labourer that would not wish, among all that broken gold, to offer back a tithe or a hundredth into the hands that formed the original fecund dust).' (1973, Hogarth Press, London)

need to be taken and big rocks hurled at the mould of what circumstances dictate.

Financial remuneration may be a poor gauge of how important our work is. For instance, paid childcare may be costly, but the unsalaried sustaining care shown by a parent or relative is of incalculable worth.*

Keeping a home together may be intrinsically worth-while, but for some people this will not be enough. They must make their mark in a wider sphere or maintain a wider perspective to keep their sanity. For others, petty irritations or the perpetual pressure of too much to be done can rob them of the continual joy in the present moment which precedes a 'happy tiredness' or even a happy exhaustion. A vocational approach to work does not exempt us from stress, but it does keep our sights on the belief that what we are engaged in is in the end worthwhile.†

---

* This was the reply of a mother of three to the dreaded question 'Do you work?': 'Actually, I do work. I'm involved in a programme of social development. At present I'm working with three age groups. First, toddlers: that involves a basic grasp of child psychology and medicine. Second, teenagers. I confess the programme is not going too well in that area. Third, in the evenings and at weekends, I work with a man aged 39 who is exhibiting all the classic symptoms of mid-life crisis – that's mainly psychiatric work. For the whole job you have to be a brilliant planner, have a "can-do" mentality and have a degree in conflict resolution. I used to be an international fashion model, but I got bored.' (Quoted in Rob Parsons, *Sixty Minute Marriage*, 2000, Hodder and Stoughton, London)

† A few years ago we were sent a letter at Christmastime from Laura Messina and her husband Brian in which she talked about their 'vision' for car-wash. I hooted with laughter. It was a job Brian had been working at, and the possibilities of expansion seemed endless. She spoke of it in glowing terms, but I found the language odd, to have 'vision for car-wash'. Years later, when they have worked hard, and he now manages a series of car-wash places, has built a house on a hill with its own land, provided security for them and their five children, and is still excited about the car-wash business, the words seem far more appropriate to me than they did at that time. Laura and Brian had the 'vision' of what it could be back then – I did not.

The world at large has a bad habit of labelling people according to what they do and assessing their value accordingly. People will often be asked on a first meeting or introduction, 'What do you do?' – or in the States, even worse, 'What do you earn?' Accordingly, you are a farmer, an osteopath, a bricklayer or watchmaker or whatever. It is self-evident, if we think about it, that this misses the point, and minimises, or hides, the person's true identity. If a person changes his job he remains at a more basic level himself, although people's expectations of him on meeting him could well be different – because of their preconceptions.*

Jim Wallis on a visit to the UK from the States was confused to hear a girl explaining to him that her brother had been made redundant. 'What do you mean?' he said. 'My brother's out of work – he lost his job.' 'And that made him redundant? How can a person be redundant?' We are so familiar with the expression that we never think to question its underlying assumption; it took Jim Wallis from another country with different use of the same language to be surprised by the word.

Some people work hard all their lives and look forward to a well-earned retirement, then don't know what to do with all their time. They feel like a spare part or lose interest in everything. This is a sure indication that they themselves had fallen into the trap of equating their

---

* One person we know was a church minister who then relocated to be a lecturer at a college, and later took responsibility for counselling at the same college. For a while he was unemployed, then took on a job as a copyholder in the proof-reading department of the local newspaper. Eventually he was offered the senior pastorate of another church. He was obviously the same person through all these changes of job (however profoundly they might have affected him). But, socially, imagine the different persons you might expect to meet were you introduced to someone as: a minister, a lecturer, someone involved in counselling, a proof-reader, or as someone who is out of work.

value with their function. They think there's nothing left to live for. The same can happen with a person who loses their job too soon to retire, but too late in life to be easily re-employed in a job with similar status.

Like the children as the school nativity play approaches, we all still want to know, 'What do *I* get to do?'

Are you on the lookout for the ideal job which matches your individual profile of abilities, likes and aptitudes? Someone who has enough belief in who they are is less likely to give up and can confidently look for opportunities others would fail to notice. With enough determination and self-discipline, and a realistic appraisal of what you can offer a client or employer, who knows what doors may open for you!* But even automatic doors only open when you walk towards them.

In pursuit of that ideal job you may risk much, and be prepared to make sacrifices, potentially relocate or retrain, and refuse other offers which could have been advantageous.

In contrast to this, you may equally well decide that there's more to life than just work. If you can find (a) a job you do not hate, (b) a tolerable or pleasant work environment, and (c) adequate pay, you'll be better off than most people!

What do you do? And how do you feel about what you do? For some people the world must be demonstrably changed or their life has been a failure; for others, to make it through the day is enough of a struggle.

---

* To identify the elements that are going to be crucial for you to look for in a job, it may be helpful to ask yourself questions about many stages of your childhood, youth and adult life: What have you done? What have you enjoyed? What have you found fulfilling? (See section on 'Who do you think you are?' on page 325.)

Culture: How then shall we live?

The TV show is focused on someone in particular, but their name does not appear in the credits. We go 'Through the Keyhole' and start to explore the house for tell-tale signs, and a general sense of what this person is about. If this was your house what would we

find? What would our impression be? What would be most noticeable? What does looking at your books tell us, for instance?*

Is there a cat flap or dog basket? A piano? A chip-pan? Or an outside barbecue? A large collection of videos or CDs? A demijohn or two with home-made wine on the go? A radio playing to itself in the kitchen? Why has the computer got a picture of Sydney Harbour as its screen-saver? Why would anyone need so many pairs of sun-glasses? There are lots of candles in the bathroom and bedroom but they have never been lit . . . There are shoe-racks full of odd sandals and shoes but not a pair amongst them – could this be a one-legged sun-lover? The records and CDs are exhaustive collections of Leonard Cohen, Dylan and Van Morrison songs – a thoughtful person, then, and we could guess at their age.

Music is full of memories. Some people make it, sing or play, others appreciate it and maybe buy it. For some of us it's very important, for others it's incidental; but it is interesting to ask, 'What is the music that's the sound-track to my life?' Sometimes it is not the most significant

---

* I remember my surprise early in our marriage when my wife insisted that we could only have a few books in our living room because she recognised that for many people it can be intimidating to be surrounded by books! I then remember visiting one couple several times and always wondering where they kept their books, only to finally realise they had hardly any!

songs in terms of their content or associations but a whole genre or style of music. Some people tune in exclusively to classical music.

It may be a negative definition of who we are, but even the things we object to can be a helpful test in establishing our cultural reference points.

> There is a popular TV programme in which the celebrity guest is invited to nominate five things they dislike to be consigned to perpetual oblivion in 'Room 101'. It might be water bills, bad spelling, other people's mobile phones, retail Christmas and the World Bank. Another week someone else might decide the world would be better off to be rid of stiletto heels, brass bands, fox-hunting, drunk drivers and party political broadcasts.

> The things we most dislike or find distasteful can sometimes provoke a stronger reaction or group solidarity than what we appreciate. For instance, in *My Fair Lady* Professor Higgins remarks,

>> 'An Englishman's way of speaking absolutely classifies him –
>> The moment he speaks he makes some other Englishman despise him.'*

The reference is not just to a communication issue. Someone from another place may be hard to understand, but the hostility, dislike or suspicion is more likely to arise from a clash or contrast between two different cultures, the assumptions made from what is associated with the differentials in speech or language. The outward signs – dress, language, lifestyle – may cause others to label someone in terms of that particular culture or 'tribe', and then place expectations on the individual to conform to their stereotype of what a Southerner/Arab/teenager/

---

* Alan Jay Lerner, 'Why can't the English' (1956, Max Reinhard and Constable)

woman driver/Republican is capable of. (Ironically, the identical not very funny jokes surface all round the world at the expense of some ethnicity or other. Irish jokes from Britain are Polish in the US and so on.)

With what money I finally have I can slowly make changes that detach me from the things I most dislike about the life I was born into. Someone whose whole family live within one street of each other may escape to see the wider world by joining the army. A newly qualified doctor with dazzling career prospects may choose to work instead in some third world country and then becomes adopted by its indigenous people and, valuing their customs and way of life, opts ultimately never to return.

A *tribe* is a group you are born into *or* identify with *or* choose. (Not every tribe will allow newcomers to join, of course.) In some societies tribes are readily named and identified.

The sorts of things which make a statement as to which tribe or tribes we belong to are these:

the music we play, and listen to
the way we dress
what we drink
what we drive

Some of these statements may be the shared preferences of a peer group or special interest group. At a young age a group of friends may start to 'support' a football team or wear their hair a particular way. They listen together to the same music which is probably not appreciated by their parents, and it will have strong associations for them for the rest of their lives. They may individuate and follow some preferences that differ from their peers. They may play chess as well as football, appreciate Mozart *and* MTV. The youngster who must have the correct make of trainers to not stand out from the crowd eventually wants to wear something distinctive and individual too, different enough to be interesting but not so unusual that it indicates migration to another tribe!*

The young are quick to identify tribes and differentiate between them because the establishing of identity is an urgent concern.

Each individual has an important voice – it is like putting the colour back in the world. Once people were respected for their social standing and character, and their personality was well known also. The post office and sweetshop, the school, the church, the hardware store were in sight of each other. Social change over the years has created a divide between public and private life so that work and leisure are two distinct worlds. At work we are measured for productivity and efficiency, and at home we are a consumer, valued for our purchasing power and sedated by endless television.

The traditional wisdom voices in society are unable to straddle the widening chasm between public and private life, and increasingly opt for the private side of the divide. The schoolmaster or schoolmistress, the village

---

* Some people choose wine at the supermarket; another tribe meets on Fridays at the pub over real ale. An observant person notices you drink Fair Trade coffee now . . . The Land-Rover is wasted in a built-up area, but it is hard to part with all it represents. A motorbike is replaced by a camper van – the driver wears jeans and a black T-shirt.

Advertisers are eager to identify tribes too and focus on them as distinct markets to be exploited and targeted specifically. So, Guinness drinkers are cool, deep, discerning – pure genius, in fact. Ski yoghurt hit the market as the 'full of fitness food' for all the family. Car commercials are a work of art. A Mercedes Benz is security and safety, gliding silently through the city, so Daddy, won't you buy? It is the dream you would be buying, not just a vehicle.

Children watching TV before Christmas are convinced their life will be over if they do not have whatever the toy was they had never heard of five minutes previously. The advertiser has them convinced quickly – unless they learn to be suspicious and critical.

priest, the family doctor, the elders in the family or village, the keepers of collective memory and many others to trust and refer to are no longer known to us. They have no public influence and our private worlds may rarely coincide. Even the trusted friend may be superceded by the familiar face of a persistent TV presenter. Wisdom is sought from the consistent companion.

So what is culture? In our society what are the elements that constitute and gener- ate culture? We think immediately of the Arts, the develop-

ment of leisure activities and facilities and the 'world' of sport. Communication is another critical element.

Language expresses and describes our experience, and loss of distinctive language muffles the articulation of that experience.* Today we are more aware of a wider world, but less immersed in our local culture and, if we hold it too lightly, are in danger of seeing its distinctives eroded. Decisions are made over our heads by distant and faceless policy makers.

More and more money and energy is poured into our leisure time and the re-inventing of our lifestyle. Arts and entertainment is a major consumer industry. Do-It-Your-self stores and garden centres become weekend shopping destinations. Labour-saving devices and ready-prepared ingredients from under-one-roof hypermarkets minimise the chore factor from tasks that for generations kept everyone busy from sun-up until bedtime. What will we

---

* The Eskimo people have many different words for snow because they know that all snow is not alike. In our own language a few new words are invented or adopted each year, but far more disappear and fall into disuse.

choose to do with all that time we have saved? When our basic needs of housing, clothing, food and fuel are covered we have, hopefully, some 'disposable income'. What will we choose to do with that leftover money? Every retailer wishes to convince us there are certain 'must-have' items on which we should spend it. We become so convinced these really are 'must-haves' that we will spend on them money that was not disposable income at all. Banks and mortgage companies, credit-card operators and car showrooms are kept in business as we live beyond our means. Advertising and availability of products influence or govern consumer choice.

Communication, the Arts and entertainment, sports and leisure, government, politics and social action: these may be the components that define culture, but it is business (money) and media that drive each part of our contemporary culture.

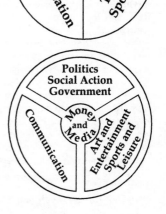

The diagram on the right is from notes I took when listening to Jim Thwaites from Australia.

Now look at the diagram again, but with money and media at the steering wheel, driving and steering our culture!

I was intrigued to learn that the word 'idiot' originally derives from a Greek one, and meant a private person, one only concerned with himself and his family. (By that definition contemporary society is producing more idiots than ever before!) Each of us has a voice, but usually it is effectively stifled, so that we set the world to rights in the safety of our own homes, but do little to influence the course of events affecting larger numbers of people.* Even our own actions and choices are not as free as we suppose. We assume that we will act on the basis of what we believe and hold to be important, but find instead that we have followed the course of least resistance.

People act on the basis of what they believe. This may be very different from what they think they believe. We unconsciously absorb the values and assumptions of the surrounding culture or even programme-makers and advertisers. You do not rule what you believe; rather, what you believe rules you.

---

* In January 2002 I was doing intensive teaching on Motivational Gifts for the staff of Burrswood House of Healing. I drew the sphere of culture diagram on a whiteboard. Joyce and Ben Williams were part of our team for those few days, and Joyce came up to the microphone and said, 'I started going to a church with my friends and I discovered God there. I entered a whole new world of meetings and teachings and healings. But looking at all those words on the diagram I realise every one of them described Ben's world, his work, his friends, his projects, everywhere he belonged and operated. I stayed close to Ben, waiting for him to stop fighting and hand his life over to God. Then he'd move across into my world. Years later he did come to faith, very much so – it was always going to be all or nothing with Ben. But he never withdrew and moved across into the cul-de-sac of church life as I'd assumed he would. His new-found faith found a home right where he already belonged, in the world of sport and arts and business and money and local government, social life and endless connections and conversations. Eventually I understood that he had instinctively done the right thing. I mentally moved out of my close church circle and stepped wholeheartedly into the world he'd never left, where our lives and faith are in constant interaction with lots of people.'

Let us take a theoretical example:

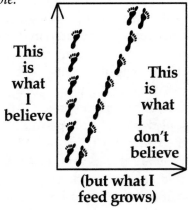

A married clergyman, someone of depth and integrity, falls into an affair and runs off with someone else's wife. Everyone is stunned and confused. How could this happen? It's against everything he has always believed.

But he acted on the basis of what he believed: 'I had a right to be happy,' he explains. Until that time he did not believe he believed that, but suddenly he acted on the basis of what he really believed, not what he believed he believed. Unconsciously he had been believing two things at once which were at odds with each other. Eventually he could not stretch any further and acted on the basis of what he had come to believe.

It is important to rule what you believe, to act on that basis. Otherwise you go through life asleep, passively smoking other people's values and assumptions. How, then, will *you* live? What kind of lifestyle will you choose? Will you determine to speak out for what is important to you? Often our struggle is not against individual people but against systems and power structures already in place. In each area, we may occupy or abdicate.*

---

* All too often disillusionment with the systems in place makes ordinary people feel powerless to make a difference, make themselves heard and alter the course of procedures. Power passes by default to those who are ambitious, stand to make personal gain from certain outcomes or have an agenda at odds

We should not stay home, then complain about the politicians other people voted in. You can fill a shoebox at Christmas for children in Romania or campaign to get the road markings changed at a dangerous corner. You might teach computer skills for an after-school club or offer to babysit one night for a neighbour. You can support local traders where possible – but each of these small things will usually begin by asking questions: Will they be on their own for Christmas? Do they ever go out together? Why are things arranged this way? What can be done to change this situation?*

If I develop a reflex of questioning, my own priorities will need re-evaluating more often. Is a dishwasher just another expensive appliance, or could it rescue premium time to be together? Could I manage without a car? What are the drains on my time and resources? Where can I more usefully engage my energies? Who is it that I would prefer to spend time with? How, then, shall I live? Does the way I live reflect my own individual tastes and interests? Or am I a drifting, undiscerning consumer?

If each individual were to find their unique voice it would be like putting the colour back into a world afflicted with potentially terminal blandness.

In addressing the culture-question 'How then shall

---

with the wishes of most people. The process is like attending an auction, surveying the goods and then leaving before the bidding commences because the items you are interested in may go for too much. The bargains are always picked up by those who wait long enough, and usually it is dealers who get their pick of whatever is on offer. If you exclude yourself from the proceedings you have no voice, you cannot make a bid.

* The questioning will often be at two levels. I see the poor have no bread. Question 1 may be 'How can I get some bread to the poor?' Question 2 would be 'Why do the poor have no bread?' Both questions are appropriate, but if we are asleep we ask no questions at all. We need to be very critical when reading news reports. We must be wide awake in our reactions to the programmes, even if we occasionally fall asleep in front of the TV.

we live?' for yourself, there are two components that are relevant. The first is *authenticity* – what is so much a part of you that you would not want to be without it? The second is *integrity* – what matters so much to you that you could not live with yourself if you ignored it?

Sometimes particular things were very important to a person at an earlier stage in their life – a teddy bear, a stamp collection, Beach Boys records, a motorbike, prawn vindaloo, a power-drill, the Rocky Mountains. Are each of these significant only for their nostalgia value? Were they left behind as life moved on as part of a valid process of growing older and beyond them? Which will go on to be part of the authentic you now and in the future? Can you still crush your own spices and fix a mean curry? Are you just itching to have your own motorbike again?

So take another look through the keyhole into your own life. What are the distinctive features that should be noticed? If it was to be mostly faded out into black and white, what would stand out in full technicolour? A guitar? A garden? A favourite whisky? A guest-room? A pair of walking boots and a warm sweater? The photograph of the youngsters on holiday you keep as your screensaver? A mirror or two in the bedroom? An old rocking chair by the woodstove? The car keys returned to their hook on the wall, the telephone ringing as you step through the door?

Are these clues to the authentic you? As Julie Andrews might ask, *are* these a few of your favourite things? If some of these elements are missing in your own picture, is it not time to go searching for them, to resurrect that interest, dig out those records or learn the language at last? Become better acquainted with the authentic you. Is your nationality or family background important to you?

Your education or lack of it? Do you work longer hours than you need because you love it so much? Is music in your blood? Do you wear your Doc Martens even in bed? Are you never happier than when you're travelling? Are you comfortable around strangers? Is your middle name Karaoke? Are you a bit of a traditionalist, conservative in your tastes? What kinds of people do you immediately relate to and relax around? Authenticity may mean breaking the mould of how someone else has expected you to behave and doing what feels good for a change!

Integrity is often about prioritising core values. Is image so important it must be maintained at all costs? Integrity in my lifestyle may mean *not* having the latest, in order to get out of debt. The habit of being critical, wide-eyed and questioning will make me responsible, concerned, and determined to find a voice.

In every area of our culture people of awareness, vision and integrity are urgently required. In the situations you are in, you could be the one to advocate change.

Being wide awake ensures that we continue the journey and that, at the very least, it is our own mistakes we make!

Fast-asleep dreams are often just our subconscious stretching itself out for a short while, but wide-awake dreams . . . these are the possibility of envisaging an altered reality. Bono from the music band U2 stood onstage in Dublin one New Year, and said, 'To the future! The only limitations are the limits of our imagination. Dream up the kind of world you want to live in. Dream out loud at high volume.'*

---

* U2 had a voice, and a vast breadth of perceptions and experiences to resonate with and articulate. They were not inclined to be silent, passive or asleep. But more was to follow. In *Walk On* (2001, Relevant Media Group Inc.), Steve Stockman writes, 'For a long time, Bono and the rest of the U2 guys were amused by the absurdity and obscenity of how important rock stardom had

Friendship: You've got a friend

So, who are my friends?

> We're trying to enlarge our circle
> of friends to include people we
> like.
> *(From an overheard conversation)*

There are people who are sort-of friends by force of circum-stance; they do the same things, go to the same places and may even have some interests in common. They live nearby and walk together to school, or do the same bus journey each day. They strike up conversation because they step outside to smoke. Or perhaps they do not par-ticularly connect directly but have mutual friends they appreciate a lot. Where a whole group of friends enjoy being together there will still be all kinds of different dynamics in their various one-to-one interactions – some of those relationships are strong and vital, others intense but uncomfortable; some depending entirely upon the group remaining intact. A group of friends can be mutually

---

become. It seemed foolish that a Dublin singer should have the clout to affect world powers, but he was recruited for the "foot in the door" job of winning over the attention of the media for the cause of Jubilee 2000. The organisers were stunned at his commitment. They expected concerts and records, but it turned out Bono's a very brilliant political lobbyist holding his own with an economist, financier or UN ambassador.'

As the millennium ended, Jubilee 2000, with significant help from Bono, had encouraged the seven richest nations to promise the cancellation of $110 billion in debt that would possibly benefit some 41 countries (though many conditions could still allow the rich nations to stall on implementing this). During their three-month Elevation tour U2 were also campaigning for action against the HIV/AIDS crisis in Africa.

Few people have the visibility that U2 enjoy, but each of us can dream up the kind of world we want to live in, and do something to shift life in a better direction. Bono's argument that the only limitations are the limits of our imagination is a compelling one.

supportive and a source of strength in any kind of trouble. There is also a comfortableness which comes from having been around each other for a long time, and having memories in common, things that do not need explaining. Most of us have had some occasion to hum away to ourselves, 'I'll get by with a little help from my friends.'

Sometimes there can be comfortableness and ease in the company of a complete stranger, as effortless as reaching for a favourite fleece. If we were to pay attention to this recognition, particularly where there is immediate mutual interest or liking, our life would be far richer in friends. Surely some pretext can be found to keep in touch or to spend some time around each other when next you coincide? Life is too short and friendship too important to ignore your instincts. As in other spheres of life, the determination should be to occupy not abdicate. (Most of us do not get to choose our families. When we move into a house we usually have very little say as to who our neighbours will be. But friends at least can be chosen.)

Obviously you may decide to choose someone as a friend, only to discover they are really not interested in having much to do with you!* A friend is not only someone you can be yourself with, but someone who is happy to spend time with you. A good friendship is worth investing time and energy in. Some friendships are the kind where if you see each other even after years you can pick up effortlessly from where you left off. An enduring friendship has more stability than many romances, and if a marriage sadly should fall apart altogether it is to their

---

* Whether it's trying to be a friend, or being interviewed for a job, if you want to be taken seriously it is wise not to try too hard. You would come across as having something to prove – or too much to lose. To be over-eager is to be off-putting.

friends that most people turn for support, continuity and a reference point.

The conflicting priorities of friendship and marriage or romance may mean some juggling is required. But rather as a plant thrives on a mixture of seasons, so most marriages are enriched by both partners also having close friendships affecting their lives, sustaining them and provoking growth.

Often a marriage is also a sort of friendship (even though, of course, you may not ordinarily be in the habit of going to bed with your friends!).

> Two people holding each other like flying buttresses. Two people depending on each other . . . and defending each other against the world outside. Sometimes it was worth all the disadvantages of marriage just to have that: one friend in an indifferent world.*

A whole genre of films known as 'buddy movies', and many reinventions of the same formula in TV series, depends upon the constant dialogue and feel-good factor of friends who travel together/solve crimes/do comedy/ drive fast cars and rescue each other. Good friendships are a warm and enduring memory. True wealth may be better measured in valued friends than in financial wherewithal.

> We call that person who has lost his father an orphan; and a widower that man who has lost his wife. But that man who has known the immense unhappiness of losing a friend, by what name do we call him? Here every language is silent and holds its peace in impotence. *(Joseph Roux)*

So where and how do these friendships occur that prove to be deep and enduring enough to last a lifetime? In

---

*From *Fear of Flying*, by Erica Jong (Martin Secker & Warburg). Reprinted by permission of The Random House Group Ltd.

circumstances that are challenging, unpleasant or disconcerting a friendship struck up with a companion in adversity can deepen significantly quite quickly. For some a lasting friendship may date back to a time spent together in prison. Those who have done military service, especially in wartime, will often name as their closest friend someone they trained alongside and came to know well. Shared experiences in a time away from home and roots and previous companions are a significant foundation for relationships that have the likelihood of being retained through later life. Those who become close friends when at college together, studying, surviving and socialising together, will sometimes make strenuous efforts to keep in touch long after their circumstances would guarantee further contact. Many people, married perhaps with grown children, or single and settled with a house and mortgage of their own, look back to times when they shared a flat or house with random occupants or with other single people from work or college. Deep friendships seemed easier to build then, and much of what went on was often unplanned, with conversations running deep into the night, impromptu meals, other people dropping in and something different happening night after night.

Sometimes a friendship is begun in one set of circumstances but cannot depend on those conditions being maintained or replicated for its survival.*

---

* Friendships can be struck up unexpectedly in all sorts of circumstances. Another couple attending the same birth class may still be in touch years after your babies have been safely delivered. You may suddenly find that you get on with the parents of your children's friends, and they become your friends, too (and of course your children are expected to play with your friends' children whenever you meet up!). Setting up a neighbourhood watch scheme can be a surprising way of getting closer to people you already knew slightly. Someone who has an adjoining allotment seems more than willing to talk, and offer

If you live in the same building for a while, or meet every day over lunch, or go for a drink once a week for a year or two, then one person moves a hundred miles away, some adjustment needs to be made. The Friday pint or few is replaced by a Sunday phone call and a visit once or twice a year. A postcard from Australia may be very fine, but is no help when what you miss is the only person who ever thought your jokes were funny. At times a get-together with an old friend may only go to prove that you have nothing left in common after the reminiscing is over. But a person who was always good company probably still will be once you have got to know them again, and a friend you were able to share deeply with and confide in will usually prove to be someone you still want to trust.

I have come to recognise that each friendship will always leave its mark on me in some unexpected way. It can be a powerful stimulus, a source of strong affirmation, of laughter and healing. The gift of friendship is to be present to each other, and this in turn can bring healing to many wounds our lives have unconsciously sustained.

There is no substitute for a really good friend. It may be that a relationship with someone half a world away or whom you meet up with only once or twice a year is still of immense value.

The friends whose company I would ideally choose may not be as available to me as previously. But nothing is to be gained by me sulking. Some new friendships may be waiting to be discovered. Every person is unique; each friendship is different, and could never be replaced.

---

suggestions. One of the local pubs has a really good atmosphere, and is a good place to pop out to for an hour or so. Would your neighbour be willing to let you take her dog out for a bit more exercise? It is maybe also becoming a priority to find a gym, and get into the habit of working out.

> I need all the friends I can get.
>
> *(Charlie Brown, 'Peanuts' cartoons)*
>
> You can make more friends in two months by becoming interested in other people than you can in two years by trying to get other people interested in you. *(Dale Carnegie)* *

Friendship is costly. It means making an effort. It takes time – lots of it, if possible. One friend is worth a hundred acquaintances. One acquaintance may be that friend you have been waiting to discover.

Let me serve you (ministry dilemmas!)

Over the years I have spent many hours talking with people whose life and work has been in church leadership or ministry of some other kind. For them the subject of giftedness is even more complicated, and it can be a crucial process to recognise which gifts are supernatural tools, what is their innate (motivational) giftedness, and what is an enabling for the task they are called to. This is made more confusing by the mix of job descriptions, real gifting and the expectations put on them by others or themselves! The scope of this book is much wider than its relevance to ministry, professional or otherwise, but the next few pages are devoted to some of the material that has been helpful in unravelling those specific confusions.

You may now want to skip the rest of this chapter, or pursue it later, and proceed to the summary at the end of this chapter (page 82).

We will now go on to see the games people play at church, and examine the intoxicating concept of 'ministry'.

---

* *Quote, Unquote,* edited by Lloyd Cory (1977, Victor Books, Wheaton IL)

Society at large defines people according to their function, but if you are a Christian – one of those practising, churchgoing, part-of-it-all people – then you really don't have that problem. You know that your identity is all tied up in being 'in Christ', being 'part of the Body'. The Body of Christ has many parts and the ear cannot say to the big toe, 'I have no need of you!' nor can either knee say to the right elbow, 'I have no need of you.' Each is a member of the Body. Each serves in its own way. Each 'ministers' to the others. Each has value and is needed. These are very familiar words to the average churchgoer, part of the pep-talk vocabulary for keeping them involved and stroked and committed and paying their dues and feeling needed. The convinced speaker continues, 'Each of us is part of the Body; each of us belongs; each of us has a ministry of some kind. Look at Wilf, he has a ministry of welcome. Whenever someone new walks in the door he's ready with a smile and a hymn book. Or Muriel, she has a ministry of visiting the sick and the housebound, and showing them that they are not forgotten, that we are all thinking about them. Or Jeff and Maggie, now they have a music ministry. When they lead the worship we are all caught up into the presence of God and can join in with the singing. Or David, he has a ministry in the Word and is able to teach us so much that we would never hear otherwise. So, you see, each of us has a ministry of some kind, and each of us is part of the Body, each of us belongs.'

What the speaker hasn't said at this time is that he has actually reached the end or close to the end of his list of people with obvious ministries. His hearers have readily identified these same people as obvious examples and have got the point: they themselves have not got a ministry that they are aware of, therefore they are not really part of the Body, therefore they do not really belong. So in order

71

to belong, in order to be really part of the Body, they had better get a ministry, quick. At this point it is interesting to observe that they never seem to try and duplicate Muriel's ministry of visiting the housebound, since this would not be visible and would defeat the object of being seen to have a ministry. Instead, they throw their energies into becoming what Arnold Bittlinger calls 'a superfluous inauthentic facsimile of someone else's ministry'.

So, does the analogy of the body have any valid application if someone was hearing it for the first time? Surely, yes. The thrust of its general argument is this: where do you function most naturally? Then find your place and you will function as part of a whole body by doing what comes naturally.

The attempt to find a valid ministry of some kind may perhaps best be made by asking:

    1. Where can I function naturally?
    2. What is needed?
or 3. Is there a gap that someone should fill?

With persistence, or by trial and error, you may then stumble into an ongoing ministry of some kind, or may cease to worry about finding any identifiable ministry and just be content to serve as best you can.

If someone has a recognised ministry they have a different set of problems. Quite properly some people will relate to them only in their capacity as a 'ministry', while others will not know them in that context and relate to them only as a private individual. A third group of people know them and relate to them in both ways, so that occasionally there can be mismatched expectations as to when they are being which, and whether they are wearing a particular hat at the time or not. There is the assumption that a professional minister, for example, is at all times available and, in a sense, is public property. This assumption may be irritating but is understandable and perhaps forgivable. Everybody knows, after all, that ministers only work one day a week! The problems really begin when the person-with-a-ministry ceases to believe they have any distinct or separate identity at all. They deny their humanity and, ironically, their innate gifted-ness. To see the problem is halfway to solving it. John Noble puts it something like this: 'I have enough people relate to me as a ministry. When I come home, I am just a husband, a lover, or plain tired. I don't go to bed with my "ministry-pips" on.'

The second box, in specifically Christian terms, would bear the label 'Ministry gifts'. But on the spine simply the word 'Jobs'. The list of probable contents would read:

APOSTLES
PROPHETS
EVANGELISTS
PASTORS
TEACHERS (or PASTOR-TEACHERS!?)

The list continues with:

ministries of helps – necessary tasks
gifts of administration – thankless task!
speakers in various tongues – for the general good
interpreters of the same – else what would be the good!
workers of miracles – any applicants?

The list then continues in large italics:

etc, etc, etc . . .

because the list is never intended to be an exhaustive list, only a list of examples. There are many opportunities to serve or do 'ministry', which may be simply putting our hand to what needs doing at the time; in another situation it might be something entirely different.

The block capital gifts or 'Ascension-gift ministries'

There are some gifts of ministry which are crucial to the development of the Church as a whole, without which its development would be stunted and impaired. Their role is to be facilitators for the whole Body to move and grow and develop with harmony between its constituent parts. We have often inherited a conscious or unconscious model of the Church which makes much of hierarchy. Ephesians 4 talks of the ascended Christ giving as gifts to the Church some apostles, some prophets, some evangelists, some pastors and teachers to equip the people of God to do the work of ministry so that the whole Body is built up in unity and faith and knowledge of the Son of God, becoming fully mature, filled to full measure and beyond. Some translations have encouraged an unfortunate mistake by adding a comma to the punctuating of the previous sentence. This means that instead of those block capital gifts being there 'to equip the people of God to do the work of ministry', we are given the impression they are there 'to equip the people of God, to do the work of ministry'. No wonder professional ministers are expected to do all the work of the Church – the comma has spoken!

What makes the block capital ministry gifts different from any others? Are they more important? No, they belong 'in the saucer' just like anybody else, and should have already sunk to the bottom if they have a heart to serve. Their gift is not more important, but it may be crucial.

Without their gifts the Church-at-large will not mature, will not be healthy, will not reach 'the fullness that is Christ's'.

The block capital gifts are distinctive in that, with the possible exception of the PASTOR, their gift is immediately relevant and recognisable translocally. The person's gift in that sense makes room for itself. Their gift is a gift from the ascended Christ to the whole Church, not just a local gathering of Christians. They will usually be ministers by occupation, or could be but have chosen also to work at secular employment part-time or for the time being. Characteristically, they have a clear sense of calling, a story of vocation. (This may not be as clear in the case of a pastor whose story is likely to be one of how his heart for the people he cares for developed, and he is just as likely to talk about them as himself and his own calling.) Their gifts are able to be recognised translocally – even the pastor whose gifts really require relationship and a charge.

Most people spend their lives living between the spheres of marriage, family, work, culture and friendship. The Church as a gathered people and its leaders are supposed to be there to serve and support those who live out their lives occupying these spheres. Too often, instead of engaging with popular culture and participating in contemporary society, the Church and its leaders withdraw and as far as possible retreat into an alternative reality with a different set of values and cultural norms. Its culture is not immediately accessible to the uninitiated. Too often it is 'privately engaging but publicly irrelevant'. Far from seasoning the whole of life and bringing out its flavour, its response implies distaste and defensiveness. Instead of guaranteeing realistic support for the faithful immersed in the world, the Church-as-gathered requires the faithful to support its own separatist activities. Its leaders look to be supported more than looking to support. However, 'The Word became a human being and moved into the neighbourhood.'*

For most people this middle box of Life-Work is taken up with working. A person (of whatever motivation) is living and working, and has access to whatever tools they need.

For the person with 'full-time' ministry as their job, the box is labelled a little differently. An equally committed ministry-person may also be giving their energies to secular employment and effectively be 'double-time'. They would probably prefer to label the middle box of giftedness:

LIFE, WORK + MINISTRY
or LIFE-WORK + MINISTRY

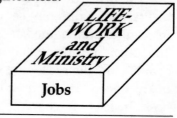

---

* John 1:14 (J. B. Phillips translation)

The challenge for many leaders or ministry-gifted people is to relocate mentally and emotionally from a church ghetto or Christian cul-de-sac, and engage with life in the real world in an authentic way. Whatever is distinctive must then unashamedly find its relevant context and response. Where their ministry giftings have hitherto been invested entirely in the church, leaders should balance this by considering at least an equal investment in some broader context of involvement. They should also, for their own sanity, be looking to have significant mutual relationships with friends who are not already Christians, and pursue other interests that are not work-related just like anyone else, without apology. They should be an example of authenticity and integrity, and encourage others to engage with life more fully and to live more generously.

It may be useful for contrast to outline the characteristics of the different block capital ministry gifts in turn.

1. APOSTLES

Gift of imparting strength and courage, recognising people's gifts and believing in them, lighting their 'blue touch-paper' or commanding them to stand, creating more space around them and helping them to recognise possibilities.

Gift of seeing where people and their gifts fit within a bigger picture.

A building gift, laying foundations, implementing or making alterations to plans in an enterprise, community or project. People of initiative. Employ strategy on the basis of instinct, prayerfulness and wisdom.

2. PROPHETS

'Wild men' (or women!). Gift of declaring vision, adjusting through a radical word. Speaks current concerns of

God's heart. Deals in revelation. It may be observed that they are often prone to extremes of circumstance . . . 'Look at the prophets limping in!' The reaction to their message is likely to be extreme and diverse also. They provoke others, unsettling them, confounding, confronting and exposing lies. They feed apostles with vision. (Apostles suggest and can apply and implement these fresh ideas, usually recognising their implications rather than origi-nating them.)

They may prophesy from a platform, by their writings (even posthumously) or by their lifestyle. Their arena may be any environment or situation. They may have long periods, even many years, of obscurity or reproach: God does not consider it a waste to spend even seventy years preparing a person for one moment of greatness.

3. EVANGELISTS

Have a concern to bring people to know God, and the ability to bring them into an encounter with him. Most of their energies are absorbed in this. Many conversions to Christ follow in their wake: it is as if any fruit that is ripe for the plucking will fall into their hand. With discipline they can give their energies to inspiring others to become involved in sharing their faith, but they need convincing in their hearts that it is valid and worthwhile for them to divert their energies into that kind of investment. They will need to make allowances for the fact that others will not share their obsessive enthusiasm for the task, nor appear to meet with so much success. To others, they seem to effortlessly win those they meet to loyalty to Christ and faith in him. They also then seem to lose inter-est in these new people quite quickly, and speed on to another capture with genuine concern. (It may be impor-tant that they recognise the need for mutual co-operation between the various complementary block capital gift ministries.)

4. PASTORS

Every true pastor is gifted to shepherd, to care for any number of individuals (a 'flock'?) or congregation, to take them into his/her heart, to lead them gently, to gather strays, to care for and nurture them, wherever they are. Pastoral gifts need to emerge in the workplace, and every other social grouping – sometimes this may be deliberate positioning; at other times it may grow organically. Pastors are those people who have this ability, not just this job-description. Pastoral gifts will often emerge locally as the person's heart becomes stretched in preparation for the task. People around them feel safe just having them around, and they in turn develop such a concern for others that often it will turn into an all-consuming task. They should rarely, if ever, be transplanted, since being there long-term breeds a relevant security in those they care for. If they are professional ministers and are ordered to move, this can be a source of tremendous emotional upheaval. (It is also worth remembering that some denominations refer to all those with charge of churches or congregations as pastors, regardless of their emerging gifting or lack of it.) A pastor functions locally as one of those in leadership, but need not be the presiding elder at all. It may also not be appropriate for a pastor to do a great deal of teaching if he or she is inept in this capacity.

5. TEACHERS

This gift is not attainable by studying at a teacher training college or even at seminary or Bible school, for that matter. It is a clear 'anointing', enabling and commissioning by

God, an ability to expound truth, including the scriptures, in such a way that people hear and understand and slowly grow in that truth. Although a gifted person with various abilities, it is this expounding and instructing they are concerned with. An authentic teaching ministry is consistent: they will teach well most of the time. (The test of their value is not some once-only A+ but a persistent A−.)

The opening sentences of the book of Luke talk about the setting down of an orderly account and investigating everything carefully so that others may know the truth. These are the characteristic concerns which develop in someone as a teaching gift emerges. They are satisfied that this is their primary calling and that nothing else must distract them.

> 'If any man be called to preach, let him not stoop to be a king.'

For example, the Bible comes alive in their hands, and they possess the gift of making people able to access its truth. Teaching is not just about the exposition of scripture passages: their ability to expound is on the full range of information to be transmitted. Application is essential: their approach is to take pains to explain, This is what it will mean for you.

They will often teach widely translocally. This may occur partially through writing, tapes, conferences and training material.

The teachers are keepers of memory. They will use the telling of stories to incarnate truth (or to echo what scripture might have said) and can somehow articulate the presence of God in our 'now' with us at this moment. They go digging in for truth wherever it is to be found, mining for it like precious metal or searching for it like hidden treasure. Their persistent bias is to ensure good provision is made for learning, imbibing, nourishing, and not towards providing blueprints or battle plans.

They are concerned with taking what is complicated or not perceived and making it understandable, so that their hearers will go away and want to find out more for themselves. Teachers add bulk and muscle as well as nourishment to the Body.

Enabling gifts

Each of the ministry gifts will naturally inspire others, to some extent. However, they need to recognise that maximum effectiveness is not measured in what they in their giftedness can accomplish or achieve. The express purpose of them being so gifted is to enable others and release them into their giftedness. If they recognise this they will not be content just to be an inspiration, but will constantly, consciously, provoke other people beyond their complacency.

Those in professional Christian work or with ambitions in that direction have a more than casual interest at stake in the content of this part of the chapter. For you here are a few key observations:

1. Do not try to ascertain too quickly where your gifts may lie in the list above. It may be that things will become a little clearer once you have absorbed the burden of the next few chapters. God may take a person of quite specific focus and gifting, which has always been there at least latently (in the bottom box), then eventually compound this with other giftings equipping that person for the tasks they are called to. The combination of these two sorts of gifting is what makes for a fascinating and distinctive overall effectiveness.

2. Examine again your sense of vocation. Where did it come from? Is it something you have held on to already through many discouragements? Is it distinctive? Or were you merely a volunteer? (Volunteers can be crucial too, by doing what they can so someone else is freed up to do what they cannot!)

3. The model for ministry that Jesus gives us is to wash feet, to learn to be a servant of his people, perhaps a servant of the servants of God if they in turn respond. Servanthood grows by example. Responsibility also is given to those who prove faithful. Is your heart towards the anonymity of the bottom of the saucer? Are you able to make real friends, or does your position make that too difficult?

To summarise this chapter

It is good to examine each sphere of your life in turn. Aim to take stock of all five spheres simultaneously to assess where you really are at. For instance, a person who has been widowed may need to acknowledge that this continues to impact the daily balance of their life years after the initial shock and grief and practical upheaval.

Too often you pay attention only to new data and shut off awareness of where you are in the other four spheres, thinking, 'No change there . . .'

So much time and energy is spent on work, and occupying the other spheres of life, it is important for us to take inventory, and prioritise our 'spending' so that if possible it reflects what is important to us. We must be authentic, have integrity in what we do, and where possible make a difference for other people.

Some moment happens in your life that you say Yes right up to the roots of your hair, that makes it worth having been born just to have happen. Laughing with somebody till the tears run down your cheeks. Waking up to the first snow. Being in bed with somebody you love.

Whether you thank God for such a moment or thank your lucky stars, it is a moment that is trying to open up your whole life. If you turn your back on such a moment and hurry along to Business as Usual, it may lose you the ball game. If you throw your arms around such a moment and hug it like crazy, it may save your soul.

How about the person you know who as far as you can possibly tell has never had such a moment – the soreheads and slobs of the world, the ones the world has hopelessly crippled? Maybe for that person the moment that has to happen is you.   *(Frederick Buechner)**

* Frederick Buechner, *Wishful Thinking* (1973, HarperCollins Publishers Ltd)

Chapter 3
Chocolate box

It is not healthy when people try to get their identity from the use of special powers. Whether this is magic or clairvoyance or 'channelling' or out-of-the-body experiences *or* legitimate supernatural phenomena in Christian experience, the emotional 'need-to' is the same. The tools, which may be spectacular in their operation, are fine in themselves, but too heavy to carry around for the sake of it. My friend John will often say that the 'need-to's' are very telling. So, I don't mind if you drink, but if you need to drink you might have a problem; I don't mind if you drive fast, but if you need to drive fast you might have a problem; I don't mind if you turn up late, but if you need to be late you might have a problem.

If we use the manifestational 'tools' as emotional props, they can be as dangerously dependence-inducing as their counterfeits.

Similarly, it is very unhealthy to try to find identity in work *(or 'ministry'!)* alone. Work may be an appropriate place to explore how we may express our innate identity: it should never replace that identity. Working hard because we enjoy it (or need the extra money to survive) is not necessarily a bad thing – but who wants the company of a workaholic? The compulsiveness indicates a problem.

We have removed both of the boxes on top of the bottom one, and you will not be surprised to see that it has a fancy name on the label: 'Motivational gifts'. On the side of the box, where there is less room to write fancy names, are written the words 'Who am I?'

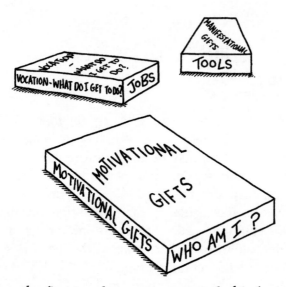

When the first two boxes are removed, this foundational box is still in its place, and it is intended to be the strong one on which the others rest. At times it may be less visible, but it has always been there. A person's job, or role in life, may change many times, but at this deeper level they remain the person they always were. That person inside may be hidden or squashed or damaged, but is still there. That person inside has the capacity to live responsibly or selfishly, destructively or redemptively. That person inside is unique, just as every snowflake has a different pattern, and no two blades of grass are exactly alike.

When we look at this bottom box, this 'Who am I?' box, we discover it to be like a chocolate box. Opening the lid and pushing aside the packaging, we encounter first of all a delicate, filmy, single sheet on which are drawings and the names and descriptions of the expected contents, the texture and flavours, the sorts of chocolates we are to anticipate. Dazzled by the words, we think, 'Well, all it's really saying is that there are some hard centres and some soft centres and some chewy centres.' And if you look at any average group of people there's a fair chance that that is true of them too!

One of the chocolates is described as a Mandarin Fondant Surprise, which seems a bit daunting until you realise it's just a fancy way of talking about an 'orange cream'. Perfectly familiar, and you've liked them all your life, just don't let the name confuse you!

In the box of chocolates is a little Marzipan whose best friend is a Montelimar. He thinks that Montelimars are the best thing that has ever been invented and wishes that he could be like his friend. He does learn a lot by being with his friend the Montelimar and tries so hard to be just like him. When someone opens the lid of the chocolate box and looks at him, he pulls himself up to his full height, all shiny and black and smooth; and thinks, 'Montelimar' as hard as he can. 'Oh what a lovely Marzipan!' they say, and he scowls his hardest. He probably knows more about Montelimars than anybody else, but he'll never be a Montelimar.

All the Marzipans are a little different, but in one sense if you've met one Marzipan you've a fair idea what to expect from another one. Not so with 'Hazelnut Clusters' – they're all shapes and sizes! Although they may be more diverse, it is still true to say that one Hazelnut Cluster has more in common with another Hazelnut Cluster than with a Montelimar or a Marzipan – or a Mandarin Fondant Surprise, for that matter!

Then we come to a fresh (though fascinating) problem. When you look at the drawing of the different chocolates you see a diamond-shaped chocolate with a line running lengthways from one corner to another. If it's a wavy line, it will be a Coconut. However, there's another sort of diamond-shaped chocolate with the line running lengthways from one corner to the other, but that diagonal line is a straight line and then you know it is a Fudge. So far so good: that's all simple enough. Until you look at the actual chocolates in the chocolate box instead of the drawing. You see, there's one chocolate sitting there and it's obviously a diamond-shaped chocolate and it clearly has a line running lengthwise from one corner to the other, but whether it's a straight wavy line or a wavy straight line is anybody's guess. 'Oh! It just has to be a Coconut Fudge,' you say in your frustration; but all the time you know, if you're really honest, that it isn't a Coconut Fudge at all, that it only looks that way from the outside, that inside the chocolate it already is a Coconut . . . or a Fudge. From the outside there really is no way of knowing. Inside it already is what it is.

All this talk about chocolates has probably made you very hungry. So, we'd better stop talking about them and look at the chocolates themselves.

The first sort of chocolate in the box is called the **PROPHETIC** chocolate. And immediately we have a problem – because we've met that word in each of the boxes. What we are not talking about is the screwdriver of prophecy that is designed for any idiot to be able to use in accomplishing a whole range of household tasks. That is a tool, not a person. Nor are we talking about the job of a prophet, in block capitals or otherwise, because someone who by nature would never say, 'Boo!' to a goose could be given the job of being a prophet and enabled to speak out boldly against injustice of some kind, or to embrace a radical lifestyle that would challenge the most indifferent. That would be a task, a job, and the most likely or unlikely person may take it on.

What we are talking about as the PROPHETIC chocolate is the person who by their very nature has always been a radical, and sees things in black and white rather than smudgy shades of grey. This person is truthful, capable of being brutally honest. They can inspire others. They are compelling, direct and sincere. They tend to be restless, interested in the next thing, wanting to pursue an idea now, or sooner. They hate compromise of any kind and would rather speak their mind than fudge the issue. Some PROPHETICs can be loud, others seem silent and withdrawn; some may be both in turn. But their intensity is what marks them out.

The second chocolate is the **SERVING** chocolate. The SERVER is a practical person who likes to be useful, to be busy, not to waste time, but to get on with the job. They have lots of energy and love to apply it. They enjoy practical problem-solving, and can't understand why other people are so lazy and so unreliable, although they have learnt that this is usually the case and that it seems little can be done to change them. It is often easier for them to do a job themselves than to enlist unwilling volunteers – besides, they don't mind working on their own, and they're just as happy getting on without someone else breathing down their neck or getting under their feet. A good photograph of a SERVER would always show them in the middle of doing something, and if you were to see them sitting down it is probably with their hands busy or when they are completely relaxed having worked hard at something and earned a good rest. They enjoy making things, mending things, helping things grow – and can turn their practical insights to almost any situation.

The third chocolate is the **TEACHING** or **EXPLAIN-ING** chocolate. This one is definitely the chewy centre in the chocolate box. They love to understand and to learn, and are interested in a wide variety of topics. They store away endless snippets of interesting information, all of which becomes slowly organised somewhere in the back of their mind. If someone presses the trigger, a lot of this is available for recall, to other people's surprise and admiration. They like to listen and observe, and they become animated when explaining something succinctly, or thoroughly and in detail. They don't like to commit themselves to anything without having thought through the implications. They can be thoughtful and considerate in relationships (if they put their mind to it).

The fourth chocolate is the **EXHORTER** or **ENCOUR-AGING** chocolate. The EXHORTER is a people person, energetic in keeping everybody happy or spurring particular people on to achieve what they are capable of. Relationship is their bread and butter, and in an informal sense they will inevitably become involved in counselling other people in situations of all sorts. They remember especially the interpersonal dynamics, and can often reconcile apparently opposite points of view. 'Truth can be cruel and untimely,' they say; 'what they don't know can't hurt them.' They focus equally well with individuals or in a group.

The fifth chocolate is the **GIVER** chocolate. They enjoy giving, not just what they can spare but what they can't as well. Possessions, time, money, emotional energies excite them: all these things are expendable resources to the GIVER, and they give as generously as they are able. They look for opportunities to meet other people's needs, noticing who has a spare wardrobe or piano they want rid of, and matching that to a mention of the desire for one when someone else is in conversation. They like to give in secret, to plan and plot surprises, but are unattached to possessions, and a chance remark or compliment may result in them making a spontaneous present of something they know you like. They protect themselves from being too close to any number of people, who nonetheless feel they are close to them, because if they once allow someone close enough access to really hurt them, they will be unable to build the necessary walls to prevent themselves being wounded again and again by that person. They are the softest of all the chocolates in the box, but they don't tell anybody that.

The sixth chocolate is the **RULER** chocolate. (These are perhaps the most diverse, depending on how much opportunity, especially in early life, they have had to use their gift to the full and be appreciated as the considerate and capable person they could be.) When asked to make a decision, they will characteristically hesitate momentarily, then reply very definitely. This moment of hesitation is the only space required to update or review their entire picture of all the relevant factors – time, people involved, consequences, reactions, weather, finance, abilities – and come up with the best idea for everybody concerned. Having now already thought about it, they will remain convinced this was the best decision, unless given fresh factors to consider. They will also similarly assess the decisions others make in organisation, almost on reflex. This makes them very helpful to consult, since their criticism will usually be perceptive. They are restive if ignored. Given the chance, they do any number of things reasonably well without ever having previously tried. They appear rarely to be spontaneous. They are sometimes accused of not having deep feelings at all: this is not the case, but they are unlikely to parade them in public.

The seventh and final sort of chocolate is the **MERCY** chocolate. (Some of these will have been convinced by now that there is probably no chocolate like them in the box, that they will not be on the list!) Their gift is that of empathising and caring, laughing when someone else begins to laugh, and crying with those who cry. They may not know what they are laughing or crying about, but they know by its taste what the other person is feeling. A MERCY knows primarily through feelings rather than words or thoughts. They are sensitive and intuitive, enjoy spontaneity and are good with people, especially if they can be with them one to one. They are good to be with when you are down or upset because they really understand what you are feeling without needing to know why. They feel what the other person feels from the inside. They are obviously a soft centre.

So, now you have heard the various chocolates described. Perhaps you think you have recognised people of your acquaintance. Perhaps you already have a suspicion which one might be you. Perhaps you are just confused. It may be you feel like a little bit of each of the descriptions was talking about you. Take heart if that is the case. Because we grow up in a world full of other people, we learn to develop lots of things by example that would otherwise not come naturally at all. This is essential if we are to be a well-rounded person. But it is wonderful to know that there will be one area which is a gift. It comes naturally, and we have never needed to try to be that way. We have more than a head start. That is our motivation.

Other people may look from the outside and think they know us from the way we behave, but they have no way of knowing how we feel about what we do. A key principle to remember in exploring motivations is:

It's not what you do but the why that you do it that betrays who you are.

If you are very clear that some of the motivations are not at all in any way like you, you could cautiously cross them off your list of possibles. This may get you down by process of elimination to two or three. Read the descriptions carefully, especially in the chapters that follow, and you will find this will help, or confuse you further. The real benefit of the material will only be felt when you have clarified which is your own motivation. You may look like a Coconut Fudge, but inside you are already one thing or another.

Some people have tried to pick out what they liked from the material, but missed the whole point in the process. This happens if you do not distinguish properly between people and jobs or tasks, but lump them together into some composite list. Believe me, it will be a waste of time pursuing this any further unless you at least try to discover one central motivation which is your own.

Some people struggle with the concept that everybody is identified as having one or another of the seven sorts of motivation listed above. They feel this must inevitably pigeonhole them in a way that is not helpful. But no two people are the same. We are each unique but share many traits in common with those of the same motivational grouping.

Imagine a group of people sheltering under one umbrella in a rainstorm. Each is standing in his own space, but because they all share the one umbrella their perspective is similar, although slightly different. They are still individuals but their perspective will have more in common with each other's than with that of anyone who is sheltering under a different umbrella a few yards away.

The motivation of either parent, or other significant people in our life, may have a profound effect upon us. We may develop habits and ways of behaving that reflect their priorities and values, behaviour that reflects their motivation and not just our own. Alternatively, we may alter the way we behave in reaction to the pressure put upon us by a strong influence we have disliked or resented.

My friend Pat grew up with a mother of a GIVING motivation and was so inspired by her example that strong giving traits are still a key part of his behaviour pattern. Pat is PROPHETIC by motivation, so partly it was his mother's recklessness in abandoning consequences into God's hands that was radical enough to incite imitation from him.

Another friend had an EXHORTER for his mother. She was always trying to fit in more projects, more people, assuming other people would always make allowances if some things didn't get done or if she was often late in arriving. In reaction, her son became wary of over-extending himself and can be punctual to the point of obsession.

Some traits of behaviour have been learnt deliberately and systematically as part of our training in particular jobs or professions. Children in large families invariably have more awareness of practical responsibility and task sharing. Sometimes we are drawn to particular jobs precisely because they seem attractive to us and give us scope to find expression for the very traits that do come naturally.

It is a helpful principle in identifying your own motivation to think back even to childhood. See which characteristics you remember as always having been there, and which feel the most 'you', before you were moulded by other people's expectations. Try to remember how you felt about what you did, and the situations that arose.

Each of the seven chapters that follow will describe characteristics of one motivational gift. Begin reading in whichever order you prefer.

Chapter 4
The Prophetic Motivation

GENERAL CHARACTERISTICS

1. Black and white
2. Intense and outspoken
3. Senses what is genuine
4. Needs only few close friends
5. Self-critical and introspective
6. Idealistic
7. Has to have a dream
8. Thinks about God
9. Wholehearted and sincere
10. Truth matters to them
11. Has strong opinions and convictions
12. Angered by injustice
13. Intolerant or dogmatic
14. Dynamic
15. Determined and compelling
16. Direct or judgemental
17. Radical
18. Restless
19. Hard to ignore
20. Tough and tender

1. Black and white

To the Prophetic there is truth or there is untruth. There's no such thing as 'sort of true'. There's no point pretending black is white or wrong is right, and they are uneasy when someone suggests that the issue might not be cut and dried. They like absolutes. So black is black and white is white – forget about all this talk of smudgy grey or blurring the distinctions! (Those Prophetics who appear more 'laid back' may have had to work hard to habitually modify extremes of behaviour or attitude.)

2. Intense and outspoken

Intensity is the natural language of the Prophetic person. Even their humour at its most memorable can be on the edge of being scary at times. They can create an uncomfortable atmosphere just by their silence when experiencing negative emotions – people feel an intensity, which is sustained and sometimes reproachful. People would say, 'You could have cut the atmosphere with a knife.'

Prophetics come in all shapes and sizes. They may be loud or quiet, larger than life and obvious or little and lethal. But watch out when they get excited and that wild look comes in their eyes!

Their directness and frankness will often be viewed as harshness or bluntness, even if they themselves are close to tears.

They frequently hurt people with their words, when they share what they think is obvious. They tend to 'blurt out' what they see because they don't know what else to do with it. It would be good to take stock first and weigh the situation before attacking or antagonising someone. Confrontation must not be an end in itself.

3. Senses what is genuine

Prophetics have the ability to pinpoint insincerity and hypocrisy and to be indignant about it. In fact, they have amazing accuracy when they follow their instincts in this area of knowing what is genuine and what is false. It is *not* through analysis but is intuitive! They react harshly to any form of deception or dishonesty.

Their contempt for hypocrisy may lead them to dismiss anything at all said by someone they despise or whose behaviour they disapprove of. This leads to deep self-hatred when they themselves act in direct opposition to their declared goals. The expression 'I can't hear what you're saying for the noise of who you are' would make perfect sense to them. They are thrilled when they see a person's attitudes and actions fall in line with higher principles.

4. Needs only few close friends

In a group situation, the Prophetic will often feel like an outsider, an observer. It is as if they stand on the edge of the circle. At times they may give off signals which cause others to gather around them or follow their initiative, but they are just as likely to be a loner or an intense observer. They may, even silently, be a jarring or even discordant element in the group. They love to spend time alone anyway, and are unlikely to go along with the crowd – and certainly not out of any need to belong. They enjoy the companionship of people they respect. They are likely either to like someone a lot or to have no time for them at all. To those who are close to them, they make a loyal friend through good and bad times. If Prophetics have once won your heart they are eminently forgivable.

Their determination to follow a particular course of action will characteristically make them want to fight for it whether anybody opposes them or not. Those around them may be blamed for throwing obstacles in their path without having any thought of doing so. It's just that they were spoiling for a fight with someone. Not everyone is prepared to stick around to be treated like this. But the Prophetic needs only a few close friends who are unlikely to take offence if he or she is hostile, self-absorbed or withdrawn. The seriousness of their outlook seems sometimes to prevent them from seeing the funny side of things, although creative imagination is otherwise a strong point.

5. Self-critical and introspective

Prophetics have a strong tendency to be inward-looking and take themselves too seriously. When they fail they are quick to justify themselves, but are just as likely to judge themselves too harshly. It all tends to extremes. They are often extremely self-critical and feel worthless when they fail or under-achieve. They can become very dissatisfied, even overwhelmed by a sense of guilt, when they fall short of their self-imposed unrealistic ideals or standards. They condemn and accuse themselves, and can be too demanding of others.

The Prophetic wants to do their best, nothing less. Their expectations of themselves are usually higher than those demanded of them by others. This is often the case with a teenager or young person who is a Prophetic. They are not frightened to be different, to live by their own standards instead of drifting with the crowd; and they may be highly indignant if underestimated or misunderstood.

When the Prophetic has a struggle with self-doubt or a self-image problem, it may be that of a Messiah complex ('the whole world is waiting for me') or of intense self-hatred. Since Prophetics have such an inner drive to do what is right, and since they are introspective and readily aware of their own shortcomings, they are quick to judge themselves inadequate. They may experience a sudden self-hatred when they realise how often the things they say hurt people. They can appear strong, even tough, not needing anyone else; but the truth is they are very sensitive people who struggle with a lot of self-doubt.

They are very open about their own faults (except in extreme circumstances) and want others around them to be equally transparent.

6. Idealistic

Most of us prefer to avoid trouble or uncomfortable circumstances and dislike disruption of any kind. But Prophetics like a challenge. The more circumstances are thrown in the air, the higher they are thrown, the more widely the pieces are scattered, the more different the situation that can result. They enjoy change. Even negative events relieve the monotony, or can be the occasion for extraordinary *angst*, something to be really depressed about.

A Prophetic is likely to see a tragic situation as interesting, a trial in someone else's life as a challenge for them, an opportunity. It is just possible that he or she will forget to be sympathetic. On a personal level they will sometimes set themselves high goals and targets (which others would prefer them to modify), then push hard to meet these ideal goals. Some of these goals or ideal standards they are able to meet, which is fine providing they do not expect others to do quite as they do. They are capable of dreaming the impossible dream and in a number of instances of achieving it. Usually they have too many impossible dreams and there is not time or energy enough to achieve all of them.

The Prophetic wants nothing to be average. (Their marriage, for example, must be completely unique, at the very least the ideal marriage. It must be a model.) But since what happens is not always the best, they are often disappointed, even if they attained more by aiming high. Everything in their thinking is epic. Holidays must be unconventional and achieve different things: there must be adventures to relate! It is important to them to envisage things in epic terms if they are to be motivated for even menial tasks.

Setting the standards or targets higher, time after time, may be satisfying: If they took up running, for example, they would have to keep on changing the goal of their exercise programme so that it was a bit further, a bit harder, a bit faster. Usually, they would set a target well beyond what they presently can reach, then push to achieve it.

7. Has to have a dream

The Prophetic has strength of personality and is not easily overlooked. If they take seriously the self-discipline that develops character and personal integrity, their example and energy can greatly impact the life of other people. They say, 'You've got to have a dream.' They love to share the vision or dream that has captured them, and this inevitably inspires others. They aim idealistically for perfection (and occasionally achieve it) and this causes others to reach higher. The Prophetic is often, by their words, action or example, a catalyst in the situation, bringing change.

> The Prophetic may say, 'Oh, what a wonderful day it is out there. I could just walk up to the top of that mountain and stand there and breathe in the morning.' It sounds such an appealing idea that the whole family decides to join him, but by the time everyone is ready, and it has been turned into a family outing, he has lost all enthusiasm for it and is impatient to return.

If people gather around the Prophetic it is usually because they each have initially been captured by the vision. Just as others are beginning to pour energy into the fulfilling of that vision the Prophetic will typically have largely lost interest. They seem to need to be always looking ahead, which is what they do to scratch the itch of their innate restlessness. In order to keep them focused on fulfilling the present vision, it will be necessary for them to add new details to existing plans, just to maintain interest. An 'on-going' now is to them a yawn! Also once their own interest is focused elsewhere, they may not remember to encourage others who are persisting in the on-going project they gave so much energy to beginning.

Since the Prophetic tends to be the one steaming on ahead, it is a good idea if he or she knows where they are going. They are so convinced and energetic that others who have begun to follow are less likely to be able to stand back and question, since just keeping up takes a fair bit of doing. Faulty vision is more of a danger to the Prophetic when he or she knowingly compromises, and is awkward about this, unable to be transparent, wary of being caught out. They may then cover their tracks, rather than risk exposure, but then a fault may run through the length of whatever is built upon it. Other people have come to depend upon him or her as true and sincere, so it can be devastating to them if the Prophetic they relied on disappoints them. The disillusionment could be just as awful if they only find out long afterwards that the Prophetic was not all they appeared to be.

The Prophetic who realises that they can take responsibility for their own actions does themselves and the rest of the world a favour. They are able to develop enough self-discipline not to aggravate people automatically, but instead to win their trust, and enlist their help in a cause worthy of their full energies. It is like shoring up the banks of the river so all of that energy is a channelled torrent. Without proper boundaries the same waters would dissipate everywhere, or flood and cause damage somewhere else. By remembering not to make an issue of things which are comparatively unimportant, the wise Prophetic ensures they are taken seriously, and that their voice will be heard and respected.

8. Thinks about God

The Prophetic is a thinker, an idealist, a dreamer, or even a visionary, one who cares about truth. (Some teachers on motivational gifts call this person the 'Perceiver'.) They wonder about the principles which hold life together. Even if they are an atheist they will often invent the concept of God to argue a point or tell an intriguing or provocative joke. Their hypothetical concept of God is often more highly developed than that of firm believers of other motivations! A Christian of this motivation may often remark, 'I wonder what God thinks of all this . . .?' and in response their companions may look baffled as if to say, 'What an odd thing to say!' Hearing from God will matter to them intensely.

Their power of influence, the power to sway other people, is great. It is important that this is used with integrity, and that they adhere firmly to their ideals of justice, fighting to make the impossible attainable. Their particular aptitude for imagining what God's perspective in a situation might be will be worth investing significant time in (whether the person specifically believes in God or not). This kind of meditation – or even intense bouts of intercession – will create a still focus at the centre of their life which is preferable to headlong indiscriminate involvement in situations. From this place of focus will come a clarity as to what and who to be involved with, and a less aggressive involvement when it comes.

It is important for them to be centred in this way, to find a peacefulness around their intensity, a focus of thought – or prayer – about others. This will also temper their tendency to disappoint by talking big then not following through. Their life will match up to their mouth.

9. Wholehearted and sincere

They operate with fits of enthusiasm. Once they 'see' a thing, it drives them into action. Once activated they have great drive – unless interrupted. Once committed to a cause they are wholeheartedly involved in it. But they need to have their imagination captured and fired initially if they are to stay the course; pragmatic reasons will not be enough to maintain their interest and commitment. Within a maintained commitment they are quick to respond to new situations and opportunities. They can be generous on occasions.

They are both tough and tender. They know the value of being bold and frank, but can learn also to be gentle and persuasive. They can insist on high standards and be very demanding, yet can forgive wholeheartedly. They are serious, a good listener at times, when they choose to give their attention to it. At other times it may seem impossible to engage their attention, silence them or slow them down.

They are often very capable, and are not afraid to attempt the impossible. They are sincere, and eager to do what is right, usually with transparent motives. They enjoy people who choose to be completely honest with them.

10. Truth matters to them

They are uncompromising. If they are going to do what is right, they will do it regardless of cost. They are honest. Integrity is their byword.

They would return to a shop to pay for an item they had accidentally not been charged for, as soon as they had discovered the mistake. They will even tell you what is wrong with an item before they try to sell you it.

They are often willing, sometimes eager, to suffer when it comes to standing for the truth or doing what is right. Usually they will fight for what they believe is right even at the cost of relationships.

However, they may ignore truth where personal need is great (for example, sexual needs).

11. Has strong opinions and convictions

They let people know how they feel about important issues. There is a tendency to be too dogmatic, too extreme, too blunt, and they overstate the situation. Prophetics are quick to have an opinion – even about something they are only hearing about for the first time.

They talk in strong, uncomplicated sentences, and get carried away with what they are saying. They don't like things to be too cautious and balanced. Complications irritate them! (They are suspicious of sentences with subordinate clauses that modify what is being said.)

The Prophetic is always in pursuit of whatever they consider to be most important at the time.

12. Angered by injustice

We should not be surprised that many Prophetics have a strong interest or involvement in politics, political causes or social issues. The context for this may be sounding off to the four walls of the living room in indignation at some news bulletin on the TV, or it could be folding or delivering leaflets campaigning for a candidate of the political party of their choice. The grand canvas on which the issues are painted is the common denominator. 'The poor you will have with you always,' Jesus said, and injustice, the need for change, concerns requiring action are unlikely to become exhausted. The Prophetic's boundless energies can be poured readily into causes that are always going to seem big.

13. Intolerant or dogmatic

Prophetics are intolerant of opinions and views that differ from their own. What they see and say may be right, but they tend to forget it is only one perspective or one aspect of the truth. Each person's view may have validity, and should at least be listened to instead of dismissed by an impatient Prophetic! Madeleine L'Engle says, 'I have a perspective, you have a perspective, but God has *perspective.*' The Prophetic often acts as if they believe that they *are* God and that their perspective is the only true one.

Often a couple with difficulties in their marriage will arrive for counselling, and one of them happens to be Prophetically motivated. The Prophetic usually has quite clear ideas what is wrong in the situation: the problem, of course, is their partner. They go on to give the counsellor all the relevant answers, expecting their opinions to be reinforced – it's what comes of knowing they are right!

The apparent strength of their conviction would cause most people to back down rather than argue a point. But, in fact, if you suggest another possibility to the Prophetic they may be surprisingly open to any alternative.

14. Dynamic

The energy and drive of the Prophetic person may feel disruptive when it is not going anywhere, but once it has found an appropriate channel it can accomplish great things and carry others along in its sway. They know what direction they are going, even if they haven't worked out what they are going to do when they get there. They like to be focused and walk in straight lines. They will characteristically say, 'What we are losing sight of is this . . .', calling people back to the original focus and intention. Of course, they may see things differently from other people. What others perceive as 'racing off towards nowhere in particular' the Prophetic may be enjoying under a mental heading of 'embarking upon an adventure'!

15. Determined and compelling

They are overwhelmingly convincing. They are persistent enough to remain convinced and 'right' in splendid isolation. Everyone else can go and be wrong and it wouldn't matter to the Prophetic at all; it wouldn't budge them one inch. And, of course, they always believe they are right at the time, even if they have to revise their opinion later.

When they are not being silent altogether, they will often talk in great detail about the matter in hand. They are not good at small talk.

But if they set their mind to influencing others, their power of persuasion is considerable because of the strength of their convictions about everything. A persuasive Prophetic will often convince others to revisit their previous opinions, and they can make a risky course of action seem plausible. At other times they can be pushy or impatient when wanting a quick response from others, and they will often press for quick decisions.

As children they are likely to have been 'headstrong' and strong-willed. When checked or reproached they would usually remonstrate and give reasons for their actions!

16. Direct or judgemental

They often jump to conclusions. Whenever they see or hear something that is wrong they feel responsible to speak out against it. It might not occur to them to ask, 'Whose responsibility is this?' or 'Do I have all the facts?' or 'Do I need to take action at this time?'

They draw conclusions from few known facts. They tend to be very impulsive and make quick judgements on what they see and hear. At times they can waver between extremes. They also tend to express their views before others have had chance to speak. Once a hasty conclusion has been reached, that judgement tends to be fixed in their minds. They then tend to look for confirming evidence, and may feel compelled to persuade others to agree with them.

When correcting others they can be painfully direct, and have no regard for the status or prestige of the one they are addressing. It does not intimidate them at all. When the Prophetic sees someone's actions are wrong, they are inclined to assume that this insight alone gives them the right to set that person straight. They then tend to denounce what is wrong so strongly that others feel protective of the culprit. Yet this exposure may be a necessary first step to reparation or a fresh beginning.

Then the Prophetic would tend to expect the person to want a complete change to take place immediately, regardless of whether the rebuke was in the person's best interest or was even fully accurate. They expect others to change direction as radically and rapidly as they would themselves. Sometimes they find it difficult to distinguish between an action, decision or attitude and the person behind it, and find themselves rejecting both with equal vigour.

17. Radical

They are bold and radical, sometimes ruthless, and will often be at the front in an initiative, moving forward loudly or visibly enough to stir others to action, like a trumpet call summoning the troops.

They will often say, 'But the important thing is . . .' to move a discussion on. Once they decide to go for something they will go for it and pursue it, regardless of the cost, and are very inclined to go over the top. Excess of all kinds is natural to them (which is why they instictively like Givers and admire their recklessness). In their pursuit of what is important, other people may be knocked over or stepped over with no deliberate insensitivity on the Prophetic's part. When they see that someone got hurt they can be suitably penitent, or may just shrug their shoulders. Keeping the peace with everyone seems like very hard work to them and not always worth the effort. It may sometimes be observed that they like to go against the crowd – even for the sake of it. They will play 'devil's advocate'. They will choose the route that involves swimming upstream. They will turn a simple task into a challenge.

They are not frightened to embrace a course of action that makes great personal demands or presents endless difficulties to overcome. Sometimes they would rather tear everything down and start again from scratch, instead of modifying and adapting what they are uneasy with.

18. Restless

Their restlessness makes them difficult people to live with. Sometimes they'll begin a task just to work something out of their system. This could be cleaning and tidying furiously, even disruptively. At best, their restlessness provokes them to useful and appropriate action. They are unlikely to become complacent. Prolonged inactivity and vegetating will make them feel nervous – or bring on a bout of self-loathing. It is a relief for them to discover their restlessness is part of their giftedness and not just sin or negativity. They are painfully aware and critical in most situations but can be bitingly negative unless they find appropriate outlets for their perceptions.

Don and Katie Fortune* tell of a 73-year-old woman being taught motivations for the first time and recognising herself as a Prophetic:

> 'If only I had heard this 50 years ago,' she said. 'I have lived all my life with a torturing awareness of what was wrong in people and situations. But I didn't know what to do with it, so I criticised. Then I criticised myself for being critical. All my life I've wanted to be different.' From that point on she accepted who she was, and threw all her energies into praying for possible transformation in people's situations.

19. Hard to ignore

It is as if their natural plumage includes a signal that shouts, 'Look at me! Listen to me!' Their intensity and energy mark them out before anyone has a chance to interact with what they wish to convey.

They have the need to graphically express their inner vision, and they are often seen as original thinkers with the ability to come at an idea from a totally different angle to what other people would expect. They will sometimes come up with a striking picture, a telling or memorable phrase, a compelling story. Even in conversation they may

---

* Don and Katie Fortune, *Discover Your God-given Gifts* (1987, Fleming H. Revell Co., Tarrytown, New York

leave an uncomfortable sentence hanging in the air in a way it is difficult to forget or ignore.

If they are the more silent, little-but-lethal Prophetic, people will be surprised that they come up with the crucial point or remark that is remembered; if they are the louder, more visible Prophetic, then it is the occasional moment of focusedness that is so arresting.

Some Prophetics will be drawn to story-telling, graphic arts or even theatre, and seem to have no shortage of original ideas.

20. Tough and tender

Strident and sensitive, passionate and disarming, they are the tough-and-tender ones. Although they may be viewed as rather 'tough' or blunt individuals, inside they are very sensitive people who can experience inner anguish over their own faults and even the failings of other people. Once they recognise they have been in the wrong, or are found out, they have the capacity to experience deep and genuine inner sorrow and to exercise a real inner brokenness or repentance.

They are often acutely aware of their personal unworthiness, to the point where they confess that unworthiness and want others to point out their personal blind spots. They see, understand and grieve deeply over sin in themselves and in others. The idea of 'sin' is quite satisfying to even the non-religious Prophetically motivated person. It's one of those words that calls a spade a spade: if you're going to be wrong, you might as well be dead wrong!

Approval from other people, the relevant authorities or even from God is very affirming and important to them, but if it's not there, forget it! – they'll do without. For children or teenagers of this motivation the approval of parents will matter a great deal.

COMPLIMENTS

The Prophetic person may be pleased to be told that what they said was 'such an inspiration!' They may be sensitive about people who call them 'cruel'.

(Some Prophetics may be quite upset about the way their characteristics are described even in this chapter, and argue that it is unjust – they would never be so negative, rude or abrasive. Their objection may have validity. Often a Prophetic has learned to habitually temper these traits with sensitivity and consideration, and can maintain their 'edge' without being obvious or offensive.)

Chapter 5
The Server Motivation

GENERAL CHARACTERISTICS

1. Alert and active
2. Practical and ingenious
3. Meticulous and thrifty
4. Hospitable
5. Finds strong emotions hard to handle
6. Reliable and loyal
7. Content not to lead
8. Available and direct
9. Needs to be helpful
10. For them, love means action
11. Goes the extra mile
12. Gets over-involved
13. Should learn to prioritise
14. Applies their energies
15. Likes immediate goals
16. Resents wasted time
17. Gets on with the job
18. Dependable
19. Sees ordinary tasks as crucial
20. Needs appreciation

1. Alert and active

A Server is well aware of the many tasks demanding their attention in their own home or workplace, but carries this same practical awareness with them wherever they go. If they are going to be in a situation anyway, then they would rather roll up their sleeves and get involved. If they can see there is a lot to be done, they may even be the first to arrive and the last to leave.

They spot all the jobs that need to be done, and often wonder why other people seem not to notice. However, they don't go looking for extra work just for the sake of it. They get involved when they are willing to, or when it seems the obvious thing to do.

Others are often not aware of all that the Server does because they are typically a 'behind the scenes' person. They will tend to do more than their share of the necessary work, voluntarily. Their measure is 'Well, I could do that'.

They concentrate on the task in hand and deal with the people later, unless they recognise that people *is* the job in hand!

2. Practical and ingenious

A Server is competent and practical, and enjoys working with their hands. They like hands-on involvement in any task they have to supervise, and don't delegate easily or instinctively. They don't mind doing jobs alone; in fact, they often prefer to work alone, to be left unsupervised with nobody looking over their shoulder. (Sometimes they may reject others' offers of help, because they know what they are doing and would like to be left to get on with it.)

Servers enjoy practical problem-solving and are usually excellent at improvising solutions. One might use a pair of tights for a new fan belt on the car; another might throw together a great picnic lunch out of next to nothing. They enjoy demonstrating things and passing on practical tips, such as the best way to effect a particular repair.

They are interested in learning new skills. They enjoy watching anyone who knows what they are doing, and, where possible, they will have a try themselves.

3. Meticulous and thrifty

The Server likes to get the job done and done properly. When allocated a task, they give great attention to detail, and this can become a distraction or a delay. They like the bench to be clear so they can get on with the job in hand. Things that might come in handy can also be a problem, as these must be stored somewhere, whether there is a place for them or not. A garage, shed, attic or scullery is useful!

4. Hospitable

The Server (like the Giver) enjoys showing hospitality. Welcoming people to their home is a great way of showing they care.

They enjoy having company and make every effort to put you at your ease. They will be interested and involved, and ready for in-depth conversation. But the next day if you met them in the street, they may seem more abrupt. They still genuinely care, but are in gear for a different set of tasks!

5. Finds strong emotions hard to handle

The Server's people-skills are somewhat uneven. They understand the world of things in a way that other people often marvel at. They like people but feel they don't always know how to cope with them, especially those most different from themselves. Some Servers even secretly compare people to things in an attempt to make sense of the people, saying to themselves, 'I wonder what needs fixing with him', or, 'Now, what made her blow a fuse?' (They are wise enough rarely to admit that they catch themselves doing this. They have a sneaky suspicion folk would disapprove.)

117

In everyday life a Server processes emotions as they go along, integrating them into the general scheme of things. So if someone else becomes very emotional, the Server may feel disadvantaged or at a loss. They don't know how to help, and feel they ought to!

They feel very deeply about some things, but cannot always unlock their responses. When their own strong emotions become overwhelming and surface unexpectedly, the Server typically finds that hard to deal with. It seems to them almost like a malfunction. They feel they should have a handle on what is happening inside of them, but instead feel awkward, angry, tearful or confused. They feel out of their depth and unsure of themselves. Afterwards, they are likely to continue on their way, with the vague sense that they have not adequately understood what all that was about. In the normal course of events, they would feel things, even sometimes very deeply, but without being knocked off balance.

A particular change of circumstances, a crisis or fresh experience may be a challenge to the Server. It is an opportunity to go deeper, and experience a new range of emotions they are not accustomed to dealing with. The obstacle to going deeper may be the Server's need to cope, since their capacity for deep emotions is extended only by getting out of their depth and experiencing what they cannot cope with.

6. Reliable and loyal

One television quiz show makes the contestants answer as many questions as they can before the buzzer goes. If time is up while the question master is reading a question he says, 'I've started, so I'll finish . . .' This little phrase is very typical of the Server's thinking. They are dissatisfied if for some reason they have to leave a job unfinished. If the buzzer goes off, the Server is likely to ignore it and finish what they were doing. Things take time, especially if they are done properly. Many Servers pride themselves on always doing what they said they would.

Similarly, they are consistent and loyal in their friendships. Servers know who they are. They are not generally threatened by those who intimidate other people.

7. Content not to lead

A Server tends to avoid positions of leadership or being upfront. They typically do not want to lead people or projects. Their instinct is to become frustrated in a position of leadership, but they are generally very supportive of those who lead. They are happy, instead, to 'do what they can' to help. They like to be loyal to those they work for (and those they work alongside).

However, a capable and well-adjusted Server makes an admirable leader, avoiding unnecessary talk or delay. But they must take care to communicate adequately to whoever is under their supervision what is required of them, and to communicate what they themselves are doing, whenever it is different to what has previously been communicated. A Server as a preacher or teacher is a pleasure to listen to (unless, of course, they get caught up in detail which to them is practical but to you is lengthy).

> Robson Rochester trained as a non-stipendiary Anglican priest. (That meant he would take on new responsibilities unpaid and still do his normal job.) His preaching was always to the point and eminently practical. In his soft Northumbrian accent he would insist: 'Jesus said, "Love one another, love one another!" So why don't we do it?' Just over five minutes. Not a word wasted.

119

Sometimes a Server is given promotion because of being a diligent worker, only to find their new role frustrating, and the change unhelpful.

Servers in managerial roles may offset the inevitable frustration by allowing themselves some small task in which they may have practical hands-on involvement. This must be in-built in the general strategy and have defined limits so it doesn't absorb all their energies. They must also refuse to be drawn by distractions. When the fire alarm goes off, the temptation would be to fix it themselves, rather than continue with what is on the desk. They find it hard not to volunteer a helping hand or become involved in tasks which it would be appropriate to delegate to others. This can lead to them not completing their own work on schedule.

Servers can make good leaders, once they make their mind up that it could be appropriate. Then if the job is worth doing, they will learn how do it well.

8. Available and direct

A Server is more interested in meeting the needs of others than meeting their own.

A Server child may ask, 'Can I help?' or 'Is there anything to do?' The offer of help is genuine and must be treated seriously. They want to be useful, not just occupied – so they will be frustrated if they are given next-to-nothing to do. If you are just glad of their company, say so. Then they will contentedly give their attention to talking.

Servers especially like it when they can do something which frees other people for tasks which are more important or which can't be done by anyone else. They love to do things, knowing that getting them done is bringing peace of mind to another person and allowing that person to be more productive.

They also are generally very direct. They can get flustered, but don't like to 'beat around the bush'. They tend to speak in straightforward sentences without secondary clauses. Their vocabulary is littered with the words 'do', 'did', 'doing', 'done', 'job', etc. – whatever they are talking about. The most complicated concepts will usually be reduced to these terms or seen in reference to them. (It becomes very noticeable in a group if they try to give examples which explain which motivational gift might be theirs.)

9. Needs to be helpful

Servers get their greatest joy by doing something that is helpful. But when the Server has already begun a job, and other people wade in to help, the Server may resent it. Suddenly they feel put upon and no longer wanted, especially if the others are only doing it because they can't think of anything better to do.

The Server needs clear directions about not only what needs to be done but what should not be done! (In their eagerness to help they could insist on walking the proverbial old lady across the road when she doesn't want to go.) A Server enjoys doing small tasks that need to be done without being asked to do them.

Don and Katie Fortune tell the following story:

At a church there was a Server lady who noticed one of the classrooms needed painting. She went to the minister about this who assured her the deacons would take care of it. Two weeks later nothing had happened, so she took the matter into her own hands and painted the whole room. Later she discovered that the deacons had decided to enlarge the room, put in wall-to-wall cupboards, etc. Then because she had used a dark paint, they had to use two extra coats of the lighter-coloured paint that had already been chosen.

121

10. For them, love means action

The Server likes to express how much they care, but they instinctively express it through deeds and actions rather than words. Not content just to be physically demonstrative, they will first look for other practical expressions of affection. They demonstrate love by meeting practical needs and showing in this way that they care.

A Server will say, 'It's easy to say the words, "I love you", but the other person may never really believe it until you do something for them.'

11. Goes the extra mile

The Server likes to do things well, and may do more than is asked, even if at times it goes unnoticed. They know they did it!

12. Gets over-involved

A Server has a hard time saying 'No' if someone could do with their help. It comes naturally to them to be helpful and they are usually good at what they do. When someone asks them to explain how to solve a particular problem, the Server's way of explaining soon turns to demonstrating, which quickly becomes doing most of the job with them or for them.

Servers easily become involved in too many activities, and may complain of lack of helpers. They may also neglect their own work and their family needs by being too busy helping others.

> Alan says, 'Someone else has asked me to go over and help them move house.' He relays the information with such enthusiasm that you'd think it had at least been an invitation to an outing or social gathering.

Over-involvement can easily put a person under stress and cause anxiety. Servers regularly disregard their own weariness.

13. Should learn to prioritise

Within a community or family, Servers are happy seeing to practical needs. They get on with the job and keep everything going with great commitment, but not just for the sake of it. It may be their way of demonstrating their love or that they care. They love to be doing, to be useful, to be dependable. A Server sees what they do as a demonstration of their loyalty to their husband or wife, family or even God. This is especially true of the ordinary things of life which other people might discount as routine or unimportant.

The Server needs to learn to put their priorities in order. They should not say 'Yes' to everyone who asks. They should not do too many things or they will be too tired to work out which things have made them too tired!

14. Applies their energies

A Server wants to do things well and may even go beyond their strength, expending all their energies on some job which they have taken on. They may not have any more energy or stamina than anyone else, but they are determined and may disregard their own weariness at times. They will sometimes keep going at things when the rest of us have collapsed and dropped out of the race! They do get slightly irritated by those who won't pull their weight or put themselves out.

15. Likes immediate goals

Servers prefer jobs that are short rather than long. It's

satisfying to see the end of one task and then have another to move on to.

A longer project needs breaking down into smaller individual tasks that can be addressed one at a time and completed. On that basis the Server will continue happily indefinitely.

A Server is a 'now' person, and when they see a need they want to meet it right away, rather than wait for a more convenient time.

16. Resents wasted time

A Server hates to have their time wasted. This will be demonstrated in their attitude to committees. Some Servers are on numerous committees, and see this as an opportunity to be really helpful. A lot of other Servers avoid committees like the plague. They are likely to sit restively, remembering all the other things they could more usefully be giving their time to.

The Server finds the needless hours it takes to come to the point and make a decision very irritating. We could picture an exasperated Server arriving early enough to fill the urn, then clock-watching through the meeting, disappearing quietly to pour out drinks and bringing them round during the meeting, clearing them away again, and returning in time for the only part of the meeting that interested them in the first place, the bit where all the talking is finished with and the jobs that need to be done are being given out!

17. Gets on with the job

A Server will get on with the job in front of them, while half a dozen other people are standing around talking about it. They would take a sly pleasure in creating the situation whereby when everybody looked for the job it was already 'been and gone'.

They will sigh with frustration over necessary interruptions, and be visibly at ease in the middle of what they are doing. They are typically more ill at ease when they are not sure what they should do or even when they will be allowed to start. This is true regardless of how simple or how complex the task is.

18. Dependable

On the whole, the Server is comfortable with routine: it gives some solidness on which to work, or a structure inside which they can get on. If you were to go away and leave a task unsupervised, the Server is one person it is unlikely you would need to check up on. They would continue to work through whatever tasks had been assigned to them, or keep a check on whatever were their routine areas to maintain.

All they would want to know is that you didn't expect anything different from them which you hadn't told them about. They would probably prefer to know whom they should consult in the event of a query. They would like to know that in an unforeseen emergency they would be allowed just to problem-solve as they saw best.

Servers and Rulers tend to work together very easily. They are both task-orientated and reasonably matter of fact.

A Server doesn't like to let someone down. (But when plans change they may forget that other people haven't been told.)

19. Sees ordinary tasks as crucial

The Server recognises that ordinary tasks are crucial to

the achievement of any goal. Consequently, they are un-impressed by status. Each cog is needed for the wheels to turn.

It would be wrong to see the Server as a general dogs-body. They may have strings of degrees and lots of responsibility. It is important to stress that Servers appear in every kind of job imaginable. Their spheres may differ but their perspective is predictably straightforward. They love to see people making wise use of the available time.

They can become very critical of others who don't see things quite the same way. For them the 'now' need is always the most important thing, and they cannot easily understand, or easily be generous to, people who have a different perspective.

They enjoy situations that reduce other people to the same common denominators. Everybody has the same basic needs at some time or another, regardless of their motivation or status. When someone needs baby clothes, or moves house, or breaks a leg, the server knows exactly what to do. Even if they weren't the one to go to their assistance, the Server is reassured by knowing the other person is going through things that are common to us all.

20. Needs appreciation

The Server may need reassurance from time to time that what they are doing to help other people is appreciated. Their work should be seen, even if *they* are not. Servers do not like to do things that no one notices or cares about. They hate to be taken for granted or treated as if they were inferior just because they do things others dislike doing! Any deprecating remark or attitude really hurts. They are in danger of being walked on, but also in danger of being resentful at times.

They get their greatest joy when others realise just what they have done and express this in some way. In quietly showing appreciation you affirm their own sense of self-worth. But they do not want much public recognition or praise. They hate a song and dance to be made on their behalf. Because their attention is on practical things, it is easy for us not to think of them as particularly having feelings. But they can be deeply hurt if they are never acknowledged.

> One Server said, 'It really hurts me when I put myself out to help someone and they never even say, "Thanks."'

Look at the Servers in your life, and make sure you really appreciate them.

COMPLIMENTS

The Server is the one others call a 'salt-of-the-earth' type, but they prefer to have it acknowledged quietly that they have done a job well. They like folk to say, 'Thank you', but preferably in private.

In the JOBS box they will most naturally be drawn to take on a 'gift of helps' (1 Corinthians 12:28). Of course, the natural thing is not what inevitably happens. Instead, someone less easily suited may become a helper, and the Server may bring their particular aptitudes and priorities to a less predictable job or area of service. Perhaps this is a deliberate dynamic (blame God!) which makes life more complicated and more interesting!

Chapter 6
The Teaching Motivation

GENERAL CHARACTERISTICS

1. Logical and systematic
2. Questioning and thorough
3. Learns with concentration
4. Backs up arguments
5. Legalistic and dogmatic
6. Objective and detached
7. Struggles with practical application
8. Uses words well
9. Factual and accurate
10. Checks the source
11. Has respect for experts
12. Informative and 'know-it-all'
13. (Potentially) self-disciplined
14. Struggles with their emotions
15. Insensitive to atmosphere
16. Has wide interests
17. Inquisitive
18. Relies on memory
19. Has few close friends
20. Hates to be hurried

1. Logical and systematic

They like logic and order, or would like everything to be logical and ordered, if it were only possible! It tends to make them feel more comfortable! They want to know events in the order they occurred.

The Teacher would like to make profound concepts simple and understandable. ('The one who says it most simply, knows it best.') They are an explaining person with the gift of making things clear. Truths must be acquired and communicated effectively if people are to learn in a meaningful way. A simple question from a friend will result in long explanations, presenting in a much more accessible way what had puzzled their friend. The Teacher can always explain, but may be too shy to do so or to teach in public. They may never have ever dreamt of teaching anybody anything, but those around them recognise their ability to listen and try to understand.

2. Questioning and thorough

The Teaching motivation could be better described as an explaining motivation, but most of all they are somebody who wants to understand, who likes to learn. They want to know, or would like to know. The Explainer is concerned about whether something is true, and will validate this by checking out the facts. Their concern is with whether information is being presented fairly. The Teaching motivation wants to ask questions all the time.

They become frustrated when anybody teaching or demonstrating is unclear or uses big words unnecessarily which some people may not understand. The Teaching motivation will typically then interrupt and ask questions they themselves already know the answer to, in order to give others a chance to understand. They will usually grasp the essence of what is being communicated, and make a mental note of any words that were unfamiliar so as to check up on them afterwards.

A Teaching person is uneasy with subjective truth. They are concerned that everything be presented in balance.

They recognise the danger of using personal experience as a foundation for truth. They will play by the rules, even if it means not finishing the game.

The Explainer will generally not rush into making statements. They tend to wait until everything has been said, then weigh each observation. They want their conclusions to be fair and accurate. For example, in being exposed to this material on motivational giftings, they may resent the idea of being 'pigeon-holed', especially hastily, and challenge your insistence that each person has been gifted with only one root motivation.

If a Teaching motivation learns that they have got their facts wrong in some way, they will not be able just to shrug their shoulders, but will want to retrace their steps to determine at what point they got off the track. They want the misunderstanding to be cleared up.

Someone may casually ask a question in conversation. If the Teaching person finds the question interesting they will warm to the subject and answer carefully, even if the other person was not that bothered.

This thoroughness applies not only to explaining tasks, but to most jobs they finally undertake. Having made the decision to get involved they wade into the task with sustained energy. But if they were unsure about taking it on in the first place, their enthusiasm will predictably dissipate quickly.

3. Learns with concentration

The Teaching person loves to understand and to learn. But they are not necessarily brilliant students. Some will learn by reading, others by listening to tapes, sitting in lectures or seminars, or by watching TV. Some learn only through conversation, but manage to have something to interject in discussions about almost any subject. They can quickly be seen to be articulate and knowledgeable, and can give the impression of having far more to say if they chose to!

If something is to be presented, the hunt for material or systematic research may be more enjoyable than the actual presentation of it. Their concern for thoroughness may sometimes mean they feel obliged to explain how they reached their conclusions, or they include too much fascinating detail which others find tedious. The proverbial wood can no longer be seen for the detail of the tree by tree account. (The Explainer, given long enough, will complete by reiterating their original summary: the wood!)

They have an amazing ability to concentrate and shut out the outside world. This can be very good: the ability to remain focused on the task in hand without being diverted by a multitude of distractions. It often enables them to keep their head in a crisis. But, if they are thinking something through, they can be totally oblivious to what is going on around them, and even ignore direct questions. Many Teaching people have the uncanny knack of being unknowingly insensitive! A lot depends on who or what they are concentrating on at the time. This is not deliberate insensitivity – just the flip-side of the intensity of their concentration.

4. Backs up arguments

The Explainer objects to unfounded statements. They will not accept ready-made conclusions. They want to know how you can say that and why. They distrust hasty judgements – even their own. A Teaching person likes a background of factual detail against which they can view whatever is the subject. They want to see something in context.

They may enjoy being argumentative or divisive, always giving reasons for the position they have adopted. They are comfortable with concepts and ideas, and will play around with ideas at an abstract level. They will follow an argument to its logical conclusion.

They like to be sure of their reasons before adjusting their stance on any issue. The Explainer appreciates the phrase, 'I have reason to believe . . .'

5. Legalistic and dogmatic

For the Teaching person, if a thing is right once, it's always right. If why we do it that way has once been explained to them, then that way we will do it.

This trait can show up even in children. They will insist on playing games exactly according to the rules – or check the instructions on the box-lid! A shortcut in Monopoly would be unthinkable. They will say, 'Play it right, or not at all.'

Similarly, if a thing has been proven, then it is true. If the logic of an argument appeals to them, they will warm to the conclusion more readily.

They will defend what they believe to be true by stating and restating it. If someone attacks their basic assumptions or underlying beliefs, they may react defensively. They can appear coldly dogmatic and unable to see beyond their own secure, proven knowledge boundaries.

6. Objective and detached

Sometimes in a crisis it will be the Teaching person who remains steady and acts normally while others panic. In day-to-day activities and situations the Teaching person usually manages to stay self-contained, even with whole-hearted involvement. This helps them to assess what is going on, without their own emotions needing to figure in the equation. But when it comes to those they care about, they are less detached, less objective. This is because they have chosen to be emotionally involved.

What often confuses other people about Explainers is that they are unevenly involved. They can listen attentively, and be truly responsive, when they are making this the priority, and can be wonderfully understanding as friends. This makes it all the more hurtful if on occasions they revert to being totally abstracted and insensitive. This is not deliberate, only a temporary preoccupation!

7. Struggles with practical application

Their head stores two kinds of scrapbooks on any given topic. One is the theory and accumulated data concerning the history of . . . plus miscellaneous minutiae. The other is the manual with step-by-step application. The manual includes the diagram of how it all works, so when they meet a new problem or situation without a previous record of step-by-step problem solving, they access into the overall diagram and begin the process of 'let's see now'. This can be very useful and is automatic.

Sometimes it is irritatingly impractical. When faced with a new situation, they may try to understand it, rather than address it.

> Once we saw a milk bottle skid on to its side on the work-bench for no apparent reason. Our friend Brenda, the person nearest, stood fascinated as the milk continued to pour all over the floor, trying to figure out how it could have slipped with no one touching it.

At other times the Explainer will respond immediately with good reason in a way few others would have thought of.

As we were crossing into Massachusetts, Brenda slammed on the brakes to avoid hitting a baby's high chair which was standing upright on the freeway right in front of us . . . One driver coming over the brow of the hill apparently did not see our hazard lights. As he continued towards us at full speed, Brenda abruptly released her brake. The collision wrecked both vehicles, but no one was killed. When we have related this story, other drivers are often puzzled and ask why she took off the brake! Brenda, with her Teaching motivation, had immediately recalled that this was what you are supposed to do to minimise the impact.

The Explainer can become a hoarder of useless information. The above example was one instance where it saved the lives of a number of people and turned out not to be useless after all! It might be 'just theory' at first, but the time may well come that demands the application of that theoretical knowledge, and then it ceases to be 'just theory'.

8. Uses words well

People with a Teaching motivation are good with words, and usually pay attention to how they are used. They are likely to enjoy quizzes and word games of all kinds. They enjoy being right or doing well, but are also storing answers for another time. Their own vocabulary expands naturally and easily. Given the task of communicating, their aptitude may suddenly become evident; sometimes they are engaging or fascinating to listen to. Their speech is measured and their words are usually carefully chosen, even in everyday conversation. Some Teaching folk can be witty, with a keen sense of humour. They also like to use illustrations to communicate more effectively. They are enthusiastic conversationalists and often enjoy parties.

9. Factual and accurate

Explainers will mentally wave aside your opinions but want to know the reasons for what you think or believe. They want to examine the facts and draw their own conclusions. Truth is always validated for them by checking out the facts. They use their minds to check out arguments. When they hear important statements, whether given in private or public, they will want to verify them. Their motivation is to confirm that the statements are true and accurate.

A Teaching person has a need to go to primary sources to validate truth. They will also use recognised authorities to further confirm statements which others make. The non-academic Explainer will often give the impression of being well-read. In fact, Explainers believe deep down that teaching, or at least understanding, is foundational to all other gifts!

Explainers are like private investigators, questioning everything and distrusting anyone who makes unfounded statements.

People of a Teaching motivation place great emphasis on the accuracy of words, right definition, pronunciation, and derivation. This coupled with their ability to use words well and their objectivity, often make them painfully aware of misspelt words, improper grammar or inadequate vocabulary.

Explainers are thorough. They enjoy finding and then communicating details which are not noticed by other people. You notice them saying things like, 'Not many people know that . . .' and 'Did you know . . . ?'

10. Checks the source

In some situations Teachers are proverbially slow to commit

themselves. If we are teaching on motivations to a group, and one person keeps the others waiting by refusing to admit their gift publicly, or disputes the assertion that each person has only one primary gift, it is more than likely that they will finally acknowledge that they had already recognised that theirs was the Teaching motivation. They wanted to be sure that they had understood, and that you knew what you were talking about.

They can be very slow to accept the viewpoint and understanding of others, and can even become argumentative. 'But how can you say that?' 'By that do you mean . . . ?' 'What if . . . ?' Sometimes the question or objection will need answering before you can continue. On other occasions it will suffice to point out that it will become clear in due course, and to explain why you are approaching the material in this order and more slowly or briskly than they would like.

Explainers will always want to 'test' the knowledge of anyone who is 'teaching' them. They always want to check out the source. They are always asking questions. They want to know the basis for everything, and they will search until the facts convince them that something is true. At the first flaw in someone's presentation the Explainer can reject what is being said, and could then refuse to hear anything more, dismissing the speaker as untrustworthy. They may also be unreceptive if they are asked to accept a conclusion intellectually without knowing how the other person arrived at it.

11. Has respect for experts

A Teacher respects learning, training and established authorities on any given subject. They prefer to consult the expert in a field, and especially like to be able to refer to the one text that is definitive, the 'bible' on the subject. It may be George Bain on Celtic knotwork for calligraphy or Wainwright on the Lakeland Fells; they always respect the expert.

Often they will check up on the formal credentials of professionals. They'll notice the letters after the dentist's name, read the diploma on the wall in the waiting room when picking up a child from their ballet lesson, have their tyres changed by a reputable firm, or choose a novel in preference to another one because it is a Carnegie Medal or Whitbread Prize winner.

Those who are not easily academic still tend to place a high value on qualifications, and may even return as mature students to repeat a year they flunked, or do night classes until they attain certificates they now don't actually need. They enjoy the course but also have something to prove to themselves.

Some are disillusioned with certification or theoretical knowledge, and place more value on experience and expertise. They still want to call on the best qualified person, but have a different assessment of what constitutes being expert or well-qualified.

12. Informative and 'know-it-all'

The Explainer can be motivated to impart knowledge and to lead others to what is established to be true. They make keen use of their minds, and are able to be informative with great attention to detail. They catch on to things quickly and are soon able to remember or précis mounds of information.

To be shown round a city or historical site by someone with this gifting could be memorable. Whatever your question, or whatever landmark you pass, the relevant information or favourite anecdote is accessed immediately, and they will become more animated as they warm to their subject and want you to understand. You would either be delighted or avoid repeating the experience.

On some subjects they may make it a priority to keep updated with the latest information. They feel gaps in their knowledge are a real disadvantage, and will sometimes avoid owning up to not knowing or not understanding. When someone else is speaking they may listen attentively, nodding or interjecting only occasionally. They will often give the impression of understanding far more than they choose to speak about. (They think, 'To not know is bad enough, but for someone to know that I don't know really puts me at a disadvantage.')

The Explainer enjoys learning something new. When others show little interest in doing the same, they think it's pitiful!

Some Explainers are inclined to give you their explanation whether you want to hear it or not! And others withdraw into silence to punish you for not having the wisdom to invite their opinion. At their most irritating they can seem smug! (Even in childhood this can create a habit of distance in relationships. The habit can be broken by being more accepting of others, and by learning to respect the right of those other people to see things differently.)

13. (Potentially) self-disciplined

The Teacher likes to live in an ordered world and, with discipline, can make sure their energies are productively applied. Some Teachers are disorganised or lazy, but only because they never got around to doing anything about it. Once these disciplines are in place, the Teacher comes quickly to depend on them and insist on their importance. They then insist on knowing what they are working towards, when they are expected to get there, and what scope they have to explore possibilities in the meantime.

14. Struggles with their emotions

The emotional life of the Explainer is a bit like a sea on which normally they sail along happily enough. Sometimes it is plain sailing; at other times the waters are more turbulent or uneasy. But storms will rarely arise from nowhere – it is a gradual build up, not something sudden. Sometimes they slump beneath the horizon, but the boat is unlikely to go up or down very quickly. Their feelings are for a reason, after all. Although the Explainer is normally not at a loss for words, emotions regularly leave them speechless, unable to convey easily what they mean. It is as if the seascape is a private world, or the location for an epic in which theirs is the leading role.

They believe it is important not to be out of control, and they attempt to remain level-headed. If they are upset, they may be determined to keep their craft afloat and will the waters to subside. On other occasions the seething or unruly emotions they are trying to ride the storm of will spill over and affect folk around them. An uncomfortable atmosphere is created, which others describe as sustained and intense. A friend would then demand that the Teacher tells them what is going on or what is upsetting them, that they access and share their emotions.

If they have outwardly given no indication that there is something going on deep inside them, the Teacher expects no one else to know. But lots of people are sensitive to atmosphere. By contrast, the Teacher relies on observation, tone of voice, recollections of previously shared experience to build up a picture of what is happening with someone else. They don't have a very sure touch in the area of other people's emotions.

You are more likely to compliment them on being 'thoughtful' than 'sensitive'.

15. Insensitive to atmosphere

The Explainer is not naturally sensitive to atmosphere, but instead will remember what is important to a person, what phrases, actions, behaviour have pleased or upset them in the past. They will empathise by listening carefully to a person's description of their feelings and imaginatively recognising their importance, as if they were their own feelings. They are thoughtful and loving, rather than sensitive and tender. They deliberately cultivate a valued friendship or relationship. A strained atmosphere can sometimes go unnoticed by the Explainer if superficially all is well. This can have its advantages as well as its limitations.

> Once, at Thanksgiving, we were staying with friends who were about to divorce. A big dinner was planned because family members were also visiting from another part of the States. The uncomfortable atmosphere was apparent to everyone – except Brenda who entered into the festive spirit of the occasion wholeheartedly and helped cheerfully in the kitchen preparing food, offsetting some of the atmosphere she was blissfully unaware of.

Some Teachers have learned to listen carefully to people's comments and tone of voice, and to observe their reactions closely. They may detect quickly any change in atmosphere by noticing other people's reactions alone. Whilst not innate, there are many intuitive gifts the Explainer can learn to develop.

16. Has wide interests

Explainers have many areas of potential interest. They willingly drop what they are doing to investigate something new or different. If you happen to be talking to them and bring up a new subject, it is likely to spark something with them. They will have read something, heard something, extracted something from a TV report . . . or whatever. They remembered because they were interested, and for them learning is stimulating.

They can also become easily sidetracked. As an exercise you could try giving them an encyclopaedia or dictionary to check something out, and before you know it they are dipping into sections all over the place. Each section is fascinating, and after a while they have almost forgotten what they wanted to know in the first place! They often have lots of half-finished projects, each set aside because something else more interesting came along. The determination to be focused in one direction is not always easy, and they seem to enjoy extending the decision-making process. The delays are not because of lack of concentration. There is an ongoing process of exploring and collating. They are continually aware that other relevant data may still come into play, other options may open up.

17. Inquisitive

The Explainer likes to know and be in the know. They will sit around anywhere when something is being explained or talked about, and they may learn something, even if it doesn't need to concern them.

Fragments of information are often their way of building a picture or forming an impression, and may equip them in the difficult task of endeavouring to be sensitive to the needs and wishes of others. (Caution should be employed then: a little knowledge can be dangerous or misleading, since we react to situations as we perceive them and not necessarily as they really are.)

18. Relies on memory

The Explainer has a good memory but invariably disputes this. They always say, 'Oh no, it's not what it should be.' But they only say this because they are aware of the limitations of their memory. They actually rely upon it and value its power more than most people. They also take notes or make lists to assist their memory skills.

19. Has few close friends

The Teacher's close friends tend to be people they can really talk with and feel comfortable to explore ideas with in depth. Some people of a Teaching motivation recognise that they could have the tendency to be a loner, and they are hungry to spend time in company as a corrective or balance to this.

But the Explainer enjoys their own company in preference to wasting time relating superficially to people they don't care to be with.

More often they are comfortable with just a few close friends. They form friendships slowly but firmly and disengage gradually when a friendship is a disappointment. Although a common interest may bring them together, eventually it is really the other person's company they choose and have come to value.

They are not easily won over or persuaded. If, after much thought, someone of a Teaching motivation becomes your friend, the relationship is likely to last through thick and thin. They are warmly loyal to their friends, considerate and caring.

20. Hates to be hurried

The Teacher takes time to assimilate facts, ideas and concepts, and hates to be hurried into drawing hasty conclusions. They dislike being hurried about anything.

They are prone to prevaricate. Explainers, once they apply themselves to a task, are likely to complete it in the determined manner of a combine-harvester, processing all that comes within their scope. However, getting them started may take even longer than their thorough progress through the job. Just where are they to start? What is the best angle of approach? Or with so many jobs to do and so little time to do them properly, which should be their major priority? It all requires a great deal of thought . . .

They don't like to be hurried and, more importantly, they enjoy not having to be hurried. The Explainer loves to have a chance to breathe, to relax, to not have time constraints, to spend time with friends. They would prefer to defer having time with someone until they can spend time together properly.

They like the opportunity to catch up, to recount a whole trip, or what kind of day they had. They have a whole string of questions they were waiting to ask you sometime 'when we can really get into it' or 'when we get a chance to talk'.

Sometimes they will even defer being upset until they have time to really get in touch with their emotions. If they are greatly affected by a situation, deferring the response does not work as well as they anticipate, since the negative emotions they are not going to get into right now still leak and affect the atmosphere for those around them.

To unpack things properly, good or bad, they like time to be open-ended, or at least with a large margin around the time they estimate it will take. Only then will they relax.

COMPLIMENTS

The Explainer enjoys being told they have made things clear, helped another to understand. Also they are always pleased to have hard work acknowledged.

Chapter 7
The Exhorter Motivation

GENERAL CHARACTERISTICS
1. Likes to encourage
2. Looks for a response
3. Lovable or enjoyable
4. Needs a sounding board
5. Gregarious and outgoing
6. Talks easily
7. A realist
8. Experience-based
9. Has great expectations
10. Discerns and challenges
11. An able counsellor
12. Practical and constructive
13. Decisive and adaptable
14. Works in spurts
15. Hates to see others in pain
16. Smooths over difficulties
17. Makes allowances
18. Compromises
19. Fascinated by moral dilemmas
20. A student of human nature

1. Likes to encourage

Exhorters like to see everyone achieving what they are capable of and living life to the full. They want to see other people happy and using their gifts. They are the most likely to be excited about motivational gift teaching and its power to unlock other people's potential! The word 'exhort' means to build up, and Exhorters are very into the building-up of people. Sometimes they are into building people together or bringing people back together. It is wonderful to them to see someone begin to put their life in order or take steps to achieve the potential they are capable of. They are more than willing to put themselves out on behalf of someone who is responsive and who will take definite steps of action or follow their advice. They will usually have confidence in their own judgement about which steps of action to advise, and can be very persuasive.

An Exhorter leader will eagerly develop full participation and encourage the insights of others. It is so important to the Exhorter for everyone to be involved that there could be a tendency to make room for even inappropriate contributions or initiatives from those participating. The Exhorter's reluctance to relinquish leadership, or to share it, will be on the basis of their doubt that others could juggle such disparate and unpromising ingredients without the whole thing blowing up. The Exhorter leader longs to be out of a job, but still loved and appreciated.

The Exhorter is unlikely to forget any teaching or resource which has proved beneficial, however long it is since it was last relevant to draw upon it. In every situation as the medicine is applied the result is carefully noted and held in store against 'the next time'.

The Exhorter is always nudging people to make the most of their opportunities. This is obvious if they are teaching or counselling, if they are leading or are part of a team, or whenever they talk with those around them. They like to make a difference, and see that they have. If there's a problem, they're likely to patch it up for now and get back to it later. They hate to see people in pain, but their built-in tendency will be to keep folk happy *for now* through a short-term solution. There are other plates to keep spinning.

2. Looks for a response

The Exhorter insists on eye-contact and checks that they are being understood. (As a child, they could find it difficult to walk consistently in a straight line if the person they were speaking with was walking beside them.) They literally look for a response. Blindfold them and they are at a disadvantage. But put them on a phone and they will soon make the best of their limitations.

They need a visible response from someone when teaching, speaking or counselling, and will work hard to get it. Especially in addressing a problem, they aim for a decision, a harnessing of the person's will to implement a definite course of action that will inevitably effect change. Their part in the process is to help the person respond, and help them take crucial steps of action that are not easy to go back on. (People welcome or invite their involvement and are unlikely to tell them to mind their own business.)

An Exhorter is like a germ – most effective when being most infectious!

Exhorters can be very persistent, insisting on a response of some kind. What they have no time for is the sort of person who asks for help or advice but never intends to put it into action. You can't help someone who doesn't really want to be helped. When the Exhorter decides this is the score, they save their energy (without withdrawing their support). That sort of thing saddens them – or irritates them.

Patience does not come easily to the Exhorter, but reservoirs of it will appear the moment someone begins to respond. They know from experience that some people will respond almost immediately; others will ignore them.

3. Lovable or enjoyable

The Exhorter is a natural encourager. Because of this, people love to be around them and feel the benefit of time in their company. Other people see them coming and run a mile; they find so much cheerfulness wildly irritating. The Exhorter inevitably draws people to them; people love and enjoy them. Their effect upon others, especially at the times that count, is typically positive and affirming.

The Exhorter can usually manage to affirm others regardless of what is going on in their own life, but this is not always the case.

> One Exhorter I know was very faithful in making visits, even to the far-flung ends of the town. If you called in on someone and he had been there it was obvious they were cheerier and well pleased. Not so on the odd occasions when he was really low; he still felt obliged to visit people as normal, but left little puddles of depression behind him instead!

People willingly make allowances for the Exhorter. They have unconsciously built up a bank of goodwill. So others are happy to be involved in many of the things they suggest. The joke about Exhorters is as follows.

> 'How many Exhorters does it take to change a light bulb?'
>
> 'Only one – they just hold the light bulb and the world revolves around them!'

This does not imply that they have an inflated sense of their own importance, only that they recognise their preferred place of function is in the thick of things.

4. Needs a sounding board

The Exhorter thinks more easily aloud. They find words come easily with someone to explain to, or interact with, which helps them get their thoughts clear and more fluently expressed. Exhorters like to have someone else around to talk through an idea with. The other person is expected to respond, rather than interrupt. Their suggestions may be noted and made use of, but the Exhorter is as likely to say, 'Thanks, you were a real help', even if they said nothing at all. The partner or friend of an Exhorter will be a frequent sounding board in this way while thoughts or feelings are being processed!

5. Gregarious and outgoing

An Exhorter is equally happy in a one-to-one situation or in a group. Crowds do not intimidate them, but they may tire of having to meet more new people (another unknown quantity) until they see the new set of people and begin to interact, or start to notice and take an interest in them. The Exhorter is a true people person. They enjoy being amongst people and quickly become interested even in the concerns of complete strangers with an ease and familiarity that often creates an immediate sense of relationship.

They are not really interested in working with things or systems or abstract ideas. An Exhorter may be happy to work on their own or be on their own, but, if so, the people-interruptions become points of relief and interest which energise them to continue.

They are usually friendly, not shy. Their genius is to be a 'trigger-offerer' for others. (They are contagious, but some people find them exhausting or complain that they are overly enthusiastic, a nuisance!)

They are likely to be a ring-leader or enabler, but prefer

to be at the back watching others participate or in the thick of things, rather than leading directly. An Exhorter is prepared to lead once they have stopped worrying that people think they are doing so because they enjoy leading. Once this misunderstanding is cleared up, they can lead happily.

6. Talks easily

They do talk a lot.

> Malcolm was struggling to identify which was his gift. To those observing, and especially those who knew him well, it was already obvious he was an Exhorter. Finally, John, who was leading the seminar asked him the $64,000 question: 'Do you talk a lot?' 'Well,' Malcolm said, thoughtfully, 'the lads at work do say I could talk underwater . . .!'

But how else can an Exhorter exhort, console or encourage? If an Exhorter couldn't speak, they'd write a lot! (And Exhorter writers enjoy testing out reactions from their readers, wanting to know in detail which bits they respond to.)

Sometimes the Exhorter has one helpful thing to say, but it is not really heard as it should be; it gets lost somewhere amongst all the other things they have already said or unnecessary things they also go on to say. Much energy can be expended and time exhausted in people-pleasing and just keeping folk happy. Words come easily to the Exhorter, and can be used to encourage or spread negativity. (They can also sound so convincing: anyone who readily thinks out loud needs to have enough integrity to guard their lips and their own heart!)

At worst, their interest in other people's lives and ease of talking about what interests them could make them interfering, or inclined to gossip, speaking out of turn or telling you things that seem confidential or inappropriate. Exhorters use examples from other people's lives as illustrations whenever they seem relevant. They will also always gladly tell you what they think, and their opinions about everything going on in your life! They have a lot to say, and a confidence in what they have to contribute.

Some Exhorters regularly interrupt what is being said in their eagerness to be helpful. They are painfully aware that to withhold help or information is unforgivable.

In speaking about themselves, they will often share something which sounds very personal but to them is already a known commodity. The first time they speak of something it may cost them, but subsequent repetitions with different people can be a way of encouraging a sense of intimacy without too much expenditure. (It could consciously be shared to offset any mistaken impression that they may be a glib or superficial person.)

7. A realist

They are concerned with experience rather than cold facts or information. The Exhorter's words are action-focused: the content of what they say should become actual or it's a waste of time. (When they talk, the Teacher aims for your head, but the Exhorter aims for your heart and your will.)

On their own, Exhorters would be too imbalanced and likely to ditch theory altogether!*

They have no time for unreality. They live in the real world.

---

* If an Exhorter were to read through the Bible they would grunt appreciatively when they reached the letter of James, which is so impatient with talk that is not matched by practical reality.

However, the Exhorter tends to be embarrassed by suffering. They will often close their eyes to hurt, and would rather not hear or know about it in the first place.

They like to be able to make a difference and avoid taking on board too many situations they are powerless to address or change. They may sometimes ask, 'Are you all right?' or 'How are you doing?' without realising they didn't wait for an answer. When this happens it is a symptom of their multi-tasking and should not be seen as lack of caring or as insincerity. On this occasion they were not saying, 'So, tell me, how you are?' but 'You are all right, aren't you? – just checking.'

8. Experience-based

The Exhorter sees real life as the most important sphere of learning. That doesn't mean everything has to be learnt the hard way. Their experience will yield valuable insights and has taught them invaluable lessons that have practical application. The time they will work 'from the book' is when tackling something for which they have no understanding.

An Exhorter reads an illustration, magazine article or a section of a novel, and says, 'That's very good. I know just what you mean!' Or if something new to their experience has a ring of authenticity, it should then be remembered and verified.

To the Exhorter, if it works, then it must be true. They dislike theory and waffle. They have no time for abstract truth or for principles that don't work out in practice. The Exhorter notices cause-and-effect sequences in people's lives and tries to learn from this, so that painful and unpleasant situations can be averted in the future.

An Exhorter is concerned about credibility. They are nervous that someone will not take notice of sound advice because it is not backed up by personal experience. They may compensate for this by drawing on other people's experiences to strengthen their argument. As it is, they tend to live full and busy lives, taking on many projects and inevitably taking an interest in all kinds of people.

9. Has great expectations

Exhorters feel that most people never achieve a fraction of what they are capable of. The problem is that people don't set their sights high enough and would rather expect little than risk disappointment.

Exhorters can often see the potential in others that others can't see in themselves. They like to see a person stretched a little and achieve what they thought they could not. The Exhorter recognises that most challenges involve moving someone beyond what they are comfortable with already. Their own skills are in helping people see that those first steps out of what is familiar are possible and just waiting to be taken, and also in encouraging them to persevere, hopefully from strength to strength. (Sometimes, seeing the possibilities is the easy part. Exhorters expect a lot of themselves, but can find immediate difficulties overwhelming and insurmountable. The Exhorter struggles to keep their focus on the solution and not just the problem. Only when trouble seems to be under control can they begin to nod comfortably at it.)

Exhorters often visualise long-range projects and goals. They present these without reference to the amount of time that will be required to achieve them. Even if they think about time-scale or difficulties, they will soft-pedal them until other people have grasped what can be achieved and the benefits for everybody.

Those motivated assume the goals will be achieved much sooner than they can be. This situation raises unrealistic expectations and can breed disillusionment.

However, once the project is underway, because they tend to think of what can be done rather than what is being done, they may then be accused of being impractical and visionary. The Exhorter makes a decision that something must be done, knowing that it can only be achieved by harnessing the considerable energies of other people, and then deliberately keeps 'under wraps' their own awareness of the magnitude of the task, letting it 'leak out' a little at a time, and then only to those who need to know. They are hopeful in problem-solving. They hold it all together, and hold their breath, realising they've taken on the almost impossible yet again. If other people realised how much could go wrong, the Exhorter would really be in trouble . . . instead, they smile, and no one knows the half!

Many an Exhorter wishes there were more hours in the day.

10. Discerns and challenges

The Exhorter tries to work out where someone 'is at'. They try to work out what the hindrances are for those who appear to be stuck or not progressing, and to give further encouragement to those who are doing OK

It's exciting to witness the change that takes place when a person responds to encouragement. And the Exhorter is well aware that their own ability to make all the difference for someone is itself a gift, not something they have had to work at. All they need to do is *allow* it to be activated. It does cost, but only to the extent that if they do a lot of it they end up exhausted for a while.

The Exhorter encourages. They don't condemn or sit in judgement. They listen. They analyse. They realise that, were circumstances different, they could have been in the same predicament. They help the person understand the problem. They keep the door open for return visits, if necessary. (The wise Exhorter is careful here not to make promises they are unable to keep, however well-intended.)

The Exhorter can also challenge or rebuke when someone's behaviour is out of order or uncalled for.

11. An able counsellor

A formal counselling relationship is not necessary for the Exhorter to function helpfully. One of the most helpful qualities of the Exhorter is the ability to be fairly real and open about their own struggles – past and present. This comes naturally to them – and so do other people. Time spent engaging with people in personal counselling is fulfilling.

Exhorters know and understand their own emotions and rarely hide them very deeply. (They only need to reach into themselves and allow these genuine emotions to surface.) Rather than accepting the role of a self-effacing, dispassionate listener, they prefer instinctively to convey the sense that they are a fellow-traveller who has experienced equivalent difficulties. They find it easier than most to 'own' their pain and to be matter-of-fact about their failures, but they are often not being as spontaneously transparent as they appear, since they are instinctively selective as to what they share. It is not their intention to mislead, and the way they make personal admissions accessible to others is certainly disarming. They desire to be as open as is necessary to be really heard. Those being counselled can readily have confidence in such a person and take courage.

One reason for their aptitude in counselling is this: to the Exhorter it is obvious how important a person's will is in any change process. They tend to appeal to the will most of the time, saying, 'It's up to you. If you don't choose to cooperate with the process . . . if you don't grab hold of the opportunity when it presents itself . . . you'll be back to square one.'

Because the Exhorter trusts readily in experience they may assume that the same steps of action will be appropriate for each person in the same situation or predicament, especially if it has worked well for others. It is too easy for them to think, 'I recognise this one, no problem! . . .' and stop listening carefully and creatively.

Exhorters are constructive and helpful, naturally. (A non-directive approach may have its place. Obviously you must permit the person to talk. He needs to express himself. You'll understand him better when you hear how he sees the problem. But more is needed than just a wise nod of the head, or other questions. Instruction is needed. And when you instruct you will instruct from what you believe to be true.) It is important for the Exhorter to be sure of their reasons for believing in the principles they apply; otherwise they are likely to give their hearer the most palatable of two options. In many situations they will need to lay the choices out in front of the person with a clear view of the probable consequences and ramifications. The wisdom you serve to others will be the best of what you have access to. It is good to saturate your whole being with reliable truth.

Exhorters (even the shy ones) are inevitably involved with people, and frequently a long and changing stream of them. They interact far more meaningfully with relative strangers than most other giftings do. The question they should ask themselves is this: What depth of experience, honesty and direction have I tapped into, I, who inevitably affect the lives of others? (As this question is addressed, the formal opportunities for the Exhorter to be part of pastoral teams, personnel departments or counselling resource are likely to increase; the Exhorter is less likely to be written off as 'superficial' by those with responsibility.)

But if the Exhorter takes on too many projects, most of which involve or focus on people, then family and friends may sometimes get the impression that they are treated as 'just one more', rather than as real people who need personal attention.

12. Practical and constructive

The Exhorter is extremely pragmatic and will look for solutions to the challenges and problems in their way. They will utilise whoever and whatever is available to accomplish this.

Exhorters are suspicious of easy answers. They like material to focus on practical application, but need convincing that it will really work. They harness logical reasoning in motivating others to action.

Three or four different Exhorters might all give different counsel to the same person if consulted by them, but they would be sure to suggest something they thought was helpful or practical. They have a desire to visualise specific achievements and goals and then prescribe precise steps of action. This may appear to oversimplify the problem, but avoids the paralysis of analysis.

The Encourager likes to simplify even complex issues in such a way that practical steps can be taken to bring about change for the better!

13. Decisive and adaptable

The Exhorter would usually prefer to make a decision and run with it so that something can be done. Once a decision is deferred, it can too easily get forgotten about. It will usually be more expedient to proceed anyway and, if necessary, adjust the direction of something that's already in motion.

On the other hand, Exhorters thrive on interruptions and often capitalise on the unexpected dynamic whilst in the middle of a project. 'Oh good, that was just what I was waiting for,' they say. Or, 'Look who's here – I was wondering when you'd get to meet them!'

Taking situations in their stride can get to be a habit for the Exhorter, especially if one situation runs into the next one . . . which overlaps with the one after . . . which is quickly followed by the arrival of another unexpected visitor . . . The Exhorter is quick to reassess and adapt, but hates to discover that things have been altered without consultation. Some Exhorters freely adapt anecdotes or illustrations to suit the occasion, with little regard for accuracy.

14. Works in spurts

The Exhorter would rather complete a project whilst their energies are already applied to it. If an idea is flowing, that's the time to enlarge upon it. Once everything is tidied away, it's harder to get it all out and start again. Deadlines could even provide an incentive. They work more effectively in repeated bursts of energy, rather than slow but steady. They like to see results!

15. Hates to see others in pain

The Exhorter is liable to put sticking plasters on anything

that really requires major surgery. They hope that the original prognosis was alarmist and that the operation will not prove to be necessary. For now, all that matters is that the person gets no worse, and at least has had some attention so they are not feeling neglected in addition to being in a bad way. With the plasters on, the problem will not look so bad in the meantime. If a major operation is required, the Exhorter will reassure themselves, and the person, by saying that it will be worth it in the end. They hate to see someone in pain.

An Exhorter, switching on the TV, might catch sight of a documentary or news item about starving children, but if they could play flick-a-switch, changing channels quickly enough, would be able to avoid and forget about it. Once they started watching, they would get upset.

Visiting a hospital or prison presents a problem for many Exhorters. It is no difficulty to them to see the person they intended to visit, no matter what they are there for. It is easy to believe that a visit will do them some good. The problem, for the Exhorter, is passing all the other sick people or inmates whose situation they can do nothing about. It is very distracting and upsetting.

16. Smooths over difficulties

If someone behaves differently towards them, an Exhorter is likely to ask outright if something is wrong, rather than tolerate an ongoing tension, and may bend over backwards to get things sorted out quickly. But with an habitually uncooperative person the Exhorter will do their best to minimise the difficulty and to stop this becoming the focus of too much attention.

> I have an irritating habit of apologising without knowing what I did wrong, in the hope that it will defuse the uncomfortableness I sense in the atmosphere. My assumption is

that if I wasn't the cause of whatever is wrong, I probably did something to contribute to it getting worse or staying wrong. I don't even mind taking the blame, as long as I volunteer for it. People eventually respond crossly with, 'What are you saying sorry for?' and I don't always have an answer!

The Exhorter is the one who can get warring factions together with each other by misrepresenting what each of them is saying to the other. This may put them in a delicate or uncomfortable position for a time, but this could prove to be only a necessary time of transition before real understanding is gained.

17. Makes allowances

Exhorters take people as they find them, rather than accepting someone else's report. They are thought of as accepting and non-judgemental, but actually form quick interim impressions which are not necessarily generous, then modify original opinions as they go. They engage more slowly with anyone they initially overlooked or dismissed, and are much more tolerant with anyone they instantly took a liking to.

The Exhorter will follow their instincts as to whether to get involved with somebody or not. Sometimes they feel they could make very little difference for a particular person, and, with no instinct for how to proceed, will back off and keep their distance. They think that maybe someone else would be the right person to engage with the ones they don't like!

The Exhorter readily sees that everyone should wear a sign saying 'Work in Progress'. No one is a complete success story, nor is anyone a lost cause, unless they choose to be that way. The way forward always has to begin from where someone is already at.

If Exhorters are given responsibility for a group which includes people who are difficult to like or help, they will grumble inside until they have got some handle on how to make a start to interact constructively; then they'll wade in and do fine.

When they choose to, an Exhorter can show unconditional acceptance for another individual, expressing love in a tangible way and allowing the other person to believe that nothing is beyond forgiveness.

Of course, Exhorters also have to choose whether or not to make allowances for themselves. Usually they are casual and matter-of-fact about their abilities and limitations, even under stress, operating with a pragmatic self-acceptance.

18. Compromises

If there is a legitimate compromise to be found, the Exhorter is the one who will find it. They manage to see both sides of an argument, try to see each person's point of view, and, wherever possible, reconcile them. They find that dogmatic statements or positions have sharp corners and hard edges which bruise people unnecessarily, and they rather feel that people matter more than someone else's boxes anyway.

They also tend to compromise fairly ruthlessly if the priority is to keep the other person from being uncomfortable. The Exhorter can be selective in what they hear, and tend to smooth over or ignore the unpleasant bits. They have learned to be diplomatic, thinking, 'What they don't know won't hurt them.'

They are the master of the 'white lie'. Often the Exhorter will have a very strong moral sense of the value of truthfulness. This is because it poses a particular dilemma for them. They will then avoid outright lies, try

163

hard never to exaggerate, no matter how useful it would be, and manage only to be selective with the truth.

If a compromise solution is possible which is not legitimate, the Exhorter will probably have seen (and dismissed!) this already. The Exhorter knows that truth is relative, not absolute, and must be treated seriously, with respect – like fireworks! If not used properly, it can hurt people unnecessarily. They've seen the casualties before.

> I once was amused to catch myself saying out loud to someone, 'I don't care if it's *true* – does it help?'

19. Fascinated by moral dilemmas

The common ingredient (other than people!) in the situations which really draw the attention and interest of the Exhorter is an element of moral dilemma. What is this person to do? It would be simple to give an answer were it not for the peculiar circumstances of the case . . . After all, what would I do once I discovered that I'd murdered him . . . ? What was he to do now he found out that his first wife was still alive after all? Whether in literature, soap opera or real life, it is questions like these that draw a response from the Exhorter. It should not surprise us that they will be filled with compassion and understanding for those who face difficult decisions about abortion, divorce, care of relatives, divided loyalties, withholding information which would lead to the arrest of a friend, and so on.

20. A student of human nature

Exhorters are rarely surprised by how awful people can be. In Agatha Christie's Miss Marple books the old lady, who is a part-time sleuth, remarks that living in a small village gives one the ideal opportunity to see life, to be a student of human nature, the opportunity for close observation. The Exhorter finds that village wherever they may be, and remembers.

Exhorters basically understand people fairly readily.

While Servers will often compare people to machines or things, some Exhorters are the opposite. They will talk to the car or washing machine that is not working and appeal to its better nature! Eventually they may lose their temper and shout at it, bang or kick it.

COMPLIMENTS

The Exhorter beams with pleasure when he/she is told, 'You're such an encouragement' – which is probably often.

Chapter 8
The Giver Motivation

GENERAL CHARACTERISTICS

1. A generous personality
2. Gives of their best
3. A secret giver
4. Loves to surprise
5. Committed and involved
6. Available and wholehearted
7. Warm and trusting
8. Given to hospitality
9. Enterprising and creative
10. A contagious advocate
11. Frugal and thrifty
12. Shrewd and resourceful
13. Not gullible
14. Creates impossible situations
15. Has extremes of behaviour
16. Spends themselves on others
17. Doesn't let people too close
18. Can't build walls
19. Sensitive and feeling
20. Understands suffering

1. A generous personality

A Giver is glad of opportunities to give what they can – whether that is their time, their energies or physical resources. They seem so ready to share what they have and support other people (or particular projects). They may give support emotionally, practically or materially.

Givers have a knack of getting hold of things which then pass through their hands and are distributed wherever they know there is a need. They are also often able to stir up other people with the end result that needs of many kinds are alleviated.

If someone is getting a new fire or cooker the Giver is likely to ask, casually, 'So I expect you traded the old one in, in part-exchange? That always helps . . .' The other person responds with the information as a matter of course, but the Giver is always on the look-out for matching what one person has spare with what another person needs. This giving gift stems from the very core of their personality. It is a special attitude that flows out of their lives. They enjoy being able to give. It is important here to look back and recall your earliest memories. Did giving come naturally? Or is it a learned behaviour? Are you sure that generosity and giving have always been your point of joy? Can you remember feeling that sweets were just made to be shared? (Who had your last Rolo?)

Givers are generous by personality. Of course, if they have money they will use that generously, but they will also be generous with whatever else is theirs. They give wholeheartedly. They give something of themselves with even the smallest gift. They despise ulterior motives in other people, and are hurt when anyone views their own generous behaviour with suspicion. In fact, often avoiding recognition, they plan how to give, even plot how to do so. They will not only give what they can spare, but often what they need for themselves.

A Giver will also notice when someone has a need and will immediately consider how they can help. Usually they will make no mention of it, until they have come up with a solution. (It is either the Giver or the Server who will be likely to notice that something is broken and needs to be mended or replaced.) Givers believe that everything they have has been entrusted to them. They hold on to whatever they own very lightly. Some things they own may have greater value to them because they were presents. To the Giver the value of the item lies in the love with which it was given to them or with which it was made for them. Of course, this does not necessarily mean that they wouldn't give it away, in turn. In fact, knowing how much they valued it would increase their pleasure in letting it go to someone else. It might be said that without fanfare they would quietly sacrifice their all. They are not reluctant givers. This fact alone sets them in marked contrast to almost everybody else.

The Giver may have reservations about how what they have given will be used, or whether it would have been better employed elsewhere, but no reservation at all about releasing it. In fact, the spontaneous pleasure of giving is like an adrenaline rush to them, whereas for most of us it requires a deep breath or a you-know-it-makes-sense attitude. The appeal system, where an envelope from a recognised charity is pushed through the door once a year and collected later in the week, is sure to identify the Givers. You know them by the way they answer the door, and say, 'I was looking out for you coming,' whilst they slip a few extra small coins into the already bulging envelope, which was waiting on the shelf by the door. In churches, organisations and support committees much of the activity depends upon money or seems to revolve around it. The Givers don't resent this at all.

2. Gives of their best

When a Giver plans a present for someone it may be to mark a particular occasion, or simply because the idea has occurred to them, but they immediately become animated with its preparation. They plan it in great detail, then go to infinite pains in choosing or making that present. They will plan such a present first of all, then take great care in seeing those plans through. The whole process is a pleasure to them, and they anticipate the person's pleasure in receiving the gift whether they see their response or not.

When you know that someone is a Giver you soon learn to be careful about casually enquiring about anything, or saying you like something, let alone need it.

When Dave and Gillian were visiting Holy Island they heard Anna sing the Keith Green version of Psalm 23. It was so beautiful. They knew that Ruth, their friend at home, liked Keith Green, so when they got back they asked her whether she had a tape with the song on which they could listen to. She said she was sure she had. A few days later she handed them the appropriate tape. They played it over and over, especially that particular song. Only when they tried to return the tape that they had borrowed did they find out that Ruth had gone specially into the town to buy it for them. She didn't want it back. It was a gift!

They don't always do this sort of thing, of course, but they do it on average far more often than anybody else does!

We called at Ken's house to pick up the car he was loaning us for a week to transport the dance team to Glastonbury. He was concerned about how much fuel there was in the car, and he sat us down to a snack lunch 'just to set you right' for the journey. Some of the children and their friends were in and out of the house, and Ferg tried to make conversation: 'Oh, is that one of those T-shirts which changes colour with your body heat?' he said, to one of the girls. 'Aren't they clever!' 'Do you like them shirts?' said Ken.

'Oh, yes, I think they're really fun, but I've never had one. I'd always be playing with it, and looking to see what it did next.' Ken was gone. 'Oh, no,' said Ferg, 'I'd forgotten – he's a Giver, isn't he?' Sure enough, moments later Ken returned with a new light-blue sweatshirt he just happened to have upstairs – the kind that changes colour with your body heat! 'I couldn't take that,' said Ferg. But he wears it often – it's one of his favourites.

A Giver values things, and can even treasure things, but still holds on to them very lightly.

A Server man was married to a Giver woman. Outside their window was a patch of land that had not been used, and the Server had the wonderful idea of planting potatoes there, and growing them. He worked enthusiastically on the soil, and looked forward to his family eating their own potatoes, instead of having to buy them as usual. Every time the Giver was at the sink, doing dishes, and remembered the potatoes growing under the window, she thought how nice it would be to take some of them as a present to . . . Well, by the time they were dug up, she had so many people she wanted to give some to, there were none left for them! Their own family ended up eating potatoes they were given by someone else.

3. A secret giver

A Giver is caring and helpful. Typically they will hear about a need, check it out, and then go personally to the person involved and offer real help. They may well then say, 'Oh, by the way, there's no need to mention this to anyone else.' At times, they will decide that it is better for help or a particular gift to be given secretly and will make the appropriate arrangements.

Givers don't want just to give. They want to give exactly the right thing. They'll sometimes check it out with a close friend, with a husband or wife, just to make sure. Sometimes this characteristic means the Giver holds back too long before going to another's rescue, waiting to be sure. Then they say, 'I knew I should have . . .'

The Giver quite enjoys operating undercover. That way no one is likely to interfere or modify what they intend. Once they have got the idea in their head, they can even see their partner as the obstacle to be got over or got round. They can become secretive and evasive, not wanting even their partner to know exactly what they have. It would be a great delight to them to economise on some spending money or other in order to have more hoarded away to use later. A Giver goes out for a drink with his friend, and his wife hands him the cash he will need. Later in the evening when it's his round he buys his friend a drink, but decides to make do himself with what he still has in the glass, and pockets the difference! Later in the week he can surprise his wife with a bunch of flowers, or pay a little extra for something they need to buy, rather than having to get the cheapest. The Giver will be pleased if they and their spouse reach the same decision or conclusion independently about how to meet a particular challenge, what they should give as a present, or how much money should be set to one side. If that money was to help someone else, they would be particularly delighted if the sum they decided on turned out to match the need exactly.

4. Loves to surprise

The Giver loves to prepare a surprise. Their eyes glow as they get everything ready for a party, and hide away whatever is prepared, thinking, 'If they only knew . . .' They like others to be involved in plotting a surprise too, and enjoy the shared secrecy. It is a way of sustaining the pleasure for longer and squeezing every ounce of enjoyment out of it. This is one of the reasons they enjoy making things, or 'doing them up'. Thinking about it is part of the pleasure, as is seeing the look on the recipient's face. They enjoy being surprised in their turn. If something has really pleased them they will play back the memory tape, enjoying it all over again. They don't feel deserving or expect much for themselves, and are likely to say, 'Oh, you really shouldn't have! There was no need.' But they are appreciative.

> Kevin had a premium bond that came up. Of course, he had no difficulty thinking of what he was going to do with the money. He already had it planned out in his mind long before he ever heard he had won. He didn't use it to pay any of their bills, either. He bought one friend a new suitcase, because he was tired of seeing the old, tatty one he normally used. He used up all the money doing similar things for other people – little jobs he'd postponed in his head for the time when he would have the means to make it possible.

5. Committed and involved

When a Giver believes that a person, project or ministry is worth supporting, they not only want to help financially but also to get practically involved in other ways. They love to provide and supply things that are useful. They will sometimes show up in person to help with the work in any way they can, and will encourage others to support. They want the projects they support to be as effective as possible. They throw themselves energetically into whatever they are involved in. Their wall calendar is probably marked with people's birthdays and anniversaries, but in big letters: HARVEST SALE AND SUPPER – CHRISTMAS

– HELP THE AGED – SUMMER FETE. All of these will be major projects with a line spanning a week or more running into them.

6. Available and wholehearted

The Giver tends to think of other people first, or at least likes to be available. Being able to help is what counts, not whether that help is actually needed.

> When Benny couldn't afford to run his car any more, what bothered him was the thought that if he passed someone on the way to work, he wouldn't be able to give them a lift. It didn't matter that he would need to walk to work every day himself!

If there's work that needs to be done the Givers and Servers are likely to be the first to respond. Funnily enough, the Server will often make a mental note of where and when to turn up, then do so without telling anybody they meant to come. The Giver is more likely to raise their hand and volunteer cheerfully in the hope of encouraging others to do the same! Not surprisingly, if the subject comes up of how important it is to give or to raise funds or to re-cycle, they begin to get forceful and 'preachy'.

When someone has identified a need, a Giver is often more than willing to come alongside and help whoever is responding to it. They like to join in and participate, and are happy to volunteer on behalf of any worthwhile cause. They throw themselves into activities such as sales of work, garden parties, yard sales, coffee mornings, which involve expending a lot of effort. Other people almost lose sight of the common ingredient in these activities which is the net result of fund raising. Not the Giver – they can have fun, work hard, and know it's all for a good cause. They usually do, or give, more than they are asked. They may enjoy walking anyway, but if they could be sponsored and do the walk for a charity of their choosing, so much the better. They won't be embarrassed to collect the money in, either. Givers tend to do everything with energy and zest. They are very wholehearted. They notice sadly the way some people never seem to make themselves available, and think to themselves, 'One of these days they'll realise how they've gone through their life wasting every opportunity to make it count for something.' They are often joyful or bubbly as leaders.

7. Warm and trusting

The Giver doesn't take things for granted. They remember to say thank you. They are extremely appreciative when someone has gone to a great deal of trouble, and may remark upon it. They are warm and straightforward in their behaviour towards other people, open and receptive when someone speaks their mind or shares their heart. They relate well to those round about them, and are usually well-liked, though rarely understood. They take people at face value and are not generally suspicious or cynical. They would rather give somebody the benefit of the doubt.

8. Given to hospitality

They are pleased to be able to be hospitable, even if people rarely come to their home. They are glad to have a home into which someone could be invited and where they could feel welcomed and comfortable. They will glance round their room and quickly assess the impression someone would get of it. If they know someone is coming, and they have time and opportunity, they will go to endless trouble to prepare and make them welcome.

On several occasions I can remember sitting down with company to a meal prepared by any of the Givers I know, and having the awful feeling that this meal is obviously to mark a special occasion that I must have forgotten about . . . is it someone's birthday, or anniversary, and everyone realises but me? Slowly the realisation dawns that just being together is enough of a reason for the Giver to treat it as a special occasion.

9. Enterprising and creative

Givers are always interested in ways of making money. Some have a taste, or even a flair, for gambling. The jackpot incentive appeals to them – the thought that for minimal outlay they could get a maximum return. This may be their opportunity for the unlikely to happen. At very least, they would have the joy of planning just what they would be able to do if theirs were the winning number!

When Kevin was to come with me on a trip to Ireland, he asked me carefully how much it would cost, what the fare would be, what spending money he would need, and then added it all up. Closer to the time, I asked him how he was placed with regard to the money. 'Don't worry about it, chappie,' he said, 'it's taken care of.' I assumed that someone had given him the money he needed, and that he was only being careful not to betray the identity of the source, so as not to embarrass them. Only later, when we were safely in Ireland, did I find out what 'it's taken care of' really meant. Kevin had not had enough money for the fare, and didn't see where it was going to come from, so he put what he had on a horse, and trusted that it would all work out. It did, and, interestingly enough, his winnings came to the exact sum that he had calculated would be needed for the trip.

Even while they are young, Givers learn to be enterprising, and may get extra money by doing small errands, washing cars, baby-sitting or delivering newspapers. They also learn to save at an early age, and choose how their money is to be spent. Givers are very resourceful and capable. Some of them are successful and enterprising in business, with a flair for taking risks with additional investments. Some will live contentedly with little or no income all their lives, and exercise their motivation within the limits of their surroundings. Givers tend to be creative, and not just in entertaining or cooking and so on. They usually have lots of ideas! They love to make and do creative things, mostly with others in mind. Many show a strong interest and aptitude in arts and crafts, and enjoy nature and the things of nature which can be touched and experienced. (Some will enjoy working with wood, or find great pleasure making things with dried flowers or stones or whatever else they can find, appreciating natural things and adopting them.)

They are good at making and mending things, making things do, making things last, making things good as new, and are enthusiastic about recycling. They like to give tangible help, not just good wishes or kind thoughts.

10. A contagious advocate

In the course of normal conversation a Giver may tell you which supermarket gives the best value, or which glue really works, how they have got on much better since they switched to a different dentist. They don't do this compulsively, but they do do it spontaneously, easily, naturally. If they believe in the product they can sell it convincingly. The Giver has a strong sense of justice, and a great dislike of seeing people hurt. They are ready to act on their behalf, and will quickly spring to the defence of those who are unjustly treated. They're concerned to meet tangible needs, and are very sensitive to other people's experiences and expressed emotions. They are prepared to speak on behalf of anyone they are convinced is genuine, and would be glad to write a reference when someone they know is applying for jobs. The Giver takes things and people as they find them, and will tell you so. If they like a product, they will heartily recommend it; if they like a person, they will speak warmly of that person.

If the Giver has come to faith in God, it is natural for them to want to share that faith with other people. It's instinctive to them to share what they have, to give it away. They will be surprised when others are self-conscious in their own attempts or are innately cautious. The Giver will not be easily discouraged in their efforts to win people.

11. Frugal and thrifty

They love value for money and hunt for bargains. They will usually cut corners in spending on themselves. Sometimes they end up with something really nice that is for themselves, but usually because it was at such a good price they would be unwise to postpone the purchase. They look for special offers, multiple buys, reduced items and other practical ways to save money. It may take a little more time, but it releases money for other things. Givers (even if they have made and spent millions) are remarkably detached from money as such; they are only concerned about what it can accomplish.

Patrick said, 'I see money not as a thing to work for, but to work with.'

The question is always 'How much of this money do I have to keep back for myself?' They would prefer to opt consciously for a lower standard of living in order to allow a greater flexibility with disposable income. This has consequences for other people. At times they will be just as mean with their family as they are with themselves. It is an extension of their own habit of cutting corners by being frugal and 'penny-pinching'. However, the family will react against their generosity towards others if the Giver does not show the same care, concern and delight in meeting their needs.

12. Shrewd and resourceful

The Giver likes to make the most of whatever they have care of or access to. They like to put assets together, and will especially be delighted if this involves saving money, expending no extra outlay or avoiding the duplication of resources!

A priest friend of ours, Tom Cass, says that in his early days of ministry he was known as an able fundraiser. It came naturally to him, and much of his energy was spent in it. He pulled together the big pilgrimages to Lourdes with special care for the handicapped, and could get money out of anybody for one of his projects. When it came to holding a big youth camp, he was more than willing for the venue to be his own parish, turning over the church, hall, school and often the presbytery as well, regardless of inconvenience. On the Friday, he informed the team not to worry about preparing a meal, and arranged a deal with the local chip shop, turning up with fish and chips enough for a couple of hundred people!

Givers handle their own finances well, being careful, cautious and sometimes even a little tight with their own spending. They certainly do not squander money, and they have an eye for other necessities as well. They always seem to notice what might come in useful. They also make great treasurers for any kind of group. They are excellent to have on financial committees, and make fastidious bookkeepers and accountants.

> We knew that Patrick was a Giver, and I had no one designated to look after the money for the team and to keep accounts. According to everything they say about Givers, it ought to be something he would be good at, or at least enjoy, so I turned the job over to him. From the first, it amused us to see how this became vitally important to him. He took great care deciding what to keep the money in, how to keep the 10 per cent for 'tithe' separate, drawing columns carefully on his sheet of paper to keep a note of everything. He counted the coins endlessly, and, as we travelled in the van, would sit in the back and enquire how long it would be before we hit the next toll-booth. The triumph with which he would hand across the exact change for each toll, and his pleasure in making a note of it afterwards, amused us all greatly. It really was his point of joy. It occurred to me that it would have been much easier to keep a tray of loose change on the dashboard for tolls, like most of our American friends, but, of course, I kept my mouth shut. (When we reached the Bronx, it was even funnier to find Patrick making complicated arrangements to carry back to Ireland a whole set of golf-clubs for the brother of a neighbour, because they were so much more cheaply available than at home!)

13. Not gullible

It is dangerous to get the reputation of being a Giver, whether that is your motivation or not. Unscrupulous people may take advantage of anyone considered a 'soft touch'. The Giver will usually notice if anyone tries to exploit them, or deliberately play on their better nature. They are unlikely to allow the same person a second opportunity.

Givers realise that money has the power to corrupt, that some people lose their sense of what is really important as soon as they have too much or are in danger of losing what they have. The Giver is a realist and knows how things work in the real world. They tend to know how much everything costs. But money matters less to the Giver than almost to anyone else. It is clear to them that the most important things cannot be bought or sold. They live their own lives accordingly, often in sharp contrast to the lifestyle of other people.

So when Givers try to help someone out, they may look for ways of doing so which will not just create a new problem. They recognise that bailing someone out all the time may also delay them facing up to reality. They appreciate the disciplines they have learned may not have been learned by others who need help. They are not easily fooled by sob stories. They are often well able to discern the real from the imagined, the genuine from any attempt at manipulation; and a person with the Giving motivation will withdraw whenever they detect insincerity. A Giver hates anyone trying to manipulate them into giving. They will firmly resist all pressure appeals. They give only as they feel and think it is right to do so. They get cross at some of the emotive begging letters that are put out these days through the post, or are annoyed when someone rattles a collecting box in their face on the street corner.

On another occasion they'd be delighted to place their spare change in the collecting tin. It all depends on how an approach is made, and whether they feel the response is allowed to be voluntary. Sometimes the Giver can be so aggravated by the way a request for help is presented that they will dig their heels in and refuse to respond. Or they will sometimes want a say in how a gift is used.

They can feel so strongly about a project or issue that they will try and manipulate others with their gift. ('I will give you £200 as long as you don't do it this way.') If they have very firm views on how a project should proceed, they make it very clear that they will support it only if certain conditions are met.

Other parties involved are dismayed at what they see as an attempt on the part of the Giver to pressurise those involved. But the Giver is determined to use the leverage they have to sway the decision, no matter how uncomfortable things become in the process. This would only happen if it was something they felt very strongly about. Givers dislike being pressurised, but will themselves sometimes use emotional blackmail to achieve what they believe is best for someone. They say, 'It would make me really happy to know . . .' or 'Don't mind me, I only live here . . .'

14. Creates impossible situations

The impossible situations a Giver causes have recurring themes of persisting regardless, not knowing when to stop, adopting lost causes and picking up 'stray dogs'. Their heart will go out to someone genuinely needy, even if that person's problems are seemingly endless. A Giver cannot be pressured into responding, but if they do respond it will be wholeheartedly.

The Giver sometimes doesn't know when to stop giving. It makes them feel more comfortable, but it may embarrass the other person and make them feel progressively more uncomfortable. This is especially true in a developing friendship. The Giver wishes to express how important the other person is to them by all kinds of presents and demonstrations of esteem. Without understanding the nature of the Giver, the other person can easily feel overwhelmed or uneasy, wondering if the Giver is trying to 'buy' their friendship or affection.

The Giver may pay particular attention to someone as a mark of honour, or because they feel that person has been left out of things. Once their focus is in that one direction, it may appear to everybody else that all sense of proportion has been lost.

> Several families from The Vine Community went on holiday together to Norfolk. Kevin was painfully aware that the children were adapting less easily to including the one new family who had recently joined the community. He tried hard to make it up to them, making a fuss of their children especially, to stop them feeling left out. At the end of the holiday one of his own sons was heard to say, 'It's as if he's been a dad to Vicky and Alex this week, but not our dad at all!'

When the Giver is focused in one direction they tend to lose sight of how their behaviour will affect other people. For instance, their own commitment to hospitality or befriending may place undue pressure on the household. They will say things like, 'Come at any time', while their partner winces even as it is being said! The Giver likes to offer an open-ended invitation, and may have difficulties defining boundaries properly. Those round about them sometimes need to protect their own interests, and sometimes should protect the Giver.

15. Has extremes of behaviour

A Giver can be shy. At times they are silent and withdrawn, and people would normally find them nonthreatening. But when they really let go, their behaviour can be wildly extrovert. Other people will seem self-conscious in comparison. They can become incredibly excited.

Prophetics and Givers are the two types of motivation most naturally inclined to go 'over the top' once they decide to go for something. This will be regardless of cost. Excess is natural to both of them. (Incidentally, Prophetics tend to like Givers and admire their recklessness.)

Givers do the most unlikely things. They never know when to stop or call it a day. Once they go for something they'll give it their all. They have a wild, reckless streak, and the ability to really let go. At their wildest this can get a little scary for other people to be around.

You certainly never know what they will do next. On the other hand, once you are told about it you are likely to say, 'It doesn't surprise me – nothing would surprise me about them any more.' Their very unpredictability is the thing you can count on.

You never know what they will have thought up next. They are full of wild plans and schemes, which they tend to start putting into operation without telling anyone who is likely to disapprove. And if a need arises they are likely to act spontaneously and radically in response.

People who are married to them say things like, 'One of these days, I'll come home, and there'll be no furniture in the house!'

One night when I was teaching on motivations with a group of people, my friend Andy asked if it would be OK to tape the session. What was funniest on hearing the tape afterwards was the responses out loud from people as they recognised their gift. Robson, a Server, who is normally quietly spoken and a man of few words, became quite vocal and excited. This was especially true when his wife, Jenny, was identified as a Giver: 'Why, of course – that explains everything! All these years I've been married to her, and I've known what she was like. But I've never understood it for a minute. Now it all makes sense – she can't help it.'

16. Spends themselves on others

Givers are warm and trusting. They are usually open, friendly and receptive people. They are very respecting of confidences. They don't find it hard to keep secrets or say nothing. In fact, they pride themselves on being able to be trusted. They absorb others' bruisings as well, sharing willingly in their pain, and stand alongside them.

Their capacity to give is so great that they can easily encourage emotional dependency in another. At its best, the net effect is one of an anaesthetic, allowing painful things to be uprooted and dealt with. It will usually then be appropriate for the relationship to change slowly, so that the Giver is still valued but not clung to. But Givers find it hard to let go of one who has become emotionally dependent. If they are not careful, they themselves develop a dependency on being needed. Generally, habitual dependency is dehumanising and not a healthy thing to allow to develop. The person who has leaned so hard on the Giver may have become so strongly dependent that, even when the Giver withdraws, they immediately seek to transfer their dependency to another person.

When the Giver has made a person or project their concern, they don't separate their response into different compartments. They will often invest themselves emotionally, but offer practical help of all kinds as well. Nothing is too much trouble. Once they begin decorating for the person down the street, the whole of the downstairs of the house is likely to be finished before the Giver decides enough is enough. Meanwhile, the tiling at home will wait for another day. They assume their own family will understand or make allowances. Sometimes they are so involved in what they are doing that they don't think about their own family at all.

It can be true that Givers will often ignore (or not notice) the emotional needs of their own family or partner. Frequently they will fail to make provision for quality time with them. At other times, they will get so involved planning or making something to please you that they forget that you would rather enjoy their company instead.

They rarely take enough time for themselves. In fact, they often feel guilty about making any space for themselves. They are good at giving, but not so wonderful at taking. It would be good to make a couple of signs for the Giver to read frequently, saying, 'Give yourself permission' and 'Take time just for you'.

17. Doesn't let people too close

Givers do not appear on the outside to be as soft as they really are on the inside. This is part of their natural defence mechanism. They don't let people get too close, just in case. They don't run the risk of getting hurt. But they give the impression of letting people get close.

They generally have a large circle of acquaintances but very few close friends. They can appear confident but often doubt their own worth. Underneath all their enthusiasm, most tend to struggle a lot with self-doubt. They are nervous of disclosing who they are, yet, at the same time, like to be accepted.

They often find it hard to receive affection, hard to receive advice, hard to receive compliments, hard to receive help from others. In general, it is easier for them to give than to receive.

18. Can't build walls

Givers will withdraw from anyone who is too demanding. Their instinct is to withdraw rather than allow or maintain cautious involvement. Sometimes a Giver will hold back from people altogether. They know what it would mean, what it could cost, to let people come really close.

Many people would tell you that they feel the Giver is close to them, and open to them, and that they feel they have shared at a deep level. In fact, the Giver lets few people get very close or intimate, because they know if someone is once allowed close enough to wound them deeply, then that person will always have their permission to do so again. The Giver cannot build a wall within a relationship once they have become defenceless. However unwisely, they would always 'be there' for the other person.

Givers may unconsciously invite an abusive relationship, and will stay in that relationship when another person would not. If their partner was consistently violent or behaved unreasonably, the Giver would object, but is unlikely to leave the relationship. This staying-put can be a good or a bad thing. Others would often give up too easily, assuming the relationship could never be salvaged. On the other hand, a Giver may need someone else to intervene for their own protection.

19. Sensitive and feeling

Givers are strongly emotional.

A Giver, like a Mercy, is a soft centre. They are in fact the softest centre of all, but are less likely than the Mercy to look like they are. They appreciate and like Mercies, but are glad not to be them. To the Giver, the Mercy appears too vulnerable and seems to be asking to be hurt.

The Giver understands emotions and will listen for hours to someone who is upset.

But if someone is in trouble, their response is as likely

to be one of practical assistance as it is to be the offering of emotional support. In fact, the emotional support may well be what they give once they have decided there is no other way in which they can immediately help.

20. Understands suffering

A Giver usually has wonderful eyes (which are, after all, the 'the window of the soul') and these betray the depths that lie beneath. A good description of many Givers would be 'deep and wise'. They will not generally be forthcoming with wisdom drawn from the depths of their being, though it is there if you search it out. They tend to be still or silent, and 'don't give much away', which is ironic considering the rest of their behaviour. When they are in extrovert mode they give little indication of their depth either!

Of all the motivational gifts, Givers have a special understanding of suffering. They will have suffered deeply in their lives, not because their circumstances are on average any worse than anyone else's, but because of the way they respond, the sort of person they are. Even their inability to build walls of protection, between them and someone who has become close enough to wound them, has probably been discovered and learnt about when it happened!

Their own experience of suffering gives them a unique ability to understand and empathise with suffering in general, as well as in particular. It is as if they have a special insight, which they are not easily able to articulate, into the very nature of suffering.

People with the motivational gift of Giving are amongst those most likely to be natural 'burden-bearers'. This means they have the tendency to 'take on board' other people's problems, griefs and distress, and become weighed down by the emotional strain. If they know someone is really going through it, they may find themselves thinking about them, or even imagining their distress until they themselves are distressed and preoccupied. They will have often done this even as children.

Givers are, of course, prone to pick up 'lame dogs' of all kinds. They long to be effective through being there for another, just when they are needed. If their help is not enough to meet the need, this makes them sad. It is when the Giver doesn't know what they can do to help that they are likely to be overburdened by another's troubles. Their concern is fine as long as it spurs them to action or support. When it makes them dysfunctional, it has probably ceased to serve its purpose.

COMPLIMENTS

The Giver loves to be complimented on their welcome, their hospitality, their availability – but the more personal the compliment, the more it may embarrass them.

Chapter 9
The Ruler Motivation

GENERAL CHARACTERISTICS

1. Instinctively organises
2. Independent and critical
3. Likes to know where they stand
4. Understands delegation
5. Takes responsibility seriously
6. Enjoys managing a project
7. Fulfilled by accomplishing
8. Has drive and determination
9. Able to be decisive
10. A good leader
11. Considerate and fair
12. Values loyalty
13. Capable of initiative
14. Strongly competitive
15. Competent and efficient
16. Does most things well
17. Provokes jealousy or dislike
18. Objective and detached
19. Appears unemotional
20. Needs to be loved

1. Instinctively organises

Whether they get the chance to do it or not, a Ruler will instinctively want to reorganise almost everything in a way that makes much more sense. This may involve re-arranging a filing system, or organising a street party, or putting a team together, or showing a neighbour how to get up a petition . . .

Rulers love things to be in order. This means that they tend to be meticulously tidy somewhere (for example, messy desk, tidy room, or vice versa). Their thinking patterns are quite neat and tidy, and seem to demand some outward expression to match.

> My father had a workroom in which all the boxes and tins were carefully labelled, and his carpentry tools hung up in size order, side by side, on specially positioned nails and hooks. They were only ever used occasionally, but he wanted to be able to find things immediately.

Some Rulers will have carefully sharpened pencils lying on their desk in exactly parallel lines. This fastidious tidiness is most likely to exhibit itself in some area where the Ruler has particular pride or responsibility. These will be quite diverse. For some, it could be their appearance.

The nature of organising demands that everything and everyone is brought together at the right time. Rulers will usually make checklists of things to do, people to ring, and so on. Some Rulers carry the list more readily in their head. They always try to ensure that everything is done as quickly and efficiently as possible. (They'd rather spend longer looking at the map and working out the quickest route than waste time and fuel going round the houses.)

2. Independent and critical

A Ruler walks into a situation and immediately notices how it is run, looks to see who is in charge, notices what is badly designed, realises what they would have done differently and what ought to be done now to put the situation right, identifies the key snags and trouble-spots the person in charge has missed.

If you are in leadership, in any situation, it is critical that you identify and win the confidence of any Rulers that you are responsible for. They will invariably notice all your mistakes and you will be wise to give them permission to point them out. Without this permission they may well let slip their observations to someone else, which can undermine previous confidence in your ability or maybe even provoke a mutiny.

Most people feel at ease with the familiar and are very resistant to change. Not so the Ruler. They rarely have any sentimental attachment to the way things have always been done. They are happy to propose radical reorganisation whilst recognising that changes may need to be made gradually or that people may need to be familiarised with new ideas to prepare them for the upheaval of adjusting to whatever is different.

Of course, in the bulk of situations the Ruler is not the person with the say, and so all the organising and re-organising they would like to do is hypothetical. Their potential aptitude for rearranging everything surfaces in the form of criticism. If not listened to, they can be difficult, uncooperative or stroppy.

They reserve the right to make their own judgements, form their own opinions, and retain independence of thought.

3. Likes to know where they stand

The Ruler likes anyone with authority or responsibility to earn their respect and loyalty. They also like to be treated with respect, and if they are ignored or patronised, will become scathing and critical. They then cast their eye sideways to see if everyone else is being patronised and ignored as well. If the conclusion is yes, then this will fuel their lack of respect for the one wielding authority. But if they themselves are taken notice of and treated with respect, they may not be as sensitive to whether other people and their opinions are being ignored. It has often ceased to be relevant (in their eyes).

Authority is important to a Ruler. They like to speak with authority. They are secure when someone else can speak with authority. They like it to be real authority, not just talk. They want to know what the relevant authority structure is, so that they know where they stand, to know what the limits and boundaries are within which they are to work. Boundaries bring security to the Ruler. They want to know the deadline they need to work against, the budget that must not be exceeded. They tend to judge for themselves just what it would be reasonable to ask of other people, but need to know who is able to be called on.

Once a Ruler knows where they stand, they will organise their patch, desk or project to their own satisfaction, even if everything else is a shambles. Occasionally, they are convinced that the bigger picture is such a mess that what they are able to do will salvage nothing. So, they give it the minimum amount of their energy and attention. ('There's not much point busting a gut over this, is there!')

Rulers understand authority structures and like clear parameters. They enjoy being consulted and feeding their insights to whoever has clear responsibility.

For anyone in leadership, a Ruler in the group is a strong and valuable ally but dangerous as a critic. When they are not the person with the authority, they tend to have lots of suggestions of how things could be changed or improved; and then react or become discouraged if these are not put into practice. But if they know that the person in leadership will always listen seriously to their insights, they are content; they feel useful and valued – even if their suggestions are eventually discarded. Rulers who are not given opportunity to lead or contribute can become preoccupied with the way other people lead. They will feel excluded.

A Ruler would rarely usurp authority. They will wait to be asked, even when they realise they could help. In a crisis or emergency of some kind, they may be convinced it is appropriate to step in. In a situation where no one is willing to lead, it may be simpler for the Ruler to take charge.

4. Understands delegation

Delegation is the efficient use of energy; if it cannot be achieved immediately, it is probably worth working towards.

Rulers enjoy delegating tasks, and will supervise those under their leadership. They instinctively know which tasks to delegate and which tasks to do themselves. They are also able to sense which workers will need more assistance than others. They are able to naturally maintain a continued accountability from their workers. (Some Rulers have rarely had responsibility for numbers of people, so will delegate far less habitually. But if you ask them to project how they would set about it, they will soon be able to tell you.)

The Ruler can make unreasonable demands and be insensitive to the schedules, weariness, or personal priorities of their co-workers. It's not that they mean to do this, it just happens. They expect others to match their own energy and dedication. They ask in the nicest possible way ('If we work through the weekend, we can get this thing cracked!') and what they ask for usually makes sense in terms of the project. It is then very hard for people to say no!

The Ruler assumes that other people understand *how* or *why* things need to be done, and doesn't take time to explain. They will make a decision, but rarely tell you why.

If anyone else will competently do what the Ruler considers a chore, it will be off-loaded without hesitation. This is logical, not lazy.

Sometimes, when everything has been appropriately delegated and just needs checking for any problems that might have arisen, the Ruler stands back to observe and seems not to be actually doing anything at all!

5. Takes responsibility seriously

Rulers are thoroughly conscientious. They take any responsibility they are given very seriously indeed, and immediately begin to organise that area entrusted to them, whether they do it on paper or in their heads. They see what will be for the best.

They are happy to take complete responsibility for a project and then get stuck into it. They dislike anyone interfering or thwarting them in their task. Should it all go wrong they are unlikely to shift the blame. It was their job to get it right, not anyone else's.

It is frustrating for them to see what could be done and be unable to harness the necessary co-operation from others.

As a child they may have been called 'bossy'.

6. Enjoys managing a project

The Ruler likes a project to be something they can really get into, that will spread over a long period, and break down into smaller constituent parts. That way they can see it all coming together.

They have the ability to visualise how people, resources and time can work together to accomplish a task. They are able to get the maximum potential out of situations. They try to be aware of the strengths and weaknesses of the different people they are working with, and position them accordingly.

Sometimes the Ruler will be more able to bring a project or scheme into actuality than the Prophetic. Both of them may be able to lead strongly or inspire, but the Ruler is especially able to break a vision down into smaller manageable parts. The big dream becomes the sum of lots and lots of little practical activities and projects. It becomes achievable; it becomes more than a dream! And, because the Ruler can see the big picture, they are able to evaluate requests and situations quickly, and make firm, clear decisions.

A Ruler likes to know where they are going, and will be restless until they find out. When they do find out, they might not bother telling anybody else – they just wanted to get their bearings. Of course, if they were asked to, they would be able to explain the situation clearly, or even eloquently.

Rulers don't work well with committees. Committees are good at hesitating and prevaricating, at seeing problems where there are none, or giving up altogether because of problems that could easily have been overcome. To the Ruler, the best committee is a committee of one!

Rulers don't see any point in doing work that is unnecessary; and so, in sorting through data or information, they are usually able to grasp quickly what is key and critical, to sift out the unimportant from the important, and decide which information needs to be conveyed in an understandable form. They always see the broad picture and can sometimes see the solution to a problem because of this.

Most situations can be adapted by harnessing their own powers of persuasion, or their energy and competence. Of course, because the Ruler has a need to accomplish, it goes rather against the grain to rely directly on God.* Such is their instinctive independence.

They know the importance of detail; but like to remove themselves from its distraction and leave it to others, so they can focus on the final goal. Typically, they will hold on to whichever jobs enable them to maintain control, are the least hands-on, or involve the most variables.

(While the Ruler is completely focused on their goal, they will easily not notice themselves beginning to 'pull strings' or to manipulate. They can clearly recognise this as a bad trait when they see it in someone else's behaviour, and it angers them. But they may not notice when they fall into the same trap.)

7. Fulfilled by accomplishing

In the Ruler's mind a job is not finished until everything is where it was planned to be. They will inspire and encourage those involved to complete a task, by approval, praise, reproof and challenge. They take pleasure in seeing all the parts come together. It doesn't matter if others appreciate the achievement, as long as the Ruler knows it was accomplished as planned.

---

* One of the essential features of Alcoholics Anonymous is that someone needing help has to acknowledge their dependency on a Higher Power to sustain them. One sort of dependency is replaced by another. This could be a difficult concept to swallow if you were a high-achieving Ruler.

With projects, Rulers usually anticipate their final satisfaction along the way, but the moment the building is handed over on time and under budget, or the first issue of the magazine is completed and arrives from the printers, or the day we really have a band and not a lot of musicians, that, for the Ruler, is the moment of joy.

A Ruler will pride themselves on pouring all their energies into what they do. But the current new project can prove so absorbing that other routine responsibilities are maintained with minimal involvement! Some Rulers resent housework as a waste of time. But if the household is their chief sphere of responsibility, their domain, not a crumb would dare to be out of place, and even the chairs at the kitchen table would be arranged in neat parallel lines! It infuriates them that some jobs just roll on continually – you wash clothes and iron them, and before you know where you are you're putting them back in the laundry basket! Predictable, routine situations present no challenge or interest, so when doing routine tasks Rulers will often use the time to focus their attention elsewhere.

> When Lydia returned from Hong Kong the only job available to her was to work in the local pencil factory on a production line. 'It's not so bad, for now,' she said. 'The work is so boring that it occupies only my hands, and leaves my mind clear. That way I can think about each of the kids back in the children's home in Chung Chau, and pray for each of them. I get paid for it, and they get prayed for. There's a lot of hours in each day.'

8. Has drive and determination

The Ruler is able to throw all their efforts into something until they see it safely through. They love a job with challenges and demands, and have a particular satisfaction in addressing tasks quickly and with no fuss, then moving on to the next area.

The Ruler knows the value of good communication, but they recognise that explaining and clarifying is, of its nature, an open-ended task which can absorb all the time available for doing the job. Sometimes they avoid explanations, in case queries arise which would inevitably cause delay.

They are likely only to allow limited time for introductions or settling in, before pushing on to get things accomplished.

Other people are sometimes overwhelmed by their drive and enthusiasm. But the Ruler recognises the 'push' that is needed to keep a job going, or to keep a project on schedule. If they push too hard, others will tend to back off and become uncooperative.

9. Able to be decisive

The Ruler is particularly adept at thinking on their feet. They are able to be aware of all the relevant factors at the same time. It is as if they already have an aerial picture of everything that's going on. Then, when something happens, it gets fitted into the picture.

To reach a decision, all the Ruler has to do is focus closely on what is important. They will simultaneously be absorbing anything new which alters the detail of the picture. Anybody else would have to start constructing a picture, then start to be objective. The Ruler's picture is already there, matter-of-factly observed and quickly adjusted.

In one sustained moment, the Ruler appraises it all. It is the habit of a lifetime to concentrate in this way and they do it almost unconsciously. All the considerations are seen at once and a decision is reached. They are then unlikely to be persuaded that their decision was hasty or ill-judged. (At best, they will modify it, and then only in the light of new information, when it is made available to them later.)

It is not always easy for them to justify a decision or explain their reasoning in reaching a conclusion. They are being called upon to reason backwards. Sometimes the way forward became obvious to them, the way that opened up whilst they were already running with the ball. Or really they knew why that choice was obviously best, but did not delay in order to justify it.

At other times they may be following an instinct or intuition about the issue in hand to be addressed or about the people involved. If the results are good, a Ruler may learn to trust their intuition more often but will then have again to 'reason backwards' that this was best for everyone. Typically, the consequences for the Ruler themselves would then be considered only after the event.

10. A good leader

Most Rulers are natural and capable leaders, and amongst their peers will tend to rise to the top, not like a dead fish but like cream does when the milk settles. People say of them that they are a 'born leader'.

Often they are popular and command fierce loyalty and admiration from their friends. They are the natural choice for a sixer at Cubs or Brownies; they may eventually be head boy or head girl; they will almost certainly captain a sports team, leading the team well and with no fuss. They have a strong team spirit, and are able to assume responsibility without drawing attention needlessly to themselves. When they *are* liked as leader they accept loyalty or admiration naturally. They care for the weakest members of the team and will be their champion. (That's what makes them heroes, after all!)

Circumstances in early life greatly affect the Ruler's self-image, likeableness, ease and success. If they happened to be good-looking, popular and good at sports, they probably emerged as a natural peer-group leader, someone most likely to succeed. If not, they probably resented not having got the great breaks, and probably felt underestimated and excluded. (One Ruler experienced both these extremes at different schools.) But, once given the opportunity to try, even the thwarted Ruler will usually prove to be competent.

Leading is often simpler for the Ruler, because that way they can simply direct people on the basis of the bigger picture they see. But without a position of authority, they must earn the right to be heard. Then they must patiently explain that all the steps which they see are required to reach the goal. (Thinking about leading is automatic for the Ruler; doing it isn't!)

Rulers usually prefer to be given specific areas in which they are in sole charge; they find attempts to lead as a team confuse things. (Don and Katie Fortune tell the hilarious story of a couple, both of them Rulers, deciding to plant a vegetable garden. They couldn't agree on how to plan it, and eventually divided it into two plots for which they took separate responsibility. Two wonderful gardens eventually thrived, side by side.)

Collegiality in leadership may have its advantages for the Ruler's protection. If they trust those they work alongside, it can protect them from the isolation or loneliness which so easily goes with the territory.

11. Considerate and fair

A Ruler is readily considerate, but may choose to act in their own interest. Because they have an overview, and are aware of what is going on, what time it is, what different people consider important, how much money there is, what else has to be done today, and so on, they can generally see what will be best for everybody. It is as if they are cursed with the gift of being naturally unselfish. You may hear them say, 'I think I'll be selfish for once.'

All they need to do to show consideration is to act on what they are aware of already. The Ruler is particularly pleased when someone picks up on a suggestion and finds that it works for the best.

When they do show consideration for others, they are glad to have this acknowledged. They are genuinely pleased to see a whole group achieve something together, and, even if they are the one who has facilitated it all, they are glad to share the credit with everyone. A job well finished is more satisfying than applause.

12. Values loyalty

A Ruler considers loyalty crucial in all things. They look for loyalty and depend upon it. Rulers need to know whom they can depend upon. They would rather it was fewer people but know that they could really depend on them, than more who might let them down.

Although Rulers are accustomed to withstanding criticism, and can usually shrug it off, they are noticeably hurt if any unsupportive remark is expressed about them by a close friend or by the person they're married to. If this is in private, they are likely to remonstrate or be indignant. But, if anything is said in front of others that implies the slightest criticism or reproach, it will always be a big deal. This is because their own love is first of all expressed through loyalty.

13. Capable of initiative

In any new situation they can quickly grasp what needs to be done and set about organising the whole group to accomplish what it is capable of. They do this instinctively and easily, so their reticence, at times, to step in and take over is perhaps surprising. But a Ruler always prefers the responsibility to be given, and is reluctant to see a lack of clear leadership as an automatic cue for them to assume charge. Often they will make a snap decision that someone needs to get things moving. Sometimes, they will have decided that the whole set-up is a waste of time, and so instead they opt out or contribute only unhelpful remarks.

Rulers can't stand bad leadership or lack of organisation. They hate chaos and disorder. 'It was a proper shambles!' they'll say. Even an informal situation can turn into a disaster, if it isn't rescued by someone who realises what's going on. So the Ruler then decides whether it's better to leave well alone, or to do something about it.

Once a project is able to run itself you would think the Ruler could slacken their pace a little and relax. Instead, they are likely to look for a different focus for their energies, something else to present them with a bit of a challenge.

They dislike routine and are not keen to repeat the same project again, no matter how successful it was the first time. But if it failed the first time, they may be persuaded to do it again, as long as they can change the things they have defined as the causes of the previous failure. (The Ruler will immediately ask, 'Why has this gone wrong?' or sometimes, 'Who was at fault?')

14. Strongly competitive

Whether they are leading or not, Rulers like to be part of

groups. (Though this is especially true if they are comfortable with whoever is in charge!) They like to be part of a team and like the team to succeed.

They love to compete. Often they are fond of sports. In whatever the activity, they love the chance to improve their own skills and to have fun! They like variety and are unlikely to pursue one activity obsessively. They often do well immediately at something new and enjoy the challenge. They laugh and are satisfied to discover how well they did. They succeed in competition by focusing all their energies at that time on the task in hand, and choose to be aware only of the factors relevant to that.

If a Ruler once accepts that in a particular activity it is crucial to win, or to do better than the competitors, they will behave differently, stepping over whoever gets in their way. They recognise this as a necessity if they are serious about coming out ahead.

15. Competent and efficient

The Ruler is likely to work hard at whatever they undertake. They don't see problems, only challenges. If there is a clear road ahead, they see no excuse for moving hesitantly. They are irritated by incompetence and muddle, by irrelevant procedures and unnecessary delays.

Rulers get frustrated when those they are teaching or working with fail to pay attention or apply themselves. They know that achieving anything demands application and hard work. They hate it when people waste time or don't give their all.

They can unintentionally be dismissive of others or insensitive to how hard a task may appear to someone else. In their eyes it was very straightforward. (Yet if they say so, the other person feels put down.)

Other people's inefficiency and disorganisation really aggravates them and they forget to make allowances. Not everyone is a Ruler.

16. Does most things well

The Ruler is a good all-rounder. They manage to do things quickly and well. They visibly expend little effort, but achieve what they have to (that and no more!). They are likely to be sickeningly competent – in the eyes of most other people – at virtually everything they turn their hands to. They are not so much 'do-it-alls' as 'able-to-do-it-alls'! Whether it is playing table tennis, driving a van, speaking before an audience, plumbing a new bath-room . . . almost always the Ruler will make a good job of it. Their manner is such that they make even complex jobs look easy!

They have a vague grasp of what everybody else is doing, especially if they were the one who delegated the jobs. If necessary, they will be able to fill in for someone who is missing or who is required for another task. They might not know what they are doing when they start but will quickly pick it up. They do most things quite well, even the first time. They may welcome a little advice if it is available, saying, 'Oh, I see. . . .'

17. Provokes jealousy or dislike

Just for being who they are, Rulers get disliked. This is not by everybody, and not all the time, but more than most people.

They are often popular, the individual around whom a whole group may revolve, but even then they can't win – they'll get disliked for being liked. Someone or other will be jealous of them. If they never get a chance to succeed or excel, then instead they get criticised for being stroppy or difficult. If they do succeed, they seem to do so easily, without the effort that other people would have had to apply. They have the irritating habit of doing lots of things quite well, even at the first try.

Of course, the jealousy is really somebody else's problem. The more other people like you, the more the jealous person resents it. The Ruler recognises that it's impossible to keep everyone happy all the time, and refuses to make people-pleasing their priority. They make affirming noises to make sure people work on and co-operate. But it is often their way to cut corners in communicating what is really going on, and instead to tell people the minimum that they need to know. Sometimes people dislike being treated in this way and become uneasy.

It isn't just instructions that need to be made clear: people need to understand the why. In fact, good people management consists of *getting them to do what you want because they want to*. The Ruler's idea of good communication is to give clear directions. When they are challenged, they repeat the instructions in detail, as if that is what you had not understood, but they do not explain their reasoning. This is why they get called 'bossy'.

The Ruler is sure that they are right. They act independently, without being seen to consult other people. They don't explain why they made the decisions that they did. Because of this they sometimes appear arrogant. You can't tell a Ruler they're wrong. If someone questions a decision they made, the Ruler will always respond, 'Ah, yes, but . . .' To them, they made the right decision, based on what they knew at the time.

And if someone makes a suggestion that the Ruler has already considered, they are liable to dismiss it with a wave of the hand, and continue what they were doing or saying with no further explanation. The Ruler finds it natural to decide and delegate without explaining why.

They will work out what is best for everybody, considering every factor they are aware of, and present those concerned with a *fait accompli*. They are then surprised if anyone questions it, or accuses them of 'playing God'. The Ruler too easily makes assumptions on other people's behalf in a way that diminishes their personhood.

Little deters them, however hurt they feel. They are thick-skinned enough to endure all kinds of complaints, grumblings and cross-currents.

One thing that is especially characteristic of Rulers is their mannerism of apparent hesitation, swiftly followed by a confident response. They momentarily draw back as they take stock, then can be immediately decisive. Others interpret this as lack of spontaneity or absence of true emotion.

18. Objective and detached

A Ruler will say, 'I see the finished picture when other people only see the various pieces.' Even if the picture isn't finished, the Ruler has an idea where it is going. Imagine a jigsaw puzzle. They would be seeing which part went with which other part, and which piece goes where, even though they themselves are one of the pieces. This ability to be aware of the overview so easily is what distinguishes them from others and helps them to respond well under pressure. They realise what will happen if you try to put a piece in the wrong place or put it in the wrong way round. They know what actions will put strain upon other parts of the puzzle. They wonder what it would be like to be as blissfully unaware of things as most other people seem to be!

Other people seem to live locked in their own subjectivity. In comparison, the Ruler is markedly detached and objective. It is a source of unease or aggravation to others, who feel that the Ruler must be insensitive and unfeeling to remain so emotionally uninvolved. (Their reticence in displaying emotion can cause others to conclude, wrongly, that they have no deep feelings at all, but are a Mr Spock character, alien, insensitive and remote.)

19. Appears unemotional

If you asked someone to describe a person they know who is a Ruler, you are likely to hear phrases like 'A bit of a cool customer' or 'Quite a private person, really'. It is as if they would struggle to put their finger on the exact quality which causes them disquiet. It is all caught up with the Ruler trait of holding in their emotions and dealing with them privately.

They rule their emotions, rather than let their emotions rule them. Part of this is the realisation that a public display of feeling will in some way affect those round about, perhaps unpredictably. This would usually be undesirable. They are aware that any display of emotion would make them vulnerable to whoever was present. Part of it is an instinctive reticence about becoming so vulnerable to other people. A Ruler will rarely, if ever, cry in public. If they do, you can be sure that they have come a long way in developing maturity as a person, or that something profoundly unusual is going on.

People would often like to see them get upset, just to be reassured that they are human. They refer to them as 'hard', 'cold', 'insensitive' or 'unfeeling'. Most of this happens because the other person is projecting their own feelings on to the Ruler. If *they* behaved that calmly, it would be because they didn't care or didn't feel involved.

Therefore they assume the Ruler doesn't care and is disinterested; and wonders what it would take to move them!

Another accusation frequently levelled at the Ruler is that they are unspontaneous. Watch a Ruler try to act spontaneously and you will not be convinced. The most casual or outrageous behaviour is by choice or design.

Ask a Ruler, 'Would you like to do this?' and they will hesitate for a split-second, then respond with a very definite decision, one way or the other. It drives other people mad. But in that split-second they have considered what they want to do, what time it is, how their decision would affect everybody else, what the weather looks like doing – and then come up with a conclusion.

The other person doesn't understand. To them, their friend is giving off conflicting signals. First they appear hesitant, then enthusiastic. Which is it? What did they really want to do? For the other person hesitation is a sign of guardedness, but when you are dealing with a Ruler you need to realise that this is not the case.

If a group the Ruler belongs to receives clear teaching on motivations, it makes a great difference to the Ruler. It is such a luxury to be understood! Others can then more readily appreciate them, more readily accept and channel their insights and energy for the good of everybody.

20. Needs to be loved

The Ruler will look to close friends or to their partner for affirmation and support. In a way, it doesn't matter if other people misunderstand them, as long as they are understood and appreciated by someone.

Rulers love people, but there are generally only a few who take the time to get close enough to find the Ruler's heart! There is too much on the outside of a Ruler for people to engage with or react to; it never occurs to them that there is more to this person than what is at first presented, that the real person, the centre, is waiting to be known and discovered.

People will readily say to them, 'Oh, whatever would we do without you!' The Ruler nods and smiles. But when someone says, 'If only you knew how much you mean to me', or is able to say, 'I do love you', then that makes all the difference in the world. That realisation, that knowledge, reaches the very heart of the Ruler. Their whole well-being depends upon it. It tells them they are loved for who they are, and not for what they are able to do.

The Ruler is immediately recognised as one of the hard centres in the box of chocolates. This is true, and not true. In actual fact, they are more like a hard centre which, when it cracks open, is discovered to have liqueur in the very middle. Recognise that inside that unemotional or reserved exterior is a deeply feeling person, and appeal to the person inside, and you will almost always find that the Ruler responds warmly. So few people ever try.

> When Joyce went to work in a new school, she immediately picked up from other staff the impression that the Headteacher was difficult for them to relate to. She observed his behaviour carefully, and especially his interaction with other people. She knew that it is dangerous to guess from the outside what someone's motivation may be, but nonetheless she said to herself, 'He's got to be a Ruler; there's nothing else he could be.'

> If he was a Ruler, she knew exactly how to respond to him: go for the heart, treat him like the warm and accessible person he probably was inside. She did so, and never had any problem relating to him at all.

211

COMPLIMENTS

The Ruler is pleased to be appreciated, especially if someone notices that a particular decision was costly and at personal sacrifice. They may hear 'Whatever would we do without you!' but the expressed love of those who know him/her is very important for his/her well-being. They would probably smile privately at the poster which reads, 'I don't need a lot of love, but I do need a regular supply.' A Ruler likes to be recognised as loyal.

Chapter 10
The Mercy Motivation

GENERAL CHARACTERISTICS

1. Tenderhearted
2. Intuitive
3. Understands the language of the heart
4. Focuses on people
5. Needs to define boundaries
6. Picks up other people's feelings
7. Drawn to the hurting
8. Cares about little things
9. Careful not to hurt people's feelings
10. Hesitant and indecisive
11. At ease among non-threatening company
12. Insincerity makes them uneasy
13. Dislikes confrontation
14. Hates unfairness
15. Dislikes pressure
16. Needs their own space
17. Spontaneous
18. Imaginative and creative
19. Likes things to be perfect
20. Struggles with self-acceptance
Appendix: The Mercy Man

1. Tenderhearted

The Mercy will be fulfilled in an environment or work situation where it is considered appropriate to be loving and caring. To express tenderness or empathy is not a chore to them – on the contrary, they are pleased to be in such a situation. The more vulnerable the other person is, the more comfortable the Mercy is to be with them, especially if that other person would otherwise seem very 'together' or strong.

Many Mercies have not been encouraged to rejoice in their giftedness. They have been hurt by criticism of being too soft, and feel there must be something terribly odd and different about them to make them so sensitive. Typically, this makes them feel guilty, rather than superior.

Their heart is very tender, but quickly overwhelmed by too many people or too many conflicting demands. They are at their best when focused on one person or situation at a time.

They enjoy music, beautiful scenery, all creatures great and small, but especially small – any of which evokes a response from them, allowing them to be themselves, not requiring them to behave like someone else, and allowing them to enter fully into that response. (Having animals of their own can be a lot of work, but to the Mercy this is often a pleasure and not a pressure.)

Spending time with animals or amongst beautiful/ natural surroundings or just the right music replenishes rather than drains their emotional energies.

> Driving over the causeway from the island where I live is always noticeably different when travelling with two or three Mercies; the journey is less a matter of focusing on traffic or conversation, punctuated as it is with concern for rabbits who may run across the road!

A Mercy can take another person and their troubles deeply to heart, but they can't do that with everybody – it's too overwhelming. More than anyone, they need to focus carefully if they are to be a channel of love and caring amongst the neediness all around. They are heart-centred, but their heart isn't big enough for the whole world.

2. Intuitive

The Mercy's intuitive abilities are more finely developed than most people's. In fact, there seem to be things going on at all kinds of deep levels inside, which they are aware of but don't fully understand. It is difficult to share these, even with a close friend or spouse, because it's hard to put feelings into words, sometimes because the things they feel are too disturbing or don't make sense, or because they prefer their inner world to remain a private domain.

> I can't remember now what it was we were talking about, but I turned to Ferg and said, 'What do you think?' He took a deep breath, then turned to me and said, 'What a *stupid* question! I'm a Mercy so I don't think: I feel. Then I try to put it into words so when someone says, "What do you think?" I'm able to give them an answer.' Ferg loves words, if they are the right ones, but it takes time for him to word what he feels.

Their primary language is that of sensing and feeling. They pick up on other people's moods and emotions as if fitted with special antennae that other people do not have, and so they empathise readily.

(If the Mercy is encouraged to pray for others, their concern is primarily for the hurts and problems they have become aware of in people's lives. They may speak out deeply heart-felt, expressive prayers of unusual insight, but they can usually only be so expressive when they already feel secure about the group of people in whose company they are praying.)

3. Understands the language of the heart

The Mercy feels first, and thinks second.

People gifted with Mercy are ruled by the heart rather than the head. Their natural language is feelings, and everything they say with words *about* feelings rarely does them justice. (Maybe a special language needs to develop to help Mercy people share the way they, in particular, experience life!) It is like translating from French to English or vice versa. Words are a second language to them.

When a group of friends are really enjoying telling jokes together, a Mercy will tend to relax into the sense of fun and laugh along with everyone else, joining in with the feeling of the moment. Half-way through the next joke they may suddenly laugh again having just got the last one. The mind was in secondary mode!

This tends to be the case when they are around as someone tells his story or shares her distress. They listen to the tone of voice far more than to what is being said, and often find they have not been listening with their head and have missed some crucial piece of information. This makes them appear stupid or awkward and often embarrasses them. It is far more likely to happen when something important is going on, and what is being discussed is charged with deep emotional significance for the other person.

Often the Mercy will make a conscious effort to remember at least the name of the person being talked about by, say, a bereaved person, so as not to appear insensitive or appear not to be really listening.

For them, feelings, senses and compassion flow in and out, coming and going unbidden – feelings and intuitions just *are*.

The Mercy depends and relies upon their emotions far more than another person would to weigh what is happening within and around them. So if they are under the weather, require medication, have hormonal difficulties or are just plain tired, they are less likely to be as objective about whatever chemical changes their body is going through and may be knocked off balance. Feelings are not chemically induced but they are chemically affected, which makes this area of critical importance for the Mercy person.

Love, for them, is an affair of the heart. They rely on senses, feelings and emotions, rather than mental processes to guide their lives. If a decision is being made on the basis of what they conclusively feel, then fact-based arguments may be dismissed as irrelevant and confusing. A Mercy does use their mind, but this is likely to be in order to inform or explain what they feel.

(Some Mercies are, of course, clever and articulate, even brilliant academics. But this is just to say that they are competent and fluent in what is still a second language. They may enjoy switching between the two!)

Because of pressure from others, they can easily bottle their emotions up – feeling odd or out of line with other people. Sadly, too many have been made to feel that sensitivity is a disability; that emotions are a kind of handicap not to be talked about in normal company. Mercy men in particular have had to put up with a great deal of negative pressure of this kind. To be seen as soft, or even caring, implies weakness, which is a slur on their manhood. The truth is they need to learn to *release* their deep emotions, and not feel condemned because of their emotional capacity.

It is important to Mercy people to be able to share their hearts. When they give an account of something they want to explain how they feel. There may be no reason for sharing it other than that they want to. It may not be relevant to any current agenda, or fit with the logical proceedings. This confuses other people, who try to reply to whatever they guess was the reason for it being said. The Mercy is frustrated and hurt – they want to be understood; they want the other person to be interested in how they felt, even if that is going off at a tangent.

One night after working long and hard on this book, we stopped and instead played a game of 'Pick-a-Stick' to relax before going to bed. Gill didn't join in and next day remarked, 'We never played games even when I was a child. I just don't like them because they are a waste of time.' I immediately responded by explaining that we had only played the game in order to switch off and relax. Gill was hurt. She knew that. She'd just decided she'd like to tell me about not playing games in her family when they were growing up, and was hurt that I didn't seem interested.

Sometimes it's important just to be listened to, and to feel that the other person is listening. They may need warning that this is what you are asking from them, not help or advice. There might be time for that later. Ferg once said to me, 'Don't try to counsel me when I'm trying to tell you how I feel.' Mercies often feel there is always somebody or other telling them what to do or be.

4. Focuses on people

There is nothing worse than sharing something you are really happy about only to have the other person treat what was really important to you in a very off-hand way. It would have been better to keep it to yourself than to have it minimised and dismissed. But share good news with a Mercy and they will be genuinely pleased, perhaps even more excited than you were. They help you to really 'own' and experience the joys that come your way.

The Mercy is people-focused. Their world is full of people, but preferably one at a time. It is less confusing; that way they can give undivided attention to the person in front of them and really enter into what is going on with them. When there are too many people about it's not as easy to know where to focus, who to be with, or just where the atmosphere is coming from.

The Mercy is better, and certainly more at ease, in a one-to-one situation. Another favourite recipe for comfort is a known group of people who are together often, where the dynamic of personalities and emotions is familiar. For them a one-to-one conversation will always be easier in a separate room than amongst other people who are talking among themselves.

5. Needs to define boundaries

Mercies like to feel safe with another person and know that *they* feel safe with *them* in return. Just to know another person really trusts them is very releasing, and they are able to open up and be themselves in that person's company. They feel the need of such trust relationships, but have learned it is not always wise to trust too easily. Closeness demands in-depth communication. They hate anything sham and superficial, and desire deep friend-ships in which there is mutual commitment. They tend to need physical closeness in order to be reassured of acceptance.

The Mercy's spontaneity may also lead them to demonstrations of affection which are not measured or careful, and compound the confusion. Mercies need to learn about boundaries. Their boundaries are instinctively defined by feelings, rather than logic. This means that, to others, these boundaries appear to shift and change for no obvious reason; they appear, in fact, to be random. But once objective boundaries are set in place instead, the Mercy feels more secure, rather than inhibited.

We all need to be loved, and the genuinely affectionate nature of the Mercy can get them into all kinds of trouble or propel them into a relationship they weren't really looking for. The Mercy behaves as if the other person was the only person in the world, giving them undivided attention which people are not used to. There is nothing wrong with so much concern, nor with how they show it. The problem is that when you're down, a Mercy is a good person to be with – they make you feel better. This feeling better confuses the other person, who often believes it means they have feelings for the Mercy, or that the relationship is deeply romantic, just because they are getting some pain relief.

Mercies would like to believe that everyone is honest and reliable; however, experience teaches them otherwise. But they do demonstrate deep loyalty to a friend, and will even react harshly to those who attack that friend.

The very nature of a person with the gift of Mercy requires close friendships. But these friendships must have mutual commitment which needs to be reaffirmed quite often. Mercy people can rarely get too much of the time and attention of their close friends. When hurt in a friendship, they will be very slow and cautious about getting into another relationship. They will wait for the other person to demonstrate they are genuine and trustworthy.

Quite often the Mercy's trust in a person is misplaced. They want to trust the person they like and want to believe in them, and act on the basis of this kind of feeling, instead of making the person earn their trust. It is sad that Mercies, who are the most sensitive to other people's hurts, are easily hurt themselves.

A lot of Mercies find it difficult to believe that they have personal rights, or that their wishes might ever take priority over other people's plans and agenda. Their space gets invaded by other people. They do nothing about it at the time but feel angry or resentful afterwards. So they should develop habits of insisting that appropriate boundaries be maintained. They need to know they have the right to say no.

Physical contact needs to be chosen and not imposed. Touch is expensive for a Mercy person. They need confidence to set boundaries they are comfortable with. In the area of emotions, desires and decisions, the blurring of boundaries happens all too readily, and the Mercy cannot always easily tell where the other person stops and they begin.

For decision-making, a good plan may be to develop the habit of saying, 'Give me 20 minutes to think about it, and I'll let you know!'

6. Picks up other people's feelings

A Mercy is a good person to be with when you're down. You don't need to explain first what's going on inside. Their innate sensitivity gives them the ability to 'feel' an atmosphere, to recognise joy or distress. They don't need to see or hear anything. They sense the vibes. In fact, the Mercy uses observation of body language or facial expressions only to confirm what they have already felt. They know if people are up or down, joyful or sad, confident or fearful, at peace or in pain.

But the Mercy person can become overly absorbed with other people's distress, saturated with it like an emotional sponge. (They should at least be wrung out, giving over to God whatever they have soaked up on the way!)

A Mercy person has the ability to sense when a remark made in conversation is really hurtful or insensitive. They want to protect the person who was hurt, and hate to see anyone put down or bullied. If someone is upset, a Mercy person is likely to be the one who notices even before it shows. They feel what the other person feels, feeling it from the inside.

7. Drawn to the hurting

Mercy people seem to attract people who tell them their problems. At any given time there will usually be someone in particular to whom they are giving emotional support. And the Mercy is generally stronger on support than solutions. Sympathy hurts *for* a person; empathy hurts *with* them. It is empathy that characterises the Mercy. They go through it all *with* them more often than solve it.

It is natural for Mercy people to feel compassion, and they are often drawn to work with or care for the weak and vulnerable. They may like to be with small children or the elderly or disabled people. Not everyone understands the Mercy person's attraction to the vulnerable or the hurting, nor can everyone handle it.

> Melissa's dad was puzzled when his daughter brought home her new school friend, Janine. They seemed to have little in common. 'No one else was going to be her friend,' Melissa explained.

8. Cares about little things

To the Mercy, little things really do mean a lot. A thoughtful action, a quick phone call, an unexpected present can turn their whole day around. (And it seems the smaller it is, the more likely it is to appeal to them.)

Relationships matter a lot to them, and thoughtfulness characterises their relationships. Some Mercy people like to make a special point of sending thank you notes, or sending a carefully chosen card, or even phoning up to say you've been on their mind. (And they probably *almost* do these things far more often!)

They are likely to have a small list of people they give special attention to, rather than too big a list which would be overwhelming. They love to do thoughtful things for others, and extend themselves in each relationship to express their love. They will create a special occasion if there isn't one around.

A Mercy will like to set the atmosphere in a meaningful way, focusing on small details. To the Mercy little things mean a lot. They focus on the particular, not the broad canvas. Just lighting a candle or having one flower in a vase apparently changes everything.

Mercy friends tend to put a lot more of themselves into a friendship. They take endless trouble fine-tuning a relationship, going over what somebody meant, clearing up the smallest misunderstandings that have really bothered them, and so on.

They sometimes feel that touch is more accessible to them than words. If you don't touch them, perhaps you don't want to, perhaps they are unimportant, awful, no longer needed . . . undesirable. Someone may lie with their words, but if they lied through their touch the Mercy would know.

They like to express love in action, word or touch. Being near to somebody makes it more natural to share in their feelings. Physical closeness is, in itself, often a way of expressing what they feel, and touch matters a lot to them. At times they prefer someone not to be too close to them, in case they feel overwhelmed or crowded, even if they care deeply for the person. A moment later the need for that distance may have passed.

9. Careful not to hurt people's feelings

Mercy people are so sensitive that the last thing they want is to hurt another person. They are nervous of causing unintentional offence. They will tiptoe around anything that could be a sensitive area for someone else. (But they do react strongly towards anyone who is insensitive to others' feelings. They become strongly antagonistic towards the insensitive person, and may try to punish them by being cold or hostile. They will even sometimes shout or rage at the insensitive person, who will wonder what they have done to deserve such an outburst. At this point the Mercy doesn't seem very sensitive to *their* feelings; they're too busy nursing the hurt feelings of the other person.)

Their quiet sensitivity, their non-threatening attitude, may be judged by others to be signs of weakness. The Mercy person may be inhibited in the expressing of their own deepest feelings for fear of hurting or offending anyone else. They feel that what they really want to say would not be well received or would sound harsh. There is the temptation to say what people want to hear, and always to be a comforting and consoling presence.

With someone very close to them, they may find it hard to stand up for themselves, because they know what they would like to say would hurt the other person. Then they would be quiet and live with their own hurt. (Some Mercies develop a habit of deferring, rather than voicing their own responses.)

10. Hesitant and indecisive

Some Mercies are so used to deferring to others, and going along with what is decided for them, that they don't know how to break out of that pattern.

Decision-making is difficult, and it could be just as hard to be firm about what they have already finally decided. Sometimes, delaying long enough will take matters out of their hands, which seems easier than making a decision which could be the wrong one.

A Mercy parent will have a horror of behaving harshly towards their children, and would naturally be too lenient or indulgent in consequence, failing to bring correction. They must learn that if they fail to be decisive, it is sometimes more hurtful in the long run. This applies in many other situations of responsibility.

11. At ease among non-threatening company

If someone in the room is upset, a Mercy may instinctively want to go to them but could be too shy to draw attention to themselves by crossing the room to do so. They may go up to somebody afterwards. That's a situation they can cope with. It may also be that they don't want to risk embarrassing the other person or risk having got it wrong. In non-threatening company they have the freedom to do what they feel appropriate.

Mercies prefer a peaceful, non-threatening environment. Many of them are shy or insecure, and need to feel really safe in a situation before they can relax and be themselves. They like accepting, undemanding company; often this means other Mercies. If they can't have that, they have a preference at least for familiar groups and situations, and for the more uncomfortable people around to be known quantities.

The Mercy needs to know their insights are going to be taken seriously and listened to, or it is just not worth taking the risk of trying to express what they feel. Their feelings, about everybody else but themselves, are usually very reliable and should be trusted.

Other people lose patience while the Mercy struggles to articulate exactly what they are feeling, and so what they have to say is usually dismissed as incoherent or irrelevant.

The Mercy hears this as 'Pay less attention to your feelings . . . Be more sensible . . . Rely upon facts . . .' and all the other worn records that all their life they have heard played for them by others. This compounds the problem, not exactly encouraging the Mercy to share what they feel the next time.

12. Insincerity makes them uneasy

Mercies themselves are sincere and wouldn't know how to be otherwise. Deception seems like an awful lot of effort for a Mercy. Their instincts may be an early-warning system which alerts them to someone who is not genuine or has a hidden agenda. They would then rather close themselves off or keep right away from anyone who makes them feel so uncomfortable.

Sometimes, when they feel uneasy in a situation, instead of trusting their impressions, they will dismiss what they feel as 'unreasonable'. In fact, their feelings about other people are likely to be reliable. (It is feelings about themselves that are subject to distortion and blame.) It is usually when they go against their better judgement or initial reservations that they are vulnerable to being exploited or hurt.

13. Dislikes confrontation

The Mercy would rather drop a hint, and hope it will be acted upon, than risk a head-on clash with anyone. This dislike of confrontation may be mistaken for timidity, but, in fact, they are hopeful for a less disruptive alternative. The Mercy may eventually explode, but only when they can't hold in what they are feeling any longer.

Mercy people hate to hear negative talk. So, if they have a complaint to voice or feelings to express, they may first apologise for 'moaning again'. They don't like to think that they are being negative.

If asked to appraise something they will always find something nice to say, even if they basically hated it. They'll say, 'I don't like it', rather than 'It's dreadful!' They instinctively don't want to hurt the other person's feelings (even in their absence).

Some Mercies have been hurt so often that they withdraw from people, and try hard to be cynical. But sooner or later they find they are reaching out and trusting new people all over again.

When they hear others speaking negatively about someone else, the Mercy person will often jump to their defence, and complain that the speaker is being unfair and not giving the person a chance.

14. Hates unfairness

They have a strong sense of fairness and fair play. Their sympathies will always tend to lie with the one who has been wronged or who is at a disadvantage. Outrage at injustice seems to give the Mercy an impetus for seeking change.

A Mercy will side with a person who has been slighted, and be upset on their behalf, especially if that person is someone they love. If a hurtful remark or comment is made and the Mercy gets to hear about it, they wince and are indignant and protective. Long after the two people actually involved have forgotten the incident, the Mercy person is still holding a grudge!

The Mercy person can also be easily hurt or offended. Sometimes they misunderstand what is said or read events wrongly, and get all upset over imagined slights that were never intended. It is good for them to determine not to be easily offended on their own account or on anyone else's.

Sometimes they take up an offence on someone else's behalf and get angry at God in the process. They don't like the way that person is being treated. They remonstrate that it's not fair. (Mercy people often struggle with the idea that a person is allowed to suffer.)

15. Dislikes pressure

Mercies like to take their time and cannot be rushed. They find hurry disruptive. They get there in the end. It has been said that 'they have only one speed – SLOW forward'!

In fact, if you push or pressurise them they can take one step back. They won't be hurried. They hate to be pressurised. They need to *feel* right about something, not because you say so, but because they sense it's OK!

Somehow, time is so different for them. They are present-in-the-now people. They live for the moment. They do things at their speed, steady but slow.

A Mercy person needs quality time to explain how they feel. They won't be rushed. When a conversation is long-finished they may come back to have their say. This is not an afterthought, but their considered response.

16. Needs their own space

The Mercy person really needs to have space of their own, a safe place to be, and time free from interruptions. This restores their energies, and gives them a sense of who they are, separate from what is going on in other people, and separate from other people's perceptions of them. This is crucial. They need real time out regularly, the way other people would say they need three good meals a day. Some days they'd like not to answer the doorbell or telephone because they feel their space is being invaded. When driving they hate to be hemmed in by other cars.

Mercy feels the anger, hurt, pain, or even excitement of others. They pick up on these things naturally, virtually all the time. Even in sleep it would seem as if this faculty never shuts down altogether. In a large group they can feel exhausted and drained, just by being there. (At a party you may find a small group of Mercies outside, getting away from the people!) Without knowing it, people can wear them out. Mercies often seek to avoid crowds or large groups for this reason. On the other hand, crowds can be non-threatening because they protect anonymity.

Mercy people easily feel under pressure or that they cannot cope. Then they instinctively long to retreat into a safe place for time on their own to recuperate.

17. Spontaneous

Mercy people can experience small joys with great pleasure and spontaneity. They are genuinely happy for other people, and are childlike in the immediacy of their response to the world. Their responses are free, genuine and unhurried. (The Mercy continues to expect the adult world to disapprove of them, so the thought of other people's perceptions of them often weighs quite heavily. The more they forget this, the more truly childlike they are freed to be.)

They are delighted by surprises. Something catches their eye as they glance out of the window. A letter from a friend arrived this morning. A small thing is enough to change the course of their whole day.

If we let them, the Mercies in our life can begin to teach us the joy that is to be found in the present moment.

18. Imaginative and creative

Creativity comes easily to the Mercy, although it can be squashed or discouraged in some. Almost anything expressive or artistic could be their opportunity. Their imaginative capacity is evident, both in their ability to be creative themselves, and in their appreciation of nature and all kinds of art forms.

Rather than make judgements, they instinctively respond to whatever is presented to them and express their appreciation or response. They expect their own work to be treated in the same way, being given freedom to create without the necessity of producing some sort of masterpiece. But their desire is to create things which are perfect, or at least executed to a very high standard.

A Mercy whose creative abilities are under-developed is definitely missing out. They have a rich imagination but are robbed of much joy if it is given little outward expression.

19. Likes things to be perfect

The Mercy person is a perfectionist. If they are going to spend time doing something, it should be done well. It hurts and upsets them when what they do isn't perfect. But living in the real world necessitates some compromises. Some areas will have to be makeshift or just OK. The Mercy has to *choose* and decide which areas it will be that they can live with being less than perfect.

The Mercy is painfully aware of their own imperfections, real and imaginary. They have great difficulty in accepting themselves, and find it hard to shrug off criticism. They are likely to take on-board inappropriate levels of guilt.

20. Struggles with self-acceptance

Many Mercies have a struggle with self-acceptance, and

all too much of the time are being told they are not acceptable – which doesn't help. Because they are so self-critical, they are in need of rebuke far less than others but still get far more than their share. They will not refute criticism easily, because the inner critic too readily re-inforces all the negatives with data from the memory banks. They are always too willing to condemn them-selves, rather than contradict someone who speaks out more loudly. (Ironically, the Mercy gift is most needed wherever it is largely misunderstand and suppressed.)

The pressure has originally come from others. People who don't understand Mercies have put them under pressure, making them feel they need to change to fit in with the rest of society. The Mercy's response is to feel guilty and wear a big label round their neck saying 'Failure' or 'Worthless'. They assume the needs of others are more important than their own and should have priority. It is hard to do it, but the label needs ripping up, so it cannot hang there again.

(The potential effectiveness of an individual Mercy in their interaction with other people's lives depends upon the degree to which the Mercy has overcome their own emotional wounds and refuses to be limited by these.)

We are told that we should love other people as we love ourselves. For the Mercy it is often easier to love others than to really believe that they themselves are lovable. They tend to feel embarrassed, overwhelmed, unworthy – full of all sorts of conflicting emotions.

The unfailing, accepting love of partner and family can make enormous difference in the Mercy's self-esteem and confidence. Where they can receive and believe in that love, they can go from strength to strength.

(In *Jesus Christ Superstar* there is a compelling scene where Jesus is surrounded by so many sick and needy people that he sends them away saying, 'There's too many of you.' The real Jesus wouldn't say that, but a Mercy might have to. They know they have not the capacity to care for all the world and its needs at one time.)

But remember, the Mercy's emotions about themselves may be less than reliable! Others feel fulfilled when they use their gifts effectively. The Mercy shares in the pain and feels shattered afterwards! They are at their most effective in being available to others. The way in which this happens means that they are at that precise time the least self-aware. They are consumed with the other person's concerns and emotions, and not their own satisfaction at being able to help. Instead, after being effective, they are likely to feel exhausted, or may even still be carrying the emotional bruises sustained by others.

Appendix: The Mercy Man

Their own characteristics run counter to society's traditional expectations of masculine behaviour, for they are sensitive, emotional, intuitive and sympathetic, caring, and drawn to the weak.

There are new pressures at work in society for men to be more nurturing, tender, strong and sensitive. The 'new man' is willing to experience and express deep emotion, and is apparently a much sought-out commodity.

But many Mercy men are still smarting from earlier pressure to be a different sort of hero, strong, impassive, resolute and utterly immovable – a sort of six-foot stiff upper-lip. Until now it has been acceptable in our society for a woman to be led by her heart or easily moved to tears. Not so a man. The man with a Mercy gift is just not going to fit into some simplistic macho mould.

Their own low self-esteem and self-worth are fuelled by being made to feel odd. They may try to learn to be someone else just to fit in. To avoid being misunderstood, they may have worked hard to over-compensate, developing whatever traditionally 'masculine' characteristics or interests they are comfortable with, in case they are misunderstood. But it rarely fools anybody. They may be chided or upbraided for taking things too much to heart, but it is still them to whom people turn in times of trouble. They are usually well-liked. Those who overlook them do so at their own loss.

COMPLIMENTS

The Mercy person is pleased to be called understanding, or sensitive. They love to hear, 'You really do care.'

Chapter 11
I am confused!

The be-all and end-all?

Some individuals may fall into the trap of thinking that motivations is the answer to everything if only they understand it in enough detail. So they consult whoever knows more about it, and hope that they will tell them what to do; they may become unable to make any major, or even minor, decisions without consultation, asking, 'What should my motivation do under these circumstances?'

Any excuse?

There is a danger of using motivations as an excuse for behaviour:

> I'm a Ruler, so it's normal or acceptable or expected for me to tell everybody what to do whether they like it or not.

or

> I'm a Mercy, so it's all right for me to sit in a corner all day, feeling sorry for everybody and weeping on their behalf.

or

> I'm a Prophetic, and I will be pig-headed, because it's right that I should be!

Pigeon-holing?

In organisations there is a danger of excluding people because of their motivation, saying, 'She's a Mercy – too emotional!' or 'He's a Prophetic – too inflexible!' without any allowance for the individual to grow through experiencing situations which may not apparently suit them. However, motivations is very useful for leaders of groups who will then be able to cultivate a better awareness of possible causes of friction between group members, and a greater sensitivity to the dynamics of the group, so that the group may achieve its maximum potential.

Motivations can be a useful and enlightening aid, if employed sensibly and not taken to overpowering extremes. Your central motivation may be a given, but the person you present to others may change; your behaviour and reactions may modify as you learn and grow through experience and circumstances. We do not remain static!

Motivations will help you understand more about yourself and others, but don't assume that any of us will always react in a predictable way. We were created unique, but, sadly, presuppositions can box everybody in so that no one's responses are free or unselfconscious. (And if someone does behave differently, others can still refuse to take note of anything that is not true-to-type.) This attitude of having people all sewn up gives them no space to grow or mature.

One of a kind?

Identifying your motivation will not diminish your personhood, but embrace and enhance it. Remember, people of the same motivation are still individuals. It's just that they share a similar perspective, rather like people who shelter under the same big umbrella.

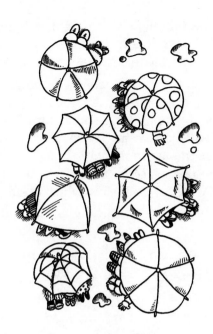

Now what?

Having read this far, you may now be asking the question:

So what is my motivation?

Typically your response will be one of the following:

A   When I came to the description of one of the motivations I just knew it was talking about me. Almost everything that was said could have been written by a fly on my bedroom wall. I am very confident that I have recognised from the description which is my motivational gift. Now I want to know what the implications of this are.

B   When I read/heard the descriptions of each motivation there were bits of each one that seemed familiar. I thought, 'Oh that must be me . . . no it isn't. Perhaps it's this one, but that bit's not right.' I don't think I can sort out which of them is me. Perhaps I'm not any of them. Is it possible to be a little bit of each?

C   I've got it down to two, mainly by process of elimination. Now I'm confused. Am I really a cross between two sorts of people? Or is some of my behaviour just learnt? Do I behave in certain ways because of the way I was trained in my job? Or was I drawn to that job in the first place because I was a certain sort of person? And how do I know which is which?

D   I'm totally confused. Can I give up and go home? Please?

Totally confused?

All human beings have a deep desire to be known and loved for who they really are, and to feel appreciated and valued for what they can do. We have an innate longing to be valued for how we impact other people's lives. We were made to be ourselves, if we can only give ourselves permission to enjoy that fact. Darrelle Marshall suggests some reasons why people say, 'I can't find my motivational gift':

1. Because I have no intention of being known for who I really am.

2. Because I am not willing to 'accept' my most obvious characteristics and would rather be some other gift.

3. Because I haven't really lived enough, or got to know me. I don't know what I want or feel; I have always just done what I've been told and not looked at what was happening inside. I need more time.

4. Because I am in a major battle right now which is consuming all my energies, so I can't see straight or be

reflective. I need to look at this again at another time, when the present crisis has passed.

5. Because I have been so damaged in the past (in childhood, through physical, sexual or emotional abuse, outlandish circumstances) that I have never yet been given permission to recognise the real me. I need to proceed very slowly.

6. Because my mental condition is not stable, and directly impinges on questions to do with my true identity anyway. This is not a good time to look at these questions.

Not learnt

By the time we have lived a while in this world it is probable that we will have learnt enormous amounts from other people – hopefully so! Often these will be people of a different motivation and therefore with different values and priorities to ourselves. This will modify and balance out our natural leanings and behaviour. We learn to do what is expected of us, as well as what we like. We achieve in areas that do not even interest us. We conform outwardly for the sake of peace, for rewards, or for the benefit of other people. From the outside it may not even be evident what interests us or motivates us. The first rule about motivations is that it is motivation not behaviour which identifies our gift:

It's not what you do, but the why that you do it that betrays who you are

Example:

A Mercy busies themselves doing many practical tasks in the background, and is mistaken at first glance for a

Server. But the reason the Mercy does this is to avoid being seen, because he/she is so desperately shy. Others, on reflection, are not surprised to discover them to be Mercy and not Server; they remember on many occasions being glad to spend time in this person's company when vulnerable or troubled.

9 to 5?

It is important as well not to confuse *function* with *being*. That is the equivalent of getting your boxes mixed up (see Chapter 3). Your job is not you; nor does your usefulness define you. How you feel, what matters to you, how you instinctively respond and behave, these are reflections of your innate giftedness – not what people expect of you.

More than one gift?

Some people who teach about the gifts confuse people by saying it is possible to have more than one motivational gift. I believe this is not true or possible; though certainly additional traits may be visible and are to be encouraged. However, identity itself should not be sacrificed, just for the sake of a few additional traits.

A better picture in response to this question was presented to us by Darrelle Marshall of Australia.* She suggests that a person's one central motivation is like the roots and the trunk of a mighty tree. Other branches may grow out from the trunk, with nourishment supplied to them by the roots. Some branches are bigger and stronger than others, but the potential for them to grow and develop is already there. Someone may be a Mercy with a

---

* See page 244 for Darrelle's picture of the tree.

strong, well-developed branch of Exhorting and a fairly strong Teaching branch – but they are a Mercy tree. To not be identified as one particular tree is to forfeit any advantage from exposure to motivations teaching.

Practice makes perfect?

Socialisation and conditioning will have affected our behaviour, and may account for even deeply engrained patterns of action and response. We do some things because our parents drilled into us their importance. We do other things precisely because we were not allowed to when we were younger – conditioning can work both ways! We emulate our parents in some ways, and dread repeating their behaviour patterns in others. (For example, with tidiness/lack of order we react against or repeat parental patterns.)

Doing what comes naturally?

When a particular motivation is our gift and not just learnt behaviour, it is recognisably the way we will be without ever needing to try. It is a matter of doing what comes naturally, precisely because it is gift. When it is not clear which of two patterns of behaviour is the true motivational gift, it is worth examining earliest memories of childhood to see which was your preferred response.

Mirror, mirror on the wall?

Sometimes a person could say yes to all the questions about a Teaching motivation *and* all those about a Ruler, for example. But to conclude that she is the one seems comfortable and sits well deep inside, whereas the other one doesn't really feel like *her*, however much she behaves that way as well. It may be that you are really

241

unhappy about the conclusion you reach, because you've always hated the sort of person you are. If you are clear that this really is the truthful identification of your motivation, start getting excited about it. It means there is one set of brilliant things you do really well without needing to try, without needing to hide it; and everyone else can be jealous of your attainment in that one area – which for them is still a struggle. We are all made differently precisely so we can complement each other's giftedness. Don't try to be someone else. They need you to be you. Be that, and by all means learn from other people as well.

Can it be true?

It has been fashionable to identify Bible characters with certain motivations. This raises many more problems than it solves, and leads to all kinds of convoluted difficulties. In real life, we encourage people never to guess at the motivation of another person, since from 'the outside of the chocolate' it is impossible to pronounce definitively what the centre will be. It is too easy to make mistakes. Even the experts do it – which is why one set of notes designates Paul as a Prophetic and another is equally dogmatic in announcing that he was an Exhorter. It is much easier to argue that Peter was probably a Prophetic since he walked on water before he thought about it, and was dramatically right and then wrong in his responses to Jesus as Messiah, with these extremes of behaviour only moments apart. Barnabas, we *may* say, was a likely Exhorter, since the name he was given by those who knew him even means 'son of encouragement', but was Martha a Server? Or would not any one of us, regardless of motivation, have been aggravated by Mary opting out of the work? And to designate Joseph the dreamer as a

242

Prophetic is not helpful. Maybe the extremes of circumstance were a consequence of his calling (i.e. his *job*) as a Prophet, and his motivation was quite different. Short of asking him, how are we to know? The most bizarre outworking of this kind of speculation accompanies the choice of Timothy as a Server. Since Paul advises Timothy to take a little wine for his weak stomach, one teacher has seriously concluded that all Serving motivations are prone to stomach disorders through addiction to hard work! We cannot demonstrate Timothy's motivation, and even if we could, why would we? And to generalise from the particular in such a way is very poor reasoning indeed.

Mercies are normally very happy to be identified with John the beloved disciple. There may be some truth in this, as it is he who exclaims, 'Lord, who will it be?' when Jesus announces that his betrayer is close by. He is immediately uncomfortable, and feels guilty just in case!

Root and branches

The picture overleaf shows a tree trunk representing a person's main motivating gift, his or her strongest gift; then the branches are secondary strengths. Usually we have two or three strong branches. Below we see a Mercy – their main gift, with strongest branches of Exhorting and Teaching.

> A tree gives glory to God first of all by being a tree. No two created beings are exactly alike. And their individuality is no imperfection. This particular tree will give glory to God by spreading out its roots in the earth and raising its branches into the air and the light in a way that no other tree before or after ever did or will do.*

---

* Thomas Merton, *Seeds of Contemplation* (1961, Burns and Oates Ltd, a Continuum imprint)

Picture supplied by Darrelle Marshall

Chapter 12
Buts . . .

Although reluctant to be slotted into a category, having my personality/motivation put in a box, it has helped me to see my 'self' as a gift from God. I've always struggled with the notion that God made me to be the person I am, for I see so much in my intrinsic self which is not of God. To understand that God has given me a character which although totally unique has certain common, identifiable features, has helped my self-image. Previously, when people talked to me about 'accepting yourself', I wasn't clear who my self was, and whether God made just the good bits or all of it!

I learnt that who I am is a gift from God with potential for good, but also potential for extremes. These extremes have been the source of confusion for I always felt they prevented God from completely delighting in me. But he does, for my essential self came from him, and although he longs to temper and control the extremes, he is pleased with who I am.

This also causes me to appreciate who I am, for I see much of value in being an enquiring person. Although I've been led to believe that thinkers like me are a burden, and few ever had any answers that didn't provoke further debate, I recognise that this motivation is of great benefit both to me and to others. *Claire Johnson * (motivation: Teaching)*

Romans 12 lists the seven different motivations in order, and then repeats the same people's motivations with instructions for each group. This is counsel to which each motivation in turn will usually say, 'That's right!' The passage then goes through the seven giftings a third and

---

* Now Claire Humphrey.

final time with a casual sting in the tail – an 'Oh, by the way . . .' or 'But, remember this . . .' – which tends to sit much more uncomfortably. This *but* highlights the particular danger area each motivation should pay special attention to.

Prophetic – verses 6, 9 and 16a

> 'Use the gifts given you in proportion to your faith. Your love must be sincere and real. Hate what is evil, turning in horror from wickedness, and hold fast to what is good.'

BUT 'Live in harmony with one another, in one accord, and have the same concern for everyone.'

The Prophetic person is often the cause of disharmony, failing to notice the hurt they cause, or not caring about the consequences of things they say and do. Sometimes, if they are bored or restless, they are prone to stir things up just for the sake of it!

If you know you can be dangerous when you get bored, then that is the time to watch yourself, and make sure you don't cause trouble or damage relationships for no reason.

Server – verses 7a, 10 and 16b

> 'Let the practical one give themselves to serving. Be devoted to one another in brotherly love, and honour one another above yourself. Be eager to show respect for one another.'

BUT 'Remember, do not be proud; accept humble duties, make friends with humble people, be willing to associate with people of low position.'

The Server likes to do, to help, to serve, to engage in humble tasks, but they hate to be taken for granted or treated as if they were inferior just because they do things others dislike doing! They are in danger of being walked on, but also in danger of being resentful at times.

The Server eventually feels they have been taken advantage of, given the 'dirty jobs'. They are taken for granted and unappreciated – maybe even treated as inferior. This can lead to resentment or anger. It isn't that they minded doing those jobs, but people's attitudes stink sometimes! The resentment builds through time and eventually surfaces. Servers especially are told to give themselves to humble tasks; and in those they will find much fulfilment. Other people may undervalue their work and overlook them, but they know it is crucial to do what they do. It is a bit like a prospector who has found where the gold is. Other people may feel sorry for him working so hard attacking the rock face; they haven't realised that he has found something.

If anything, the Server should try harder to be identified with those whom other people despise and overlook. When they do come alongside the poor or disadvantaged (whom they would not naturally seek out) they are able to help in all kinds of ways, and are received more readily because they are matter-of-fact and don't have a patronising attitude.

(When a Server is responsible for a team of people, they will never be happy remaining at a distance from those in their charge. They will need deliberately to be as involved as is possible with the most non-prestigious people on the team if they are to lead well, feel identified with everyone else, and not have the job drive them mad.)

Teacher – verses 7b, 11 and 16c

'Use your gift of explaining. Work hard, and do not be lazy, never lag in zeal and earnest endeavour. Fervent in spirit, be aglow and burning with the Spirit of God. Serve the Lord with a heart full of devotion.'

BUT 'Do not think of yourselves as wise. Never over-estimate yourself or be wise in your own conceits. Do not be conceited!'

The Teacher or explaining person is inclined to think too highly of their own opinions. They accumulate knowledge and observe carefully. They like time to assimilate what they take in, but often feel they know better – to their satisfaction. They take themselves very seriously!

Can you really cope when someone has a joke at your expense? This is a good litmus test! Learn to laugh at yourself and allow others to join in, especially those you love, without you feeling threatened. Keep telling yourself, I mustn't take myself quite so seriously!

Exhorter – verses 8a, 12 and 17a

'If your gift is to encourage others, you should do so. Let hope keep you joyful; be steadfast and patient in suffering or trouble, and pray at all times.'

BUT 'If someone has done you wrong, do not repay them with a wrong. Repay no one evil for evil.'

The Exhorter is likely to be extra-nasty back when someone says or does something that is hurtful or uncalled for. This can be in self-defence or on others' behalf, but it tends to lead to much unpleasantness. The Exhorter, when roused, has an amazing capacity for aggressive or vindictive behaviour. Make it a rule never to *begin* to retaliate, and it will not get out of hand.

Memorise the phrase 'extra-nasty back', and avoid putting it into practice. If necessary, draw up a wince-list or catalogue of unpleasantnesses that have been caused by sticking your oar in, instead of letting things pass. When you feel the indignation coming to the boil, deliberately unplug it from its source, so you're not giving it any power, rather than letting it simmer. (Don't pretend to yourself that you've unplugged it when really you have just shifted it on to the back burner.)

Giver – verses 8b, 13 and 17b

> 'Contribute what you can in simplicity and liberality . . . Practice hospitality. Share your belongings with the people in your life already (especially when they need you to), and also open your homes to strangers.'

BUT 'Be careful to do what is right in the eyes of everybody.'

The Giver tends to go overboard in their generosity until the thing gets out of hand, leaving someone else with less or feeling badly done to – especially the Giver's own family!

Your joy comes from wading into a need or situation. and you hate to let the opportunity go by. It is hard for you to keep a sense of proportion when you are so involved that nothing else matters. Try not to see other people as wet blankets or obstacles in your way, but bear in mind what you know they would say if you consulted them. Try more often to involve and include them in the process, so that they can share in the joy and satisfaction too! *Don't* just do what you can get away with, and blow the consequences.

Ruler – verses 8c, 14 and 18-20

> 'With diligence, give help and oversight. Be zealous and be single-minded (i.e. with intense eagerness and effort, earnestness, haste, speed and determination). Bless whoever persecutes you, bless them instead of cursing them, and ask God to bless them too.'

BUT 'As far as it depends on you, live at peace with everyone and do not take revenge. It is God's business to show anger and judgement, not yours, so leave room for him to do so, if he is going to! For your part, when your enemy is hungry, feed *him*; when *he* is thirsty, give *him* drink; and it will be as good as giving *him* lighted coals from your own fire, so *his*, too, can burn and keep *him* safe and warm.'

The Ruler can see when someone acts unfairly, and may see an apparent occasion for retribution.* They may then act strongly or even ruthlessly, and can also make enemies without meaning to – just by being themselves. They see how, given the same situations, they would have said or done the same things again that antagonised others, and for the same reasons. The Ruler must then refrain from

---

* It's almost a case of 'Vengeance is mine,' says the Ruler. I remember my own father as consistent and loving, competent and well organised. He was quick to reprove when necessary, firm but unruffled. In an emergency he would be calm and resourceful. I quickly noted that only one thing seemed to disrupt his equilibrium – and it would happen at every mention.

Years before, money had been raised towards the cost of an extra building for children's work he was involved with. The building never happened, and the money sat in another account. Every now and then someone new on the scene would, very understandably, ask what that sum of money was for and then attempt to sideline it for some other unrelated project. But at such times my dad would cry openly, speak angrily and loudly. He would object vehemently, and with evident emotion.

lashing out and becoming bitter towards those in whom they arouse hostile reactions.

The lashing out is crucial precisely because any such 'outbursts' are likely to be infrequent – but alarming to those who observe them, especially as they seem to be so 'out of character'. It is important to observe here that Rulers differ greatly in experience, mainly in proportion to the opportunities to achieve and excel that they have been given or denied. The high achievers are more likely to be admired and resented, the low achievers to be underestimated and resentful. (Either way, you recognise what an asset you really are – even God ought to be pretty grateful if given the opportunity to have the Ruler on his side!)

Avoiding lashing out at opponents is only half the task in hand. If someone resents you or is jealous of you, why not attempt to win them over by being their friend, and deliberately preferring them, seeking out their company, showing that you value their opinion and take seriously what they have to say?

Sometimes their strong sense of loyalty is the trigger for a fierce response as the Ruler rushes to intercept an apparent injustice.*

---

* I was on holiday in Norfolk with four families from the Vine Community. We had all driven into Sheringham, and getting out of the cars some of us were standing opposite a fish and chip shop. Absentmindedly I was leaning against a car, thinking it was one of ours – until I noticed its driver glaring at me. He was obviously offended, but responded civilly enough when I opened the car door to apologise. Just then his wife crossed the road from the fish shop, carrying their chips, so I held the car door for her. She got in and angrily slammed it shut, to my obvious dismay and her husband's embarrassment. I let go of the door as they drove off. But suddenly out of nowhere Brian came flying down the street and beat on the roof of the car as it sped away, shouting to the astonished driver, 'You shouldn't have been parked on the double bloody yellow lines anyway!'

Brian's family and the community he led stood open-mouthed. Nothing had ever made him lose his cool before.

That swift judgement or outburst is perhaps the one time the Ruler is truly spontaneous, and ironically it is the one time they are more likely to miss something important and get it wrong.

If you are a Ruler who does not relate to the warning about displaying anger and judgement, do not be concerned. These incidents are rare. But don't dismiss it just because it hasn't happened yet!

Mercy – verses 8d, 15 and 21

> 'Show mercy with cheerfulness, and with joyful eagerness. Share in others' joy, and weep with those who weep.'

BUT 'Do not let evil overcome you; instead, overcome evil with good.'

The Mercy person can become overly absorbed with another person's distress, unable to give it over to God. If they lose their own cheerfulness, then two people are down instead of one, and no one is helped. The Mercy person may also get so low in times of depression that it is hard for them to get out of it. This is because they are intuitive, and trust their emotions far more than others would. Usually this is helpful, but their emotions about themselves may be less reliable. Mercy people can experience small joys with great pleasure and spontaneity, but have a special drawing to the weak, the suffering and the hurting. They need to remember the goodness of God.

Chapter 13

Contrast and comparison

Hospital visit

Someone is sick in hospital, and seven different people come to visit. See if you can guess from what they say which is the motivation of each one of the seven . . .

1. 'Are you going to be in rough shape, financially, with being off work for so long, or is that all taken care of?'

2. 'I can't begin to tell you how I felt when I learned you were so ill. How are you feeling now?'

3. 'I'm not surprised you ended up in here. I must say it serves you right. You've never taken enough care of your health. You'll have to make some adjustments when you get out of here, if you don't want this to happen again.'

4. 'Here's a little gift. Now, I've brought you your mail, and I fed the dog, watered your plants and washed the dishes that were still to do.'

5. 'Don't worry about a thing. I've assigned your job to four others in the office until you get back.'

6. 'I did some research on your illness, and I believe I can explain what's happening . . .'

7. 'I keep wondering how we can use your experiences here, everything you're going through, to help other people in the future.'

(Answers: 1 = G, 2 = M, 3 = P, 4 = S, 5 = R, 6 = T, 7 = E)

Adapted from an illustration by Bill Gothard

Dropping the pudding

Eight people who know each other well are having a meal together, and just as one of them is carrying the dessert through from the kitchen, it tips on to the floor. They all see it fall, but are unable to stop it happening. It just so happens that the other seven people sitting round the table are each of a different motivation. (Now isn't that surprising!) See if you can guess from what they say which motivation is which, and why they say what they say.

1. 'That's what happens when you're not careful.'

2. 'Don't feel badly – it could have happened to any-one.'

3. 'Let me help you clean it up.'

4. 'I'll go out and buy a new dessert.'

5. 'Next time, we'll serve out the pudding at the same time as the main course.'

6. 'Jim, would you get the mop? Sue, please help clear it up; and, Mary, help me fix another dessert, would you?'

7. 'The reason that it fell is that all the weight was on one side.'

(Answers: 1 = P, 2 = M, 3 = S, 4 = G, 5 = E, 6 = R, 7 = T)

The Prophetic wants to correct the problem. The Mercy wants to relieve embarrassment. The Server just sees a job that needs doing, and wants to get on and do it. The Giver wants to give to a tangible need. The Exhorter wants to learn for the next time, to avoid the unpleasant happening again. The Ruler wants to achieve the immediate goal of the group. The Teacher wants to discover why it happened. *Adapted from an illustration by Bill Gothard*

By now you may be laughing at how accurate these responses are, or objecting that these are stereotypes, not real people! Obviously, any one of us would offer to clear up the pudding, not just a Server, and not just a Mercy would ask someone ill in hospital how they are feeling. It is also my experience that about half the Prophetics rightly object that they would never say anything so insensitive and judgemental. Please take it as caricature and exaggeration, and not as accusation!

Who started it?

If there are difficulties that have arisen within a given group, and we know who was at the root of it, however unwittingly, there are certain dynamics we may predict. Look out for the danger. This is what happens with each of them – at their worst!

Prophetics	breed trouble
Servers	breed lack of communication
Teachers	breed discontent
Exhorters	breed compromise
Givers	breed over-balance
Rulers	breed rebellion
Mercies	breed confusion

The restlessness of the Prophetic is at times disruptive. Servers will rush to the rescue, but forget to tell anybody where they went or what they've done – even if they were the one in charge. Teachers get chewed up when they don't know what they are doing or are unhappy with the situation. They may not be sensitive to atmosphere, but their own is quite contagious. Exhorters would

255

compromise too often, and may insist things are OK when they are not. Givers act with no sense of proportion, then let others deal with the consequences. Rulers can spot errors of judgement a mile away, and should beware of mentioning them whenever such observations have potential to undermine or to erode confidence. Mercies are usually the least coherent when they feel strongly about something, and the most expressive when they don't know what it is they are trying to say.

What sort of chocolates?

Remember the analogy of the chocolate box given in Chapter 3 (see page 85)? This is a list of what sort of chocolates each motivation may be compared to:

Prophetics	are hard, strong tasting
Servers	are firm, hard centres, but less likely to break your teeth
Teachers	are chewy centres
Exhorters	have a soft liquid surface, but are hard underneath
Givers	are, surprisingly, the softest centres of all
Rulers	appear the hardest of all, but inside the hard exterior there is liqueur in the middle
Mercies	are soft centres, and usually look like they are

Not really believing others are different

One of the stresses in dealing with people of other motivations is that we really can't believe that everyone is so different, that they are not really just like us and only *pretending* to be so wacky.

The Server gets really *cross* at people's laziness. They are convinced it's impossible for others to really not have seen what needed to be done.

The Ruler is still *baffled* by other people's blindness and lack of objectivity, and can't understand why people can't get a handle on their emotions.

The Mercy finds it hard to believe that others are not aware of what *they* are feeling – and will even *apologise* for negative attitudes nobody knew about!

The Giver is *indignant* when food is wasted, or things are thoughtlessly destroyed instead of being put to good use.

The Exhorter gives people practical steps of advice, and is *frustrated* whenever someone seems unable to follow through.

The Prophetic is *impatient* because people carry so much baggage and take so long to get started.

The Teacher is *convinced* that everyone knows some things – the sort of things they consider basic to safety and survival – that should go without saying (although they say them anyway). It puzzles them when people look blankly when they refer to the most basic information.

Languages of motivations

Prophetic:	intensity
Server:	action
Teacher:	information
Exhorter:	relationship
Giver:	generosity
Ruler:	decision, drive and detachment
Mercy:	immediate emotions

Without these they would not really communicate. Intensity is the language of the Prophetic. For the Server, actions speak louder than words. Observation and information are what the Teacher traffics in. When you talk relationships you are speaking the language of the Exhorter. The Giver expresses generosity through spending time and energy, through being available or making things happen. The Ruler's involvement says a lot, even if it is against their own better judgement. The Mercy's real language is their immediate emotions, however these may be expressed.

I think the image of speaking about language is helpful. Each motivation has a language of its own, or at least a recognisably different dialect – as different as broad Glaswegian would be from Cornish. Most people are able to communicate to some degree with one another; but when those of the same motivational type are around each other they find the noticeable ease of communication very relaxing.

In some people's language we know only enough to get by, and are limited to a few words and popular phrases. Communication can be enhanced by simplicity, clarity and slow speech. If we really want to be able to get through to someone of a different language group it will take effort. We try to understand what's important to them; we may visit them at home and learn through interactive dialogue. The more both people work at it, the better the communication. If we are to remain fluent we need to keep using what we've learnt. (This certainly is what needs to happen in marriage.)

There are stages to how a sensitivity to motivational gifts can help our communication. It often will go like this:

1. Striving to understand and please others, often operating 'in the dark'.

2. Exposure to motivations teaching leads to retrospective analysis and realisations.

3. A tendency to caricature the different motivations, and exaggerate these differences as if there is a clear separation. This can indulge and reinforce our own selfish traits in the short term.

4. A genuine desire grows inside us to really meet other people. The meeting will not be in 'no man's land' as before; instead it will be in the overlap between our motivation and their own. It will be typified by graciousness and sensitivity. We see it can happen, and we want it to.

5. It happens, or begins to . . .

Love is . . .

Charles Schulz has given us an unforgettable model for unpacking what Paul attempted to write about to the Corinthians.* His cartoon series is called 'Peanuts', and has many imitators. Love is a feeling to be learned, he tells us. But what do people of different motivations have to say about that? Here is our attempt to find out what they understand, what they are drawn to, and what they may exhibit.

Prophetic:	'Love is all that matters.'
Server:	'Love really cares.'
Teacher:	'Love is important . . .
	Love needs a great deal of thinking about . . .
	Love is very important.'
Exhorter:	'Love is a choice . . .'

---

* 1 Corinthians 13

Giver:	'Love has no limits.'
Ruler:	'Love is loyalty.'
Mercy:	'Love is strong and tender.'

Heritages *

A short story by Amy Le Feuvre

The golden gates of the city were open; the glorious sunshine seemed dazzling to those who were outside; the brightness of those gates was almost overpowering. Under the shade of some beautiful trees was a radiant throng. They were all gathered there in the sunshine on top of that wonderful golden hill. Such a long, long line of white-robed little children, ready to go down into the big, busy world below. The King was there Himself, and by Him was an open book, and one of the King's trusted servants was writing in it. Then one by one the children were called before their King, and the page in the book was opened which bore their name upon it. They were sorted into little bands, and each band was given a banner, and before they marched down the hill, the King put up His hands and blessed them.

The first band which started out was the knights, and the King said to them:

'I send you forth to fight against the evil powers, to be champions of the weak and oppressed. The fight will be long and hard; for cruelty, injustice, oppression and tyranny will last as long as the world lasts. Your heritage is warfare; a crusade against all that is wrong; the world has need of you. Go, and your banner reminds you that I am with you.'

---

* 'Heritages' story printed in the novels *Robin's Heritage* (1907, Hodder and Stoughton) and its sequel *Tested* (1912, Partridge), both by Amy Le Feuvre

Their crimson banner bore the words: 'Be strong, and of a good courage. I will be with thee.'

The next band was the labourers.

'Your heritage is labour,' said the King. 'I send you forth to labour; your life will be spent in it, and labour of mind and body is an honourable calling. Work with content, remembering that it is your heritage, and that your work will not be in vain.'

Their banner was a blue one: 'Be strong and work, for I am with you.'

The knights had marched away with strong purpose on their young faces: the labourers marched after them with the same sturdy joy, and now came a band of children with wonderful shining eyes.

'Your heritage is genius,' said the King. 'Go down into the world to quicken the intellects, to cheer the sad, to find cures for the many evils that surround you, and to ennoble the aims and ambitions of the dull and slothful.'

Their banner was a silver one: 'The wise and their work are in the hand of God.'

They marched away and the company of children became smaller. The next band was called to the heritage of teaching; and on their tiny faces was already the stamp of holy gravity. The King reminded them of their high calling, their possibilities of influence, their power for good and for evil.

'You go forth as My teachers, to teach of Me and to draw whosoever will into My Kingdom.'

Their banner was a snow-white one with the words: 'I will be with thy mouth and teach thee what thou shalt say.'

Then came the band which was called to the heritage of rulers. There was already the stamp of dignity and strength upon their soft baby faces.

'Go forth and rule,' said the King; 'and let your rule be

an ever just and righteous one, suppressing evil, and maintaining My laws. Live for those you rule, and let their rights be considered as your own.'

Their banner was a purple one, and bore these words: 'Whoever ruleth over others must be just, ruling in the fear of God.'

Another band there was who marched away from their King.

'Go down into the world,' He said unto them; 'there are many who will need your pitying, loving care: little ones who know no parents' love; old people nearing the valley of the shadow of death; the sick, the poor, the weak and the erring – all are waiting for those who will take care of them. It may not be great work; it may not bring you fame; but it will bring you these words of commendation when your work is done: "Inasmuch as ye have done it unto one of the least of these, ye have done it unto Me."'

And these words were upon their green banner as they marched away; and their eyes were full of love and pity for all the world who wanted tender care.

Then the last little band came up; and over the King's face came a wondrously soft and tender smile.

'My little ones,' He said, 'My chosen ones, I have called you to the highest heritage of all; it is the heritage of suffering. No other heritage will bring so much gain and glory as this, and it was the heritage that your King's Son chose Himself, and took upon Him when He went down to tread the busy world below. Go forth and suffer, and with every pang you feel, remember that it is the highest service for your King.'

Their banner was a golden one, and the shining glory of it almost hid the words upon it: 'Rejoicing that they were counted worthy to suffer.'

Before they marched away, the King did what He had not done to the others: He called up each child separately, and laid His hands upon each one's head in blessing.

And this little band trod the downhill path with some of the glory of their King reflected in their faces, and not one of the weakest and smallest of them there would have changed their heritage for all the world; for had not the King given them the heritage of His Only Best Beloved Son.

Children in order of appearance

1. Prophetic – heritage of warfare
2. Server – heritage of labour
3. Exhorter – heritage of 'genius' (not intelligence, but the holding of keys which can unlock stubborn doors)
4. Teacher – heritage of teaching
5. Ruler – heritage of rulers
6. Mercy – heritage of caring
7. Giver – heritage of suffering

Chapter 14
Tie breakers

If you are already clear which motivational gift is your own you may now prefer to proceed to Chapter 15 or 16.

If you are genuinely confused as to which of two may be your true motivation, these questions are for you. Try to see the contrasts between **(a)** and **(b).** If you identify with both, try to work out which reflects the earliest responses you can remember, rather than being the product of any later conditioning. In the end, you have only one gift as your innate motivation, and the questions are another attempt to help you identify quickly which it may be.

(a) is always the first motivation named in any contrasting pair, and **(b)** the second. The questions only present scenarios where the *typical* responses of two Motivations are able to be contrasted. They are by no means foolproof, and only serve to help you get a feel for the differences. If a particular question is confusing, discard it.

Prophetic/Server

- To accomplish a task am I happier working **(a)** fast and furious? or **(b)** slow but steady?

- Do I **(a)** like starting things but weary of them when the end is almost in sight? or **(b)** prefer jobs I can see that I will be able to complete?

- In the middle of the job do I think about **(a)** what I am aiming for? or **(b)** what I am doing?

- Am I **(a)** more aware of the bigger picture? or **(b)** concerned with the details closer to hand? Would I **(a)** see the bridge? or **(b)** notice the welding?
- Is my idea of sorting somebody out **(a)** to challenge them about their behaviour? or **(b)** to help with the backlog of chores?

Prophetic/Teacher

- When I'm insistent that something is right, is it **(a)** what I think at the time? or **(b)** what I consider to be established and proven?
- If I continue to insist that I am right do I become **(a)** extreme and vehement? or **(b)** dogmatic and legalistic?
- Do I **(a)** scour through what I read for anything that might be important, and ignore the rest? or **(b)** try and absorb whatever I read and give it a fair hearing?
- Do I tend to be **(a)** impulsive? or **(b)** cautious?
- **(a)** Do I trust my gut response? or **(b)** am I hesitant to commit?
- **(a)** Do I consider everything urgent, and want to do things now? or **(b)** am I prepared to be patient, and get on with what I can while I can?

Prophetic/Exhorter

- Am I **(a)** very uneasy about compromise of any kind? or **(b)** always on the lookout for constructive ways to compromise and include people?
- When a compromise is called for am I likely to be the one who **(a)** resists it? or **(b)** suggests it?
- Would I naturally **(a)** stand by the principle in question no matter who objects? or **(b)** say that people matter more than principles?

- Am I likely to be **(a)** out in front, or else observing from the edge of a group? or **(b)** amongst everybody else, and identified with them even if I lead?
- When someone comes to me for advice do I **(a)** tell them the truth, even if they won't like it, and hope for some sort of breakthrough to change the situation? or **(b)** make sure they feel totally affirmed and accepted first of all, then give practical suggested steps of action to begin to make a difference?

Prophetic/Giver

- **(a)** Am I mostly spontaneous when it comes to surprising someone? or **(b)** do I enjoy planning a surprise for someone well in advance?
- Do I **(a)** struggle to be involved in group activities which I am not leading, and always find myself on the edges? or **(b)** love to be part of things, and join in things that have already been organised?
- Do I **(a)** like to make things happen? or **(b)** enjoy keeping things going?
- Am I **(a)** inclined to be ruthless? or **(b)** always prepared to make allowances?
- When someone with an ongoing problem wants help, which is likely to be my first reaction? Do I think, **(a)** 'Unless they are prepared to help themselves, there is no point me trying to help them'? or **(b)** 'Nobody has ever given them a chance'?

Prophetic/Ruler

Am I **(a)** more than willing to admit I made a mistake, and to say, 'I was wrong! It was my fault'? or **(b)** inclined to say, 'It was the right decision based on the information available'?

Do I **(a)** feel guilty about all kinds of things? or **(b)** rarely have regrets or feel guilty about anything?

When I make an unpopular decision, am I more likely to be accused of being **(a)** harsh? or **(b)** unfeeling?

When I have no more energy left to give to a project, am I likely to **(a)** ditch it? or **(b)** delegate it to someone else?

Do I want what I do to be **(a)** better than anybody else's, the biggest, the loudest, the most striking? or **(b)** as good as it can be, just excellent?

Prophetic/Mercy

- Is it easier for me **(a)** to lead? or **(b)** to follow?
- When someone finds it hard to keep up, am I **(a)** frustrated by them? or **(b)** patient with them?
- Do I **(a)** reach for the impossible dream? or **(b)** want everything to be perfect now?
- If I know that someone dislikes me, do I **(a)** shrug it off as not that unusual? or **(b)** find that it cripples me in their company?
- Will I **(a)** sacrifice people on the basis of principles? or **(b)** do anything to stop someone being hurt?
- Do I **(a)** have big dreams that need painting on a large canvas? or **(b)** like to sketch everything on a small canvas, and get the colours just right?

Server/Teacher

Am I more interested in **(a)** the task? or **(b)** the thinking behind a task?

If something isn't working right, and I check the instructions, do I **(a)** only glance at them quickly, in case it saves time on the job? or **(b)** absorb all the information thoroughly, then go straight to what I think is the root of the problem?

Would I rather **(a)** start a job and see how I get on? or **(b)** consider carefully which would be the best approach before beginning anything?

(a) Do I value hands-on experience? Do I need convincing that someone knows what they are talking about? Or **(b)** do I expect most from the most highly trained, and take note of people's qualifications?

Server/Exhorter

- Am I likely to **(a)** sneak out and do the dishes without anybody noticing? or **(b)** spend as much time as I can with the people, or perhaps talk with someone while doing the dishes at the same time?

- When I say, 'Actions speak louder than words', am I **(a)** saying something I really believe strongly? or **(b)** using it as a qualifying statement, reminding me or someone else that words on their own could be seen as empty promises?

- Do I express love **(a)** through action? or **(b)** through words, and then touch?

- Is most of my energy spent **(a)** on jobs and things to be done? or **(b)** on people?

- Would I rather **(a)** work with my hands? or **(b)** use my mouth and speak?

- If someone didn't follow my instructions properly would I want to **(a)** just go ahead and do it myself? or **(b)** explain it to them more thoroughly?

Server/Giver

- When I get involved in a demanding situation, **(a)** do I reach a point where I say, 'Enough is enough, there's a limit as to what I can do'? or **(b)** do I need someone else to tell me it's getting out of hand?

- When I really make myself vulnerable to another person, and they get close enough to hurt me, do I **(a)** learn to be more guarded if they wound me too often? or **(b)** just get hurt over and over again?

- Would I say, **(a)** 'I'm not really a very deep or complicated person. What you see is what you get'? or **(b)** 'I really don't understand a lot of what goes on inside of me'?

- When other people don't pull their weight, **(a)** do I get cross? or **(b)** am I prepared to give them the benefit of the doubt?

Server/Ruler

- Would I say, **(a)** 'Delegation really isn't my word. Even when it's my job to give other people the jobs to do, I'd rather be getting on with the work myself'? or **(b)** 'Once I start to delegate, it's easy. Then I can put my energies into other things, and just check from time to time that there aren't any snags'?

- Does it come more naturally to me **(a)** to let someone else lead? or **(b)** to be the person leading?

- **(a)** Do I concentrate on what I am doing, and just think about the task in hand? or **(b)** am I always aware of how whatever I am doing fits into the bigger picture?

- When things go wrong do I **(a)** grumble at how it's affecting me? or **(b)** become critical of whoever was in charge?

- Do I **(a)** take things as they come? or **(b)** plan ahead?

Server/Mercy

- Would I say, **(a)** 'You could never call me lazy. I like to be doing'? or **(b)** 'I'm always frightened that people will think that I'm lazy. When there's things I know need to be done, I struggle not to feel guilty if I leave them until later'?

- Do I **(a)** find other people's emotions surprising and hard to understand? or **(b)** easily sense what people are feeling?

- When someone comes to the house do I **(a)** do what I can to make them feel comfortable? or **(b)** feel embarrassed whenever there's an awkward moment?

Teacher/Exhorter

- Is it my goal to **(a)** grow in my understanding? or **(b)** become a more understanding person?

- **(a)** Do I really come alive when I am explaining something I know about? Do I really come alive when I finally grasp something I have been struggling to understand? Or **(b)** do I really come alive around people?

- Do I **(a)** intend to see a thing through to the bitter end? or **(b)** take short cuts when possible?

- Do I accomplish more working **(a)** steadily? or **(b)** in spurts?

Teacher/Giver

- Which statement is true for me: **(a)** 'I am careful and hesitant about giving and spending'? or **(b)** 'I give wholeheartedly or not at all'?

- **(a)** Is it important to me to understand what has happened? Or **(b)** am I concerned with living in the now?

- **(a)** Am I careful and hesitant before committing myself wholeheartedly? Or **(b)** do I willingly join in without pushing myself forward?

- When feelings are strained or there is an awkward atmosphere, am I **(a)** likely to only engage with what people actually say, and likely to be slow to recognise that something is going on under the surface? or **(b)** one of the first to sense that something is wrong?

- **(a)** Do I have difficulties in beginning to relate with someone at an emotional level? Or **(b)** am I at ease around other people's emotions, and my own, and able to be sensitive to them?

- **(a)** In forming relationships, am I initially guarded, having to dismantle the walls with which I protect myself from being hurt? Or **(b)** do I hold part of myself at a distance (even though I relate freely and sensitively to everybody) because an intimate relationship is especially costly for me?

Teacher/Ruler

- In any given situation **(a)** do I concentrate on the details of the aspects that fascinate me? or **(b)** am I immediately aware of all the dynamics involved?

- In making a decision **(a)** do I like to take my time and ask more questions to be sure I have considered everything? or **(b)** can I do so quickly because I evaluate everything as I go along anyway?

- Do I **(a)** sometimes bore other people by telling them about things when they're not interested? or **(b)** easily get bored when things become routine or predictable?

Teacher/Mercy

- **(a)** Do I take things as I find them? Or **(b)** am I very sensitive to atmosphere?
- Am I more comfortable dealing with **(a)** ideas? or **(b)** feelings?
- Do I **(a)** question what I am told? or **(b)** accept what is presented to me?
- Do I **(a)** find people a distraction from my work? or **(b)** find work a distraction from people?
- Is decision-making **(a)** a matter of careful consideration? or **(b)** difficult for me?

Exhorter/Giver

- Am I interested **(a)** mainly in people? or **(b)** in lots of things?
- Am I excited **(a)** when I think about people I know meeting each other? or **(b)** when I find something I know another person was looking for?
- When it comes to organising some fundraising event, am I **(a)** pleased to see people working well together? or **(b)** excited to be involved, and enthusiastic about the cause the money is going to?
- Do I instinctively encourage people by **(a)** relating my own experiences? or **(b)** giving them practical help and support?

Exhorter/Ruler

- Am I more concerned with **(a)** the people involved in a project? or **(b)** the projects people are involved in?
- When I am the obvious leader in a situation, do I **(a)** get concerned in case people think I prefer to always

lead, and worry in case it distances them from me? or **(b)** quite enjoy leading and do it easily and with no fuss?

- When I am in the middle of a task and the phone rings, am I pleased to hear from somebody? Do I **(a)** thrive on interruptions? or **(b)** resent them as intrusions?

- At each stage in the completion of a task **(a)** do I want someone to know about it? or **(b)** is it enough for me to have completed it?

- **(a)** Do I often need to think aloud with someone else as a sounding board? Or **(b)** am I self-contained in my observations.

- When I am involved in a complex task, do I **(a)** often get bogged down with people dynamics and with details? or **(b)** always have the overview in mind?

Exhorter/Mercy

- Am I concerned more with **(a)** how things are? or **(b)** how they feel?

- Which statement is true for me: **(a)** 'I get on well with people, and am equally at ease in small groups, bigger groups, or on one to one'? or **(b)** 'I am much more comfortable being with one person at a time'?

- I hate to see people hurting. Do I **(a)** avoid situations that I know will only distress me? or **(b)** identify emotionally with those who suffer?

- Which statement is most true for me: **(a)** 'I am able to give sympathy by imagining what it must be like to be in the other person's situation. I want to help'? or **(b)** 'Around someone in trouble, I feel the hurt as my own. I am involved'?

Giver/Ruler

- **(a)** Do I sometimes 'go overboard' and 'not know when to stop'? Or **(b)** am I always measured in my response?

- Would people who know me consider that I **(a)** act sensibly most of the time, but delight in occasionally doing the unexpected? or **(b)** always act according to what is rational and logical?

- Which statement is most true for me: **(a)** 'If I get hurt by somebody very close to me, I am unable to protect myself by building inner walls'? or **(b)** 'If I get hurt by somebody very close to me, I construct walls of defence until it is safe to dismantle them'?

- In most activities would I rather **(a)** join in? or **(b)** organise and arrange?

Giver/Mercy

- Do I **(a)** mostly stand back just enough to not get hurt? or **(b)** quickly get hurt, then become wary of letting the same thing happen again and again?

- Do I **(a)** keep my head down when I get into trouble, and wait for things to subside? or **(b)** take the blame and apologise, because I feel guilty whether it was my fault or not?

- When asked for help, do I **(a)** give what I can't spare as readily as what I can? or **(b)** give what I feel I can?

- Do I care more about **(a)** what people need? or **(b)** how people feel?

Ruler/Mercy

- Which comes first for me: **(a)** thinking? or **(b)** feeling?

- Do I ask myself **(a)** what I feel about what I think? or **(b)** what I think about what I feel?

- **(a)** Am I usually confident about my actions and decisions? or **(b)** do I worry about whether I did the right thing?
- **(a)** Can I always find reasons rather than excuses for past choices? or **(b)** do I find it difficult to shrug off feelings of guilt?
- **(a)** Am I able to see what's going on, and plan ahead? or **(b)** do I feel there is too much going on, most of the time?
- **(a)** Even when I feel things deeply am I able to stand back from what I feel, and view things objectively? or **(b)** do I find it difficult to detach from my feelings, and be objective about most things?
- Does leading **(a)** come easily? or **(b)** worry me?

Chapter 15
Combinations

We hope that these little observations may be helpful, though it is always dangerous to generalise from the particular! We have tried to recognise common traits in combinations of the differing motivations.

Our data is gathered primarily from recurring elements in marriage relationships, and the language used reflects this. Similar dynamics would often be at work in friendships, family ties or close working relationships – use a little common sense and imagination to see how differently they apply. Even in marriages these paragraphs do not *sum up* or characterise the relationship at all, but only identify which dynamics in it are in common with most couples who share the same combination. There is no such thing as a good or bad combination, only predictable dynamics amongst the elements that keep a relationship interesting.

Prophetic/Prophetic

If both are agreed, they can work together in harmony with full energy and provide a strong lead for others on any issue. Only one may be actively involved, the other supportively but with full commitment. But when they clash, it can be strongly or reach a deadlock! Each needs time alone.

Prophetic/Server

The Server tends to work around the Prophetic. When the Prophetic gives a strong lead the Server can become involved in whatever the dream or scheme is, and help make it practical. A lot of the time the Prophetic may prefer to do their own thing, or doesn't know what they are doing; so the Server just gets on in the meantime. If what the Prophetic is doing is worthwhile, the Server is happy just to let them do it, or support them, or even to do enough work for two, in order to release them. They tend to go their separate ways, and are accepting of that; then they meet together to confer. (In some cases, their relationship with each other may be all they have in common, rather than shared interests or activities. This needn't be a bad thing; their time together can be uncluttered and focused on each other.)

Prophetic/Teacher

Both are inclined to be loners, and enjoy their own space. Both enjoy silence sometimes, but like to talk. Both want to communicate about things they consider important. Both may be great readers. They are ideas people, concerned with vision, concepts, even abstractions. This is interesting or exciting for them, though they can be practical when they have to.

Prophetic/Exhorter

Both have powers of influence and persuasion; and together they are a strong presence, a force to be reckoned with. They are fine as long as they are both pulling in the same direction. Both really want to have their own way, and they may end up doing different things which are part of the same bigger picture, rather than working on things together. In areas that concern them both, the Exhorter really cannot function without the Prophetic's co-operation. The Prophetic doesn't think the same way, and sometimes presents the Exhorter with a *fait accompli*. Together, they could be strongly inspirational for other people, given the right circumstances. There is a lot of personality there, if they can get their act together. Both have their own projects on the go.

Prophetic/Giver

Often they are drawn to each other by their ability to let go, to go to extremes. The Prophetic enjoys this wild streak in the Giver, and admires it. The Giver enjoys the radical nature of the Prophetic. Together they may engage in radical lifestyle, extreme courses of action, even sacrifice or asceticism. In their own way, both are idealists. The Prophetic is hard but emotional, and can be ruthless. The Giver is soft but with an energetic exterior. Both have high drive. A fiery combination.

Prophetic/Ruler

Both like to achieve and to excel. Both are concerned with vision or large pictures, but with different perspective. The Ruler is more reasoned and measured, less erratic, more pragmatic. Both are high energy. Both may be leaders or instead observe everything from the sidelines. Together they are a strong combination. There is the danger of pulling in different directions, as both are capable of leading easily and instinctively. The Prophetic may like to argue, but the Ruler will only reason.

Prophetic/Mercy

A very frequent combination, both in friendship and (especially) in love. It often seems to be that a Mercy woman is married to a Prophetic man. They complement each other, as opposites attract. This conforms to very traditional sexual stereotypes; and it may be for this reason that this combination is more often found than its reverse. The Mercy admires the intensity of emotion in the Prophetic. It's a bit overpowering, but at least they know where they stand. The Mercy quite likes to be a follower and the Prophetic usually doesn't, so both will feel comfortable with that, in the short term. However, if the Mercy is constantly overshadowed by the Prophetic, and does not develop further in his/her own individual interests and identity, there can be problems later – or the Mercy may never find out who they really are.

Both are strongly emotional. Both enjoy spontaneity; the Prophetic thrives on immediacy, the Mercy on not being dictated to by time constraints. Both are particularly troubled by inappropriate levels of guilt, though for different reasons: the Prophetic because they are an idealist, the Mercy because they are a perfectionist. Both enjoy time alone, separate from each other. Mercy needs time to know their own mind; otherwise they may end up going along with whatever the Prophetic decides, and then be uneasy about it afterwards. If they refuse to be hurried, it drives the Prophetic mad.

The Prophetic, if they are wise, will learn from the sensitivity of the Mercy. In turn, the Mercy will learn not to get swamped. But they will not lack a sense of direction with a Prophetic to follow and to disagree with. Both care about injustice.

Server/Server

Happy in each other's company, they are able to work alongside each other, to agree upon tasks, and to enjoy a similar view of life. Both are willing, and hard workers, but will not take each other to task for that; instead they will support one another. They are happy to facilitate things for other people. They are likely not to be overrun with company, but to get great satisfaction from being quietly hospitable. Their guests are happy to come again. Conversation may be a hobby, and they enjoy good company. Communication is not their strength, however, and it is easy for them to neglect to talk about things that are important. If one of them was having a problem in the relationship the other might not know!

Server/Teacher

The Teacher is likely to do more of the talking. The Teacher adapts to the Server's practical organisation, and is appreciative of the Server's practical insights. They are likely to encourage each other in practical interests or hobbies. Both are very consistent, predictable, and perhaps a trifle unimaginative. But they are able to tackle the unexpected in a matter-of-fact way, and to co-operate with each other, taking most things in their stride.

Server/Exhorter

The Exhorter becomes very efficient. Both take great pride in hospitality – an area of overlap between practical caring and involvement with people. They would not by nature have a great deal in common (but presumably met somehow!), so both need to indulge the other's very differentness.

Server/Giver

A frequent combination. Practical and caring. Both like to throw their weight into tasks and projects. Neither is typically keen to lead, or to take a very prominent position, but may do so when necessary or appropriate. Both are team players, and by combining their efforts can make a significant impact on the workload of any project. Both are very committed to hospitality. Neither really communicates easily.

Server/Ruler

A frequent combination (especially with woman Ruler and male Server). Both are matter-of-fact, and especially recognise the complementarity of their gifts, so neither considers one or the other superior within the relationship. They are able to shelve or postpone emotional issues. Both are task-orientated. For each, their well-being and sense of value is closely associated with work or achievement. Both like to see things finished. Each is practical and pragmatic. Both are private about their emotions, but will enjoy knowing they can give their emotional life free rein within the safe boundaries of a trusting relationship. They will let off steam, but are unlikely to fight.

Server/Mercy

Happy behind the scenes, they work together well. Happy quietly pootling on. But the Server's lack of communication drives the Mercy mad – it is uneven at best! – and especially what the Mercy sees as the Server's inability to access feelings adequately. The spontaneity of the Mercy keeps life interesting for the Server. Both can avoid taking a lead, even in their relationship.

Teacher/Teacher

A deliberate and thoughtful relationship. Both will learn to anticipate the other's responses and rely on their predictable patterns of behaviour. They will explore and memorise the differences between them, their tastes, their likes and dislikes, and will highlight these. They will pursue whatever interests they have in common. Their own relationship may work very well, so that they are very at ease in each other's company, but this relationship does little to equip them for the kinds of sensitivity required in relating to some of the other motivations. They are appreciative of consideration from each other. They enjoy exploring emotional responses, but are also content to be quiet together.

Teacher/Exhorter

Quite a good combination. They communicate well, because one or the other will insist upon it. They tend to get quite a lot done. Both like to have a people dynamic in their life, but the Teacher tires of people more easily, and is happier for them just to be by themselves.

Teacher/Giver

Communication is a struggle and takes a great deal of effort. Both will talk easily about practical matters, and be understood, but conveying deeper things is more problematic. The Teacher feels things and labels what the feelings are, then sums it up and throws out words to convey the nature of their feelings. The act of speaking is in itself an attempt to organise their feelings. The Giver finds it hard to look at feelings as if they were concepts, like the Teacher does. Feelings to them are something you swim in. The Giver enters deeply into their own experience, but can rarely articulate it. Instead they throw out clues, descriptive one-word passports to their inner world. The Teacher wants them to explain and they can't. It is hard for the Teacher to resonate with the clues the Giver puts out. Sometimes they both try to speak out, but the words just fall to the ground. Both pick up what they can and try again. Both are patient and persistent, prepared to persevere. They are prepared to work hard at the relationship.

Teacher/Ruler

Seems to work well as a combination. They are able to put energy into their relationship with each other which they take very seriously. But they are also able to be matter-of-fact and detached in the way they address other things that come up. They easily sort out task sharing and job allocation. Even emotional things can be shelved until more immediate and practical concerns have been addressed. They have an objectivity about their subjectivity which surprises other people. In other words, it is as if they have in their heads an updated report of where they are at in their relationship with each other. They enter into everything fully, but keep assessing where they are at.

Teacher/Mercy

Very different from each other. The Mercy is frustrated by the Teacher's ineptitude in accessing internal emotions. The Teacher is frustrated by the Mercy's mood swings and lack of objectivity. In other words, both complain that the other does not articulate emotions well. The Teacher oversimplifies, and the Mercy becomes incoherent. Both complain that they are obviously supposed to be mind-readers: the Teacher because they don't know what the Mercy is feeling, and so are accused of being insensitive; the Mercy because the Teacher expresses their feelings as if they were press releases rather than really telling them why they feel as they do. They talk together a lot to establish a satisfactory base of relationship.

Exhorter/Exhorter

Very strongly involved with people, and available to others. This means they are usually over-committed, with too many people and projects in their lives and not enough time for each other. Both thrive on interruptions, but their relationship does not. They will have many longstanding friendships, and accumulate new ones as well.

Exhorter/Giver

They complement each other quite well. Although they are very different, they don't clash. The Exhorter often finds it hard to get the Giver to really talk. It seems as if there are gaps in the Giver's communication. They struggle to say the things that mean the most. The Giver seems to have different compartments – in some ways words come easily but not for important things. Both will pour all their energies into a given project, but the Giver prefers one project at a time, while Exhorters tend to have several on the go. Both enjoy being quiet together.

Exhorter/Ruler

An interesting combination. In both there is a balance between hard and soft, outside and inside, and both can switch equally well between the two which brings much texture to their relationship. They are each capable of organising groups of people, and both will prioritise whom they spend time with or pour their energies into. They see who they can influence for the better, whose potential they can encourage or develop. They are strongly involved with people, but remain objective. They are project-orientated and unlikely to disappear into a sea of subjectivity. The Exhorter tends to put more energy into communication. The Ruler tends to assume; the Exhorter wants to be sure. They should beware of having enemies in common or taking up offences on each other's behalf. Both are fiercely loyal.

Exhorter/Mercy

A people combination. The canvas of both their lives would have people as its major feature, but the Exhorter's would be a crowd scene in comparison to the Mercy's. The people they are drawn to, and feel they can help, are likely to be the same people the other would look straight past. Both give priority to relationship, and especially their relationship with each other. The Exhorter tries to keep too many plates spinning. The Mercy prefers one plate with not too much on it, but usually gets a little more than they would have liked. The Mercy will act as the brake for the Exhorter.

Giver/Giver

Often quiet. Then share with few words. They are able to have fun, and to join in with numerous activities. They may commit together to radical long-term projects, most probably in the area of fundraising or facilitating causes. They find ways of expressing the deepest things of all. They encourage and enjoy each other's creativity, and create a warm and trusting environment for others.

Giver/Ruler

This relationship requires both to do a lot of accommodating. Both are intensely loyal, but also recognise that 'if it's worth having it will cost you'. They function together in practical things very well. The Ruler is exasperated by the Giver's strange sense of logic, their tendency to go to extremes, and appreciates their creativity and handiwork, but wishes there wasn't so much of it. The Giver in turn accepts that the Ruler cannot cope with the Giver's wildest dreams and will impede many things the Giver otherwise would do. Both are practical on the outside, but soft in the middle.

As an aside, it is interesting to note that it is Rulers and Givers who tend to gain most from motivations being taught to those around them. They are the least likely to have been understood. Their behaviour may be open to examination, but their inner scenery is less open to view and more likely to be misunderstood. The constructions others put on their actions and reasons are profoundly different from their internal reality, into which others are now being given insights.

Giver/Mercy

As two soft centres they have a safe and tender relationship. This becomes a safe environment into which other people may come, in small numbers or usually one at a time. They like to feel their hospitality can be taken for granted. Each tries to be indulgent of the other, the Giver's extremes of behaviour, the Mercy's love of spontaneity. Both are terminally likely to take on 'lame dogs' of all descriptions, and find it hard to say no to appeals for help.

Ruler/Ruler

They are able to do anything they put their energies to. It is important for them not to compete, except by agreement (for example, at sports of some kind). They are both capable of being strongly critical and truthful in their assessment of each other's work. They can share very deeply, at a heart level too. They enjoy and appreciate each other so much – the inside as well as the outside – that it could become a mutual admiration society. Two Rulers either really clash or really get on. When it works, it seems almost too good to be true. Other people are likely to be even more threatened by the two of them combined than by either one.

Ruler/Mercy

The Ruler's strength is in their objectivity, the Mercy's in their subjectivity. This makes them perfectly complementary, but the relationship hard to work at. There again, the Ruler likes a challenge. Mercies complain that the Ruler is the one sort of person whose emotions they cannot easily access. The Mercy, in turn, is one of the least logical of all people, and continues to amaze and surprise the Ruler. The Ruler inevitably has to accommodate the Mercy and their notions or mood swings. Some Rulers do this only when absolutely necessary or from time to time; others accept that plans will always be liable to change, and constantly work around the Mercy's inclinations rather than override them.

Mercy/Mercy

Their relationship is fine as long as they are not both down. If one goes down it tends to drag the other one down as well. Otherwise it is a peaceful relationship, a real safe haven. They can talk about mercy things together – dreams, feelings, how insensitive other people are, how they both cope or don't cope in various circumstances. Their decision-making is tentative but gets easier with practice. Areas of hurt requiring healing have permission to surface. Both want the perfect relationship. They say things like, 'I'm a terrible parent', because not to be perfect is to be terrible. They keep having to reassure each other. Their ideals are not something to aim for, but something they feel they should never have fallen short of.

Chapter 16
Application and growth

Playing on your strengths

Certain activities and involvements come more naturally to us, and are easier to apply ourselves to. These are in line with our own motivation, and are likely to be more immediately fulfilling for us. Why give everybody the jobs they hate? When we are able to be ourselves, and play on our strengths, we are happiest! As we move in these natural abilities, we will experience a sense of relief: 'this is what I was made for'. Then we will have *minimum weariness* and *maximum effectiveness*.

When we do things that don't come naturally, and step into areas normally the concern of someone with a different gift, it is prudent to recognise that we are out of our depth. If I am an Exhorter pretending to be a Ruler I'll not get very far, but if I do Ruler things in an Exhorter kind of way, acknowledging to myself that this is what I am doing, the end result may be fine – although different from what the Ruler would have come up with.

Remember Darrelle Marshall's picture of the tree. The roots and broad trunk correspond to my central motivational gift. Other branches grow only out from the main trunk and from the same roots.

Let us imagine that the tree is a Mercy tree, with Mercy right down to its roots. It may have branches of exhorting, teaching and so on, but it is Mercy through and through.

A Mercy person will exhort a person from a Mercy motivation.

A Mercy person will teach through their Mercy motivation.

> A Mercy person will give, serve, perceive and organise through their Mercy gift.

There is *minimum weariness* and *maximum effectiveness* in all these activities *when* we approach them through our motivation. The reverse is true when we try to imitate someone else's motivation. We are not very good at *being* them-doing-what-they-do-best. It is also exhausting to try. We are better at being us, and learning from them instead.

The marzipan will never make a good montelimar, but could be great as her press agent!

Innateness

In distinguishing what is a person's root motivation, we frequently run into an initial confusion. Overlaid upon their innate motivation are other responses and reactions, which are a result of conditioning or training. These may have come from absorbing the values of parents and friends, or from careful training in preparation for a job or profession. (In both cases, the conditioning is only really considered effective when the person will act/react as required on reflex.)

In consequence, we need to ask ourselves:

What is my innateness?

and then, in contrast, the question:

What is my developed self?

The distinction between the two answers is important in the process of self-discovery. Bear in mind that the developed self, whilst not innate, is also authentic.

Growing and stretching

A number of years ago, I taught motivations to the mission team with Sion Community. Michelle Moran was helped a great deal by recognising her Ruler gift. It made sense of so many things. It might not have been what she would have chosen, but that was beside the point. We don't get to choose our motivation! She was apprehensive at first, in case the whole teaching would tend to 'put someone in a box' and restrict them. Instead, she quickly found the potential was just the opposite. What especially appealed to her was the illustration of the three boxes representing sorts of gifts – motivations, ministries and manifestations – it was all so clear! 'Instead of being put in a box, I feel I have lots of room to grow, and that I will grow through the other boxes.' She had no say in the basic sort of person she already was; but she could choose which jobs she agreed to. She could negotiate areas of vocation, and through work experiences extend the range of her abilities. As she remained spiritually receptive, her abilities could be augmented and enhanced by the use of the supernatural 'tools for the job'. The possibilities were endless.

When we exercise our motivation through our calling, any relevant spiritual tools are made available to us. We are not to pursue these tools as an end in themselves. It is more important that we recognise and affirm our own motivational gift, and find the areas of service through which we can most effectively express it.

Combined gifts?

It is very unhelpful to become muddled in our thinking and try to hang on to two or more motivational categories as our own. I may be an Exhorter with a 'strong Ruler branch', but all that does is give me some limited sensitivity to where Rulers are coming from – it doesn't make me at all like a Ruler. It is just possible that if no Ruler was present I would be the person to ask a question which would have occurred automatically to the Ruler. But I am an Exhorter through and through, not a hybrid. I am a poor Ruler substitute, but I am only fully released when I recognise this. The idea that I could have a combination gift is not helpful; it is a nonsense and doesn't fit the facts.

Compounded gifts?

But . . . in addition to our motivation, there is enabling that comes with the tasks we are called to. When someone is called to a new line of work, a new area of service, it is legitimate to say, 'I can't do that without help'. Vocation literally means calling. For someone to test whether they are truly called to a significant task, whether they really have a *vocation*, they should ask themselves:

1. Do I feel an excitement, a challenge, and a drawing to this task?
2. Do I feel that it is bigger than me, that I couldn't do it on my own?
3. When I try not to respond do I become ill at ease?

The fourth question can be asked only after the event: Did it work out all right?

New anointing

For people whose life is taken up with 'ministry', and who operate beyond their natural ability, it is very helpful and important to clarify where one stops and the other starts. They may be able to make a distinction on the basis of before and after:

'I was never like that.'

'It didn't come naturally.'

'I'd never have thought I'd end up making this my life.'

There is a principle that 'where God appoints, he anoints'. This 'anointing' is more than imagination. It extends into many secular situations as well. The person who is genuinely inspired to take up a work they seem ill-equipped for will often testify that 'the strength came from somewhere'.

My friend Pat at first was not sure which was his motivational gift – Giver or Prophetic. His mother had been a Giver, and as a boy he had been so inspired by her example that Giver traits remain with him to this day. As a Prophetic, extremes of behaviour did not alarm him but found an echo in his heart. He didn't like to be cautious. When he became a priest it was not immediately clear in what way his radical nature would find expression. Then a new enabling began. He discovered that in the parish to which he was assigned, whenever he had contact with people only loosely connected with the church, or those of no faith at all, through conversation and example he was able to challenge them to belief and to personal encounter with God.

There was a marked numerical growth during his time there – especially from amongst those with no Catholic background. As time went on, this gifting in the area of evangelism weighed heavily upon him. His dream became to set up a community facilitating the work of evangelism amongst the lapsed or unchurched, as well as those within parish congregations whose faith was only nominal. The dream became a reality and inspired others to similar action. Was his ministry in speaking out in this way that of a prophet? No! It only seemed that way because his motivational gift was Prophetic. He was now gifted and empowered as an evangelist – but his personal energies and motivation were those of the Prophetic.

Once Pat's community came into being, it became evident that all kinds of personalities were being gathered to work together in evangelism. Pat's motivation came more strongly into focus as they all began to interact and pool their resources. The other gifts began to balance his own, whilst being fired by his drive and intensity.

Motivational cocktail

The nature of a group will almost always be determined by the mix of motivational giftings which it comprises.

The most well-rounded group imaginable would be one with equal numbers of each of the motivational gifts – and perhaps of both sexes. In real life, any group you find will usually have a mixture, but not evenly distributed and perhaps with some not represented at all. The nature of the group, and the likely ways in which it addresses situations, will probably be determined by its motivational ingredients.

Certain professions are likely to draw particular motivations in greater proportions. If you did a seminar on motivations with a group of nurses there would be a higher proportion of Mercies than amongst a group of barristers or engineers. Journalism or politics will draw higher proportions of Prophetics. This is only to be expected; but obviously each of these groups will have those of different motivations as well.

Many groups may be exposed to motivations teaching: a project team, a community, a group of leaders, a class, or members of a family. As soon as their individual motivations are recognised it will also become evident that the group is strongly weighted towards the emphases of those gifts which are more strongly represented numerically. They may already have 'felt the draught' from the absence of a certain gift or gifts, without having recognised it consciously.

A group with too many Prophetics will be very strong on vision, and may have clashes over which direction to take, but will tend to move ahead very strongly and quickly. Other gifts in the group may struggle to consolidate what has been achieved or attempted.

Missing persons

Years ago I was sharing a house with John and Linda Skinner in Berwick. All kinds of people visited us there, and we found our different motivational perspectives entirely complementary. Usually all three of us would be around during the time someone was with us. But should one of us be absent, the other two consciously compensated for the missing person, thinking, 'What would John say if he was here?' or 'How would Linda respond to this person?' or 'What would Andy do in this situation?' That way there was a consistency to the kind of help and support we were able to give. It seems the particular combination of Prophetic, Mercy and Exhorter was an ideal mix for assuring people of acceptance, and helping them experience and integrate truth and healing in their lives.

If John (the Prophetic) was missing, Linda and I would be no substitute for him. But together we could consciously try to challenge the other person more directly, and confront any patterns of self-deceit, as well as offering support and encouragement. That same pattern can be exercised on a larger scale as we seek to fill in the gaps whenever the whole range of giftings is not represented.

Across a range of circumstances each perspective is helpful and necessary. Where one person is the entire delegation into a situation, they should capitalise upon their own insights, strengths and perceptions, but also attempt to see through the eyes of the other gifts, especially those most different from his or her own.

Bias or equal voice?

The leadership of a group will usually strongly determine its emphasis. Other gifts may eventually feel uncomfortable with this emphasis, especially if it is at war with what their own emphasis would be. Some people have no desire to lead, but have very important things to say about the way things are run. Perhaps the organisation is very efficient but unfriendly. It may be that the pace is too fast, and that people are becoming weary and exhausted. The leader may not have noticed that some people are always put upon because others are too lazy to tidy up when they've finished a task. A leader needs to *listen* to concerns of this kind, and hold each of these in tension with his/her own priorities.

It is wise to give special attention to any Rulers in the group, and assure them that their observations will be noted and valued. Also, those who are less articulate in any given group are not as likely to be represented or heard. The Mercy may have surprising insights as to how things could be differently arranged; but it would probably take someone else to see how anything they suggested could actually be implemented.

A Mercy at the helm brings values of consideration and sensitivity towards individuals and their needs, but may move everything else forward more slowly.

Chapter 17

Character development

Buffet table

Listen very carefully, I will say this only once!

Character is not the same as nature

Therefore, character qualities need to be reached out for, grasped and allowed to develop. Like muscles, they will grow stronger with use. Character is about maturity, rather than something you are born with.

Imagine a buffet table at a select party or banquet. It is laid out with half a hundred dishes of mouth-watering beauty. The table itself is round and is almost completely covered with food of every conceivable variety on display. The broad perimeter of the table is left clear, lest anything should fall accidentally to the ground and be wasted. As so often happens on these occasions, people stand around in groups, making conversation and trying to mix. At some stage, each of the guests takes the opportunity to admire the food on display, and carefully notes the most appealing dishes. Their thought is to decide in advance what they most want on their plate, so when the time comes they can reach for those items first of all, rather than trying to load their plate with too much and just appearing greedy.

The host appears to have read their minds with regard to the difficulty of standing around, or circulating, whilst balancing plates of food. He suddenly suggests that they pull out the carved stools from beneath the round table and sit to eat instead. He invites them, one at a time, to choose their seat at the table. Each makes their way, shyly but without hesitation, to a particular place – closest to the particular foods they had intended to reach for first. The surprising thing is that each would have thought that they are choosing the exact seat that everyone would want. Instead, although eventually every seat is filled around the whole table, each person's place is the very one they would have chosen from the start.

All the dishes are available to each guest. The most attractive and appealing dishes are the ones immediately in front of you. Others are available, but you'd need to reach out further, or have someone help you reach them. The character qualities are like that; the hungrier you are for maturity, the more you'll get.

Instructions

1. Read carefully each **definition** on your own place setting.

2. Answer honestly whether you have taken hold of what is described, or not.

3. Then look to see its name.

It may be helpful to have someone else ask you these questions, so that you don't sneakily look at the names.

Character qualities that are usually important to the motivational gift of the PROPHETIC.

Have I reached out to develop these qualities in my life?

P-1 Earning future trust by reporting past facts accurately.

P-2 Fulfilling instructions so that the one I am accountable to is fully satisfied.

P-3 Eagerness to do what is right – and with transparent motives.

P-4 Allowing my life to influence others for the better, in spite of my past failures.

P-5 Confidence that what I am going to do is right, and that what I have to say is true.

P-6 Clearing the record of those who have wronged me, and not refusing to love them.

P-7 Using words which predispose the listener to recognise that I am telling them the truth.

Character qualities that are usually important to the motivational gift of the SERVER.

Have I reached out to develop these qualities in my life?

S-1 Being aware of everything that is happening around me, so that I know what my response should be.

S-2 Cheerfully sharing food, shelter and refreshment with whoever comes my way.

S-3 Allowing others to feel the benefit of whatever goods or money I have.

S-4 Remembering that I can make a difference in other people's lives.

S-5 Not having my heart set on ideas or plans which could easily change.

S-6 Juggling what I had planned to do, so I can help out when I'm needed.

S-7 Drawing on inner strength to keep going until the job is done.

Character qualities that are usually important to the motivational gift of the TEACHER.

Have I reached out to develop these qualities in my life?

T-1   Responding without delay when I know I should act.

T-2   Recognising with gratitude that the events and people in my life can be character-building.

T-3   Visualising each task as a special assignment – just for me – and using all my energies to accomplish it.

T-4   Realising that sooner or later everything will have to be accounted for.

T-5   Doing what I promised to do (even when it becomes more than I bargained for).

T-6   Structuring my life around what lasts for ever and cannot be taken from me.

T-7   Not becoming agitated when I can't see the end to a difficult situation.

Character qualities that are usually important to the motivational gift of the EXHORTER.

Have I reached out to develop these qualities in my life?

E-1   Relying on spiritual insight to understand and respond to the happenings of each day.

E-2   Finding the ability to understand why things happen to me and others.

E-3   Looking for a purpose in each situation, and co-operating with what I see could happen.

E-4 The ability to avoid words, actions and attitudes which are only going to cause trouble.

E-5 Really caring for other people (and not just because it makes me feel good).

E-6 Applying both wisdom and practical insights to a need or task.

E-7 Expressing inner joy about what I think or feel.

Character qualities that are usually important to the motivational gift of the GIVER.

Have I reached out to develop these qualities in my life?

G-1 Putting to good use what other people would normally overlook or discard.

G-2 Only allowing money to be spent on that which is necessary.

G-3 Deciding that I have all that I need to be happy.

G-4 Showing respect for other people, and not wasting their time.

G-5 Viewing every person as valuable and unique.

G-6 Knowing how important right timing is in whatever needs to be done.

G-7 Making sure others know in what ways they have been good to me or helped me.

Character qualities that are usually important to the motivational gift of the RULER.

Have I reached out to develop these qualities in my life?

R-1 Arranging my life and surroundings so they are not a hindrance to what should be happening.

R-2   Recognising and doing what needs to be done, before I am asked to do it.

R-3   Knowing and doing what others are expecting from me, and what integrity demands.

R-4   Recognising that I am not God, after all.

R-5   The ability to make choices confidently and without delay.

R-6   Purposing to accomplish what you set out to do, however long it takes and whatever the opposition.

R-7   Demonstrating the depth of my commitment by remaining true in times of difficulty.

Character qualities that are usually important to the motivational gift of the MERCY.

Have I reached out to develop these qualities in my life?

M-1   Caring enough about a person to give their words and emotions my undivided attention.

M-2   Being tuned in enough to respond to other people.

M-3   Looking at how each person affected by a decision will see things.

M-4   Wanting people to be healed from their hurts, no matter what it costs me.

M-5   Being quietly considerate towards other people.

M-6   Setting limits on how I will talk or behave, so as not to offend some people.

M-7   Not insisting on what I feel I have the right to expect.

You may now be interested to see the usual names given to the character qualities we have defined.

P-1   Truthfulness
P-2   Obedience
P-3   Sincerity
P-4   Virtue
P-5   Boldness
P-6   Forgiveness
P-7   Persuasiveness

S-1   Alertness
S-2   Hospitality
S-3   Generosity
S-4   Joyfulness
S-5   Flexibility
S-6   Availability
S-7   Endurance

T-1   Self-control
T-2   Reverence
T-3   Diligence
T-4   Thoroughness
T-5   Dependability
T-6   Security
T-7   Patience

E-1   Wisdom
E-2   Discernment
E-3   Faith
E-4   Discretion
E-5   Love
E-6   Creativity
E-7   Enthusiasm

G-1   Resourcefulness
G-2   Thriftiness

G-3 Contentment
G-4 Punctuality
G-5 Tolerance
G-6 Cautiousness
G-7 Gratefulness

R-1 Orderliness
R-2 Initiative
R-3 Responsibility
R-4 Humility
R-5 Decisiveness
R-6 Determination
R-7 Loyalty

M-1 Attentiveness
M-2 Sensitivity
M-3 Fairness
M-4 Compassion
M-5 Gentleness
M-6 Deference
M-7 Meekness

It is important to reach out for the character qualities that are immediately before you and that have natural appeal. That's more than enough for one person to have on their plate at first. You can always go for seconds!

Of course, all of the character qualities are up for grabs, although some of them may not appeal to you a great deal. In fact, developing character qualities relating to some other motivations may be as hard as breathing under water – it's even scary to hear the descriptions. You can go back and read them now if you would like.

Other people may need to pass you things from the table that you cannot reach yourself.

It is usual for most people to recognise how they have at least begun to reach out and develop most of the character qualities relating to their particular motivation. Where they have not, it means that *that* quality will not have been integrated into their character. Seeing the value in these things may come naturally, but growth in character must be developed. It is *not* innate.

When someone does not relate to one of 'their own' character qualities, and has not reached to make it part of them, it usually highlights an area where that person has been hurt or damaged significantly. It would be useful to consider this quality more carefully (or *prayerfully*?) to gain understanding as to what may be the problem.

Now we come to what we call the 'see-saw' effect. Each character quality has a corresponding negative, or 'see-saw'. This means that, for the person whose motivation it relates to, the negative is what they fall into instead. These dangers only apply in the group of character qualities relating to your own motivation.

For example, whenever a Prophetic does not reach out for *truthfulness*, they fall towards *deception*. (Another person who doesn't reach out for truthfulness may only be evasive or non-specific.) The Prophetic cares so much about truth that to not reflect this is the same as to deliberately deceive.

Joyce Williams has said, 'I find it easier to take the negatives, and turn the question round into a statement.' So with the Prophetic-related character quality of *obedience*, the negative see-saw is wilfulness; and the statement Joyce develops from it would be:

(As a Prophetic) whenever I do not fulfil instructions so that the one I am accountable to is fully satisfied I fall instead into wilfulness.

Using the definitions and the negatives from the list relating to your own motivation, try turning the sentences round in a similar way.

Here are the lists of negative 'see-saw' qualities for each motivation.

P-1	*Truthfulness*	vs	deception
P-2	*Obedience*	vs	wilfulness
P-3	*Sincerity*	vs	hypocrisy
P-4	*Virtue*	vs	impurity
P-5	*Boldness*	vs	fearfulness
P-6	*Forgiveness*	vs	rejection
P-7	*Persuasiveness*	vs	contentiousness

S-1	*Alertness*	vs	unawareness
S-2	*Hospitality*	vs	loneliness
S-3	*Generosity*	vs	stinginess
S-4	*Joyfulness*	vs	self-pity
S-5	*Flexibility*	vs	resistance
S-6	*Availability*	vs	self-centredness
S-7	*Endurance*	vs	giving up

T-1	*Self-control*	vs	self-indulgence
T-2	*Reverence*	vs	disrespect
T-3	*Diligence*	vs	sloth
T-4	*Thoroughness*	vs	incompleteness
T-5	*Dependability*	vs	inconsistency
T-6	*Security*	vs	anxiety
T-7	*Patience*	vs	restlessness

E-1	*Wisdom*	vs	natural inclinations
E-2	*Discernment*	vs	judgement
E-3	*Faith*	vs	presumption
E-4	*Discretion*	vs	simple-mindedness
E-5	*Love*	vs	selfishness
E-6	*Creativity*	vs	under-achievement
E-7	*Enthusiasm*	vs	apathy

G-1	*Resourcefulness*	vs	wastefulness
G-2	*Thriftiness*	vs	extravagance
G-3	*Contentment*	vs	covetousness
G-4	*Punctuality*	vs	tardiness
G-5	*Tolerance*	vs	prejudice
G-6	*Cautiousness*	vs	rashness
G-7	*Gratefulness*	vs	unthankfulness

R-1	*Orderliness*	vs	disorganisation
R-2	*Initiative*	vs	unresponsiveness
R-3	*Responsibility*	vs	unreliability
R-4	*Humility*	vs	pride
R-5	*Decisiveness*	vs	double-mindedness
R-6	*Determination*	vs	faint-heartedness
R-7	*Loyalty*	vs	unfaithfulness

M-1	*Attentiveness*	vs	unconcern
M-2	*Sensitivity*	vs	callousness
M-3	*Fairness*	vs	partiality
M-4	*Compassion*	vs	indifference
M-5	*Gentleness*	vs	harshness
M-6	*Deference*	vs	rudeness
M-7	*Meekness*	vs	anger

A number of years ago we had just begun using the character quality lists as developed by Bill Gothard.* One friend who is a Ruler by motivation was asked if he had appropriated and developed each of the seven character qualities relating to his motivation. He responded very positively to each. Just for interest the corresponding see-saw list was read out to him at the end. His colour drained as he recognised the entire list as the catalogue of faults his then wife accused him of. He had developed plenty of character, but was inconsistent in applying what he was capable of.

If you really want a horrifying picture, read out loud the entire list of negatives beside the character qualities your motivation relates to. Fortunately, some of these are traits we have not developed or have left behind by developing a good character. There is the danger that we say, 'Oh I can't help that – it's just the way I'm made. That's my motivation – it came with the package.' But to recognise our full negative potential is no excuse for bad behaviour.

Prophetic people are not insensitive – only the ones who haven't grown up! Nor are Exhorters afraid to tell

---

* The lists of seven character qualities associated with each motivation, their opposites and references for prescription all came from a card game from the Advanced Seminar from the Institute of Basic Youth Conflicts, now Institute of Basic Life Principles, Oakbrook, Illinois. Another spin-off is a schools programme called 'Character First!'

someone the truth. We must not assume that a Mercy is so sensitive that it is impossible not to hurt their feelings. I have known people to take the qualities and the see-saw relating to their own group and day by day observe and adjust their behaviour.

Sometimes we need to confess our bankruptcy in the area of internal change. Our minds need to be renewed by different values and patterns of thinking. Our hearts, too, are sometimes in need of radical surgery. Where we have been damaged, fresh tissue needs to replace the raw edges. We cannot change ourselves, only adjust our behaviour. The alcoholic attending an AA meeting is introduced to the concept that he/she is in need of the help of a higher power than just good intentions. Our negative behaviour and heart attitudes in these and other areas are just as stubbornly incurable as addictions of any other kind. We are rotten through and through. There is a tension here. We were not created with a flaw in the design, yet our problem is not just skin-deep. It needs addressing more than cosmetically. Shifting the blame will not help, either. We could visit a psychiatrist and decide, 'It's all my mother's fault that I am so screwed up', but that would be only an explanation, not a valid excuse. We can predict patterns of behaviour in terms of our motivation; but it becomes dangerous to say, 'Oh, that's just the way I am', and to reinforce habits that hurt and bruise other people.

Paul of Tarsus, who, after all, wrote Romans 12, is a good example of a man with very great potential. He used it in being convinced it was right to persecute and kill those whose beliefs were different from his own. He was a very strong man and a force to be reckoned with. (Our giftedness is not morally selective. The influence *we* exert can also be for good or for evil. We have been created with limitless potential for good or evil.) Something happened to him which broke his strength and changed him abruptly. The very people he was on his way to seek out and terminate were now to become his family. As a Jesus-follower, his strength and conviction were more extreme than they had ever been as the executioner. It was as if Hitler had overnight become Mother Teresa!

The crucial change that happened for Paul involved seeing God in a whole new way. Our picture of God profoundly affects how we act. He saw God as angry, harsh and demanding, unable to forgive; he acted the same way. When he saw God differently, he was a changed person.

Most people haven't even worked out what their concept of God is. Remote? Absent? Very like one of my parents . . . totally accepting of me . . . Many have had experiences they find it hard to explain, when something bigger than themselves has felt close enough to touch, or has intervened in their circumstances. For Paul that something – that Someone – changed his life in a moment. For a lot of us the turnaround is not so extreme, especially if we are not extreme people to start with. Falling in love can be quite dramatic, but the love that sustains a relationship over many years is what really matters, not how we got into the relationship in the first place. Love believes we are capable of anything; it is not blind. Real love wants to reach out, and free us to be truly ourselves.

The story of the gate

Kevin's dad had painted their front gates. There was the big gate, big enough to pull back whenever the car needed to get in. Then there was the little low gate next to it – the one Kevin went in and out of. The gates were all shiny now, with clean, new white paint. It was the big gate Kevin looked at when he went out to play in the street that night with his friends. Funny, really, how he never thought about the gate usually, but tonight, with it being so shiny and new-looking, he couldn't help but notice it.

It turned out to be quite a night. First, he got in a fight with some of his friends, and one of the neighbours came out, and it was Kevin who answered back and told them to mind their own business. By the time it was all sorted out and they got back to their game, it was getting late, but nobody wanted to go home. So then he was late in, and the neighbour had already been on the phone, complaining to his dad.

He expected to be in big trouble, of course. But what happened was really strange. His dad didn't shout at him, or ground him for a week, or stop his pocket money. Instead he sent Kevin to where his tools were kept, to bring a big hammer and one of the black nails out of the tin. He told Kevin to take the hammer and bang the nail into the big white gate. It didn't even matter where. Kevin did it on the inside. Nothing more was said. But every time he got into trouble after that his dad did the same thing – sent him to bang another nail into the big white gate.

In a few weeks it began to really bother him. He had liked the gate being all new-looking and white and shiny. Now, whenever he went out, he had to look at all these black nails spoiling how it had looked at first. From the outside it still looked shiny and white. But even if Kevin glanced across at it, on the outside, when he was out in the street, he knew what it was like on the inside, and it bothered him. He started worrying in case any of his friends came to call for him and noticed what a mess the inside of the gate was. It would be very awkward to explain.

One day it really got to him. By now the gate was so covered in nails it was like a black gate with white patches round the edges. He went to his dad, and got straight to the point. 'Dad, can we stop doing this? I'm tired of looking at those nails. Couldn't we take them out?'

Kevin's dad went with him to where the tools were kept. They chose a big, black pair of pliers and went to the gate. The nails came out quite easily and his dad threw them in the bin. But in every place where a nail had been, there was a hole in the gate. It was less noticeable but in some ways it seemed worse.

They didn't speak about it again. Every time he looked at the gate, Kevin felt sad. He wanted everything to be as it had been before, as if the nails had never been there.

When he came in from school one night that week, his dad had a surprise for him. 'Say, Kevin, how would you feel if we were to have a new gate fitted, instead of the one with the holes in it?' The new gate was all shiny and white, and together they hung it in place. His dad said that it was very expensive to replace a whole gate, but he thought it had been worth it.

Prescriptions from the doctor's surgery

If one of the see-saws is a particular problem for you, here are suggested prescriptions. Swallow at least once a day, until you are better!

P-1	Put away lying. Speak truth with your neighbour. No one is an island. *Ephesians 4:25*
P-2	Put your own ideas to one side. Listen. Don't be stubborn and independent. *2 Corinthians 10:5*
P-3	Strip away any pretence and self-deception, and choose to be known for who you are. Choose to love. *1 Peter 1:22*

P-4 Trust God to wipe the slate clean, and lean on His power to walk with confidence in right choices. *2 Peter 1:3*

P-5 Rise above the threatening situation, even for a moment, and see how it looks from a higher perspective. *Acts 4:29*

P-6 Be kind to others, open your heart to them, and choose to forgive. You have not just been forgiven when you deserved it. *Ephesians 4:32*

P-7 You must not strive. Instead, think of yourself as a servant. Be helpful in what you say, and considerate. *2 Timothy 2:24*

S-1 It is not enough to be willing. Look out, and see what is really happening around you. *Mark 14:38*

S-2 Don't miss the opportunity to do what you can for people you meet. Who knows how important that visitor may be! *Hebrews 13:2*

S-3 If you only sow a small crop, that's what you'll harvest. *2 Corinthians 9:6*

S-4 Remember you have much to be grateful for, and if you are happy inside let your face know about it. *Proverbs 15:13*

S-5 Look for the things that will last for ever. *Colossians 3:2*

S-6 Everybody wants to do their own thing. Do you really want to live like that? *Philippians 2:20-21*

S-7 Don't be weary in well-doing. Everything in its season. Don't give up before the harvest is ready. *Galatians 6:9*

T-1   See that your old selfish ways no longer control you, but are put to death. Rely on God, and be released into a new pattern of living.
Galatians 5:24-25

T-2   Don't think of imitating ruthless people who have no respect for anybody. In the end, all wrongs will be righted. Hang in there!
Proverbs 23:17-18

T-3   Remember that nothing you do goes unseen. If you are pleased when you do a good job, think how much more satisfying it is for God to see you being so wholehearted.   *Colossians 3:23*

T-4   It is wise to learn all we can, and to listen very carefully.   *Proverbs 18:15*

T-5   Say what you mean, and do as you say. Keep your promise, even when it costs you. *Psalm 15:4*

T-6   Don't work for food that goes bad. Being alive on the inside matters more.   *John 6:27*

T-7   Get excited about troubles, because troubles teach you patience. And all these experiences, and the patience with which you endure them, show you that there is always hope in the end.
Romans 5:3-4

E-1   Reverence God, and that is the beginning of wisdom. To know him is to understand.
Proverbs 9:10

E-2   Don't just look on the outside; try to see through to the heart.   *1 Samuel 16:7*

E-3   To have faith is to be so convinced about what hasn't happened yet that you plan around it.
Hebrews 11:1

E-4   If you are wise, you will see evil coming, and hide; it is the simple who keep on going, and walk right into trouble.   *Proverbs 22:3*

E-5   If I give away everything I own to those who have nothing, and even die for what I believe, if I do not love it does me no good at all.
1 Corinthians 13:3

E-6   Don't just conform to the world around you and its values. Dare to be different. (Being brainwashed isn't such a bad idea, when your thinking is worn and dirty.) Let true wisdom change the way you think, and transform you.
Romans 12:2

E-7   Keep joy alive inside of you. Be open to inspiration!   *1 Thessalonians 5:16, 19*

G-1   Waste not, want not. If you are faithful in little, you'll be faithful with much.   *Luke 16:10*

G-2   If you are careless with money, which doesn't matter, who will trust you with more important things?   *Luke 16:11*

G-3   If we have food in our belly, and clothes on our back, that's enough.   *1 Timothy 6:8*

G-4   Everything has its season, and there is a time for everything.   *Ecclesiastes 3:1*

G-5   Learn to love, to value and appreciate everybody.   *Philippians 2:2*

G-6 It is not good to be uninformed. Look out! If you hurry, you could run into trouble.

Proverbs 19:2

G-7 Everything in life is a gift. You have much to be thankful for, but nothing to boast about.

1 Corinthians 4:7

R-1 Let everything be done properly, and in an ordered way. *1 Corinthians 14:40*

R-2 Don't be overcome by evil; instead, you must overcome evil with good. *Romans 12:21*

R-3 We are all accountable in the end – to God, if not to anyone else. *Romans 14:12*

R-4 Help is available. But the proud won't acknowledge they need help of any kind; it is the humble who recognise their need of God.

James 4:6

R-5 If it is wisdom you need, ask God, and he will show you. He won't let you down. *James 1:5*

R-6 It's not just getting off to a good start that matters, but staying the course, and completing the race. *2 Timothy 4:7-8*

R-7 There is no greater love than this, than to lay your life down for your friends. *John 15:13*

M-1 Don't let your mind wander. You know better than that. Listen when someone is talking to you. *Hebrews 2:1*

M-2 If someone is happy, be really happy for them; if they are sad, share in their sadness.

Romans 12:15

M-3 Treat other people the way you would wish to be treated. *Luke 6:31*

M-4 If you see someone else's need, and turn away when you have the means to help, then how can love find a home in you? *1 John 3:17*

M-5 You should be gentle in your dealings with other people, just as a mother is protective of her tiny child. *1 Thessalonians 2:7*

M-6 If eating meat, or taking a drink (or a having a smoke?) is going to cause problems for someone, it's better not to do it in their company. Avoid causing them offence. *Romans 14:21*

M-7 Let go, let God. *Psalm 62:5*

Chapter 18
Questions and answers

Can a person choose which motivation they are going to be?

No, they're stuck with it as their starting point. They already have one foundational motivational gift which it is useful to recognise. They can, of course, set out to develop in other areas as well, to extend their insights and abilities. But, remember the story of the marzipan who wanted to be a montelimar! (see Chapter 3). Motivation is innate – essentially, you can trade *with* it, but you can't *trade* it.

Are people of one motivation all alike?

The answer is more No than Yes. Obviously, they are likely to see things in a similar way. If it was raining, and people gathered under big umbrellas, those under the same umbrella would have a similar perspective; but even then their viewpoint would not be identical. Nor is there any guarantee that they would *like* the others sheltering under that same umbrella. It is probable that what they dislike about each other will be their own faults, or what they have worked hard to overcome in themselves.

Could it be that I am a person with more than one motivational gift?

No. Only one is your motivational *gift*. The other areas have been learned or developed, and will be of great advantage and value to you. But the roots of your personality are those of one single motivation. A different dynamic is at work when a Mercy encourages to when an Exhorter does it, for example.

Are motivations hereditary?

I don't think so. Time and time again we meet people who identify strong *secondary* characteristics in their behaviour and outlook as being 'inherited' by virtue of the strong influence of one or the other parent. (One Prophetic has many traits of the Giver which he has consciously embraced and developed after admiring them in his Giver mother.) Where a child grows up *very* like a parent in values, personality and behaviour, this is often *because* they're of the same motivation, and they develop these characteristics in a way that other children of the same family do not.

Is it not appropriate that I exhibit traits from all motivations?

Please don't pick all the most unfortunate aspects of each, will you? Yes, it is important that we learn from each other. When several people live or work alongside each other, they learn to depend on each other's strengths. If a person you know well is absent, you may say to yourself, 'What would they do (or say or suggest) if they were here?' Someone who has lived a long and full life will often have assimilated many of the insights and skills of others they have learned from or observed closely.

May my motivation change over a period of time?

Hopefully, in time you will learn not to compulsively repeat destructive or unhelpful behaviour patterns. Also, you may learn with difficulty to embrace the qualities you find admirable in others, but which come so much more easily to them! Fortunately, you will not be prone to develop their innate difficulties and areas of potential overbalance. So, you may mature by reflecting on your instinctive behaviour, and modifying or reinforcing it as appropriate; and you may also deliberately develop in areas that are harder to assimilate or make your own. But learnt behaviour will never replace or eradicate instinctive responses.

Is it always dangerous to guess another person's motivation?

Yes, it is. Outward behaviour can be misconstrued or be misleading. It ain't what you do, it's the *why* that you do it which betrays who you are. If I suspect someone is of a particular motivation I can *project* all kinds of expectations on to them, and judge how they behave, and totally misunderstand them. That's not fair, and gives them no chance to be themselves. (Even if someone admits to being, for example, a Teaching motivation, that does not mean that all general characteristics of Teaching motivations will be specifically true of them. They may, for instance, set *no* store by paper qualifications, having found that on-the-job experience is often a more reliable measure of ability.) One of the most hurtful things in life is when people misjudge our motives. Understanding of motivations should be a corrective of this, not a contributory cause! Discipline yourself not to speculate.

Isn't motivations just a way of putting people into boxes?

Yes and no. Some years ago, a friend called Michelle Moran observed that she disliked anything which tried to categorise her or box her in. But she found motivations very freeing. It explained why she felt as she did about life and other people, why some things came easily, and why other things seemed hard for *her* that others took to with no effort. She could also learn from other people, and had a whole lifetime to grow through the other two boxes – giftedness expressed in service, and the use of the supernatural manifestations which are tools to help us be effective in what we are called to.

Once I've discovered my motivation does that mean I should try to find a job or career suitable to it?

Not necessarily. Knowing your motivation might help you to recognise what would be satisfying or difficult for you in a particular job, or why you feel as you do about your work. Finding the job for which you are most obviously suited might not be of great importance, especially if you are settled in your current employment. It can be stretching, and sometimes just as fulfilling, to learn what doesn't come naturally. And there may be many other outlets for aptitudes related to your motivation in the rest of your time when you are not at work. Lots of people go through life doing jobs that are all right, but not what they would most like to do. If they are able to provide for their family and have enough time left over to do the things they care about, they are more than satisfied.

The SIMA Institute takes this question a stage further. They suggest that a person's working life absorbs so many hours of each week that it is a shame for them to be doing anything other than work which is uniquely tailored to their specific pattern of abilities and aptitudes. The approach they take in consultation is to develop a unique profile of the individual, more focused even than classification by motivation.* Nick and his colleagues in the SIMA Institute take seriously the challenge to explore the unique 'system of integrated motivational abilities' which is fulfilling for an individual person. They aim to help that individual to recognise what elements are necessary for them to be fulfilled, and to be in their ideal position in the workplace. This can now also be explored on a self-help basis with the exercises contained in a recent excellent book by Nick (Isbister) and Martin Robinson, *Who do you think you are?* (ISBN 0 551 0131700).

Coincidentally, on a recent retreat I was given a sheet which says:

> In all the world there is nobody like you. In all time there has never been anyone who laughs in exactly your way. You are the only one in the whole of creation who has your particular set of abilities. Of course, there is always someone who is better at one thing or another. But God has a job for you to do that nobody else can do as well as you can. Only one applicant is qualified. Only one has the unique and right combination of what it takes: you

This raises the question: What *is* the job? just being you? or finding some uniquely fulfilling occupation? Maybe it's idealistic to assume that the perfect opening awaits every individual? Certainly, when it does happen, it's great.

> A number of years ago I read a report about John Irving in *Time* magazine. His novel *The World According to Garp* was being filmed with Robin Williams in the title role. As a student Irving had two main interests or passions. One was writing novels and the other was wrestling. A contemporary, who remembered him as a student, was asked what his

---

* For further information contact Nick Isbister at SIMA (UK) Ltd, Clock-house Barn, Sugworth Lane, Radley, Oxford OX14 2HX, 01865-321123 (info@sima.co.uk).

> writing was like in those days, and said, 'His stories were mostly about 158-pound wrestlers.' In the film of *Garp*, Irving played a small role himself, as the college wrestling coach.

The key thing is to hold on to the seemingly disparate elements of our dreams.

Where do you get all this from?

For my own account of gradual exposure to Motivations, read 'How it began for me' starting on page 11. The material is based on the Christian scriptures, in particular on the twelfth chapter of the letter to the Romans.

The first letter to the Corinthians 12:4-6 distinguishes between different sorts of gifting. We would say that this refers in turn to manifestations, ministries and then motivations. In principle, a reading of the Greek text (here and in other relevant passages) allows but does not demand this interpretation. Certainly, three different words are used. We then correlate 1 Corinthians 12:7-10 with manifestations, 1 Corinthians 12:28-30 and Ephesians 4:11-13 with ministry, and Romans 12 and 1 Peter 4:7-11 with motivations.

(Don and Katie Fortune draw an interesting distinction with regard to 1 Timothy 4:14. They say 'the gift that is in you' refers obviously to motivation, which is innate, and that the next phrase is better translated 'which was brought forth, or spoken of, by prophecy'.)

If all this about motivations is true, then why have we heard so little about it until now?

Gene Edwards, in his book *Climb the Highest Mountain*,* talks about truths being rediscovered progressively in

---

* 1984, Seedsowers Publishing, PO Box 3317, Jacksonville, Florida 32206

each generation. He uses the image of mountain climbers trying to scale peaks and claim them. Often they would struggle painfully to a summit only to see a cairn or a flag showing that someone else had already got there. With some mountains that seem unconquerable all we can do is move the flag a little higher up! Perhaps more people becoming familiar with Motivations teaching will give us the understanding to help us allow others to be different and still be at peace with one another. That would really be moving the flag higher!

After going on a Myers-Briggs weekend, don't I know everything there is to know about me, anyway?

Any construct which enables us to examine ourselves and others, and then to recognise that we are *so* different as to make direct comparison pointless, is very helpful indeed.

The Myers-Briggs indicator is based on Jung's Theory of Personality Types. He distinguishes between people who are extrovert and introvert, then between those who are instinctively thinking or feeling people, and finally between those who rely on the evidence of their senses more than on intuition. The combination of these choices gives eight possible permutations. Robert Innes in *Personality Indicators and the Spiritual Life* * writes:

> To be fair to Jung, I do not think that he expected or even especially welcomed the great interest that has been shown in his theory of eight types. In the foreword to a later edition of his work on psychological types he suggested that he had merely offered the types as a means of organising the

*Grove Books Ltd, Ridley Hall Road, Cambridge, CB3 9HU, www.grovebooks.co.uk

empirical material, and he warned those who sought to 'type' people that 'this kind of classification is nothing but a childish parlour game'.

Two women named Myers and Briggs introduced a further distinction between judging and perceiving, and there were suddenly 16 types, with a long series of questions to identify where a person fits in this classification.

It is like a mirror reflecting back the combination of what you have presented to it. The image you see may surprise you, or may reflect just what you expected. If I confess to having ginger hair and eating bananas, it will tell me, quite frankly, that I am a ginger-haired banana-eater (which, of course, many people are not).

Motivations claims rather more than this. If certain traits are identified, there are words of encouragement and warning which will be applicable to you (see Chapter 12).

The Myers-Briggs indicator is interesting. You may have much in common with someone of the same one of the 16 groups as yourself. If two more sets of distinctions were added, you would logically have 64 classifications, and anyone who was then in the same group as you would have even more in common with you.

How is this different from the Enneagram?

The Enneagram designates nine different sorts of people in contrast to the seven Motivations.

The teaching has its positive aspects: it points out that people are different from each other, and also suggests a process of change.

The spontaneous comment that has arisen from many people who have become familiar with both Enneagram and Motivations is that Motivations is so much more positive in its approach because it focuses primarily on giftedness. In contrast, the Enneagram is negative in its focus, and speaks continually of our compulsions. Indeed, in the Enneagram it is your compulsion that defines you.

Its origins are shrouded in mystery. Is there some significance in insisting on calling people by numbers as their 'name'? The alternative seems to be, if you go deeper into the Enneagram material, to refer to people as 'the Dog', 'the Monkey' and so on.

The fruits of Enneagram teaching are mixed. It causes people to become reflective about their life, but more usually it tends towards introspection. Writing on the Enneagram is largely academic, perhaps because it was introduced in the US by Jesuit scholars. Whether by book or by seminar, there is always the unmistakable air of someone needing to be *initiated into* the Enneagram.

George Gurdjieff was a student of occult practices travelling through Afghanistan in 1897. There a Sufi mystic is said to have introduced him to a monastery of the Sarmouni sect, where he learned their mystical dancing, psychic powers and the Enneagram.

Robert Innes (see above) points out that no solid evidence has ever been found outside of this story to support its existence in ancient times, but rumours of the Enneagram's antiquity serve to give it an air of authority. By 1912, Gurdjieff was teaching in Moscow. Usefully, he recognised three centres in a person – head, heart and gut – and taught various exercises designed to bring these into harmony with each other.

He also taught that everyone has an essence and a personality. The essence is the material of which the universe is made, whilst the personality is a mask of compulsive behaviour which covers this essence. Personal growth consists of recognising and shaking off this compulsive personality so as to return to the essence.

The Enneagram featured prominently in Gurdjieff's teaching and in the writings of his followers. They were particularly interested in the numerological properties of the Enneagram (which is a circle with nine points on it) and its relation to the mystical 3 and 7 which was held to give it a truly cosmic significance.

Through two men called Ichazo and Naranjo, Gurdjieff's work came to be developed in its current form in the 1960s. In the early '70s Helen Palmer was one of their students at the Esalen Institute, and Fr Bob Ochs also introduced it at the Loyola Seminary. And so it became widely known, firstly amongst Catholics.

Naranjo also correlates it to nine of the psychological mechanisms of defence in Freudian psychology (although Anna Freud had already developed this work with ten mechanisms of defence, not nine). But the number 9 figures strongly in Gurdjieff's teaching of numerology; and Sufis speak of 'the nine manifestations of the Divine'.

The different Motivations sound a bit like star-signs, don't they?

No. Our experience is that people's Motivational make-up has *no* connection with what time in the year they are born! The only similarity is that Motivational and astrological teaching both say you are born with it. Sometimes, twins have different Motivational giftings to each other.

Couldn't people use Motivations as an excuse for lazy, inconsiderate behaviour?

Yes, this is a danger. We have found this sometimes with older children. In an environment where most people are familiar with Motivational Gifts, the children find it easy to recognise the differences, but not always to appreciate that differentness. So it becomes, 'Oh, what would you know? You're just a Mercy.'

At worst, the Motivational tag becomes a put-down, so that if an Exhorter says, 'You did well', you don't believe it, in case they just wanted to make you feel better. And the Prophetic thinks they have a right to be rude and outspoken, feels the pressure to be radical and extreme, and makes no effort to be considerate.

Nothing in the teaching gives us the right to say, 'Oh, I can't help it; that's just the way I am.' Motivations gives us insights that alert us to possible dynamics so we can avoid the pitfalls, not write them on the calendar!

Wouldn't the best way to identify someone's Motivation be a questionnaire?

A questionnaire would help most people quickly to reach a conclusion. Experience proves that, however good the questions, a high proportion of people initially reach the *wrong* conclusion, and have a tortuous and confusing time sorting it out later on.

These are the problems:

- A questionnaire is in too much of a hurry.
- If the wording of a question or statement is confusing, the respondent isn't sure how to answer.
- Life circumstances may clash with the assumptions made in the various questions. A Teacher who doesn't read, a Ruler who has few opportunities to lead, or a Giver with little access to money, would give misleading responses to 'When you do this . . .' types of question.
- Instead of impressions or instinctive response, questionnaires usually rely on numerical scorings which can easily point to the wrong Motivation. (It is hard to

develop statements that only one Motivation will assent to, when some characteristics overlap with those of others' gifts.)

- Numerical scores are misleading. Some people conclude they must be 60 per cent Teacher and 40 per cent Exhorter (instead of 100 per cent Teacher with Exhorter traits overlaid).

- Most questionnaires fail to distinguish adequately between behaviour and motive, so a well-rounded person might easily score highly for each Motivation.

- There is no guarantee that the statements for each Motivation are equally weighted; so a quantified response to them is inaccurate.

- People's training and work-experience almost always affect their responses, and inevitably distort the scoring when a questionnaire is used.

- You can't actually reply, 'Well, that depends . . .' to a questionnaire. It requires a tick on a multiple-choice or sometimes even wants a Yes or No answer.

To determine their gifting it is more useful to ask someone about the different points made in describing one Motivation, and then notice the way they respond. Do they seem to resonate with it readily?

Are there more people of some Motivations than others?

There is no reason to believe this is the case.

Don and Katie Fortune tried to research this one and concluded that there are many more Mercies than anything else, and very few Teachers indeed. Statistics may be impressive, but they can also be very misleading. It is an amazing conclusion until they explain their methodology.

Their potential respondents were taught Motivations in large gatherings, and asked afterwards to mail back a response-card. I could have predicted that more Mercies than anybody would do as they were asked. It's also very predictable that most Teachers would want to check it all through again slowly before sending the response-card back – and then, once it's delayed, it could easily never be posted at all.

It's interesting that when someone asks this question it's because they know plenty of people of some Motivations but almost none of another. What varies is which they are reporting a shortage of!